ISLAM IN POST-SOVIET UZBEKISTAN

In recent years, the Uzbekistan government has been criticized for its brutal suppression of its Muslim population. This book, which is based on the author's intimate acquaintance with the region and several years of ethnographic research, is about how Muslims in this part of the world negotiate their religious practices despite the restraints of a stifling authoritarian regime. Fascinatingly, the book also shows how the restrictive atmosphere has actually helped shape the moral context of people's lives, and how understandings of what it means to be a Muslim emerge creatively out of lived experience.

Johan Rasanayagam is Lecturer in Social Anthropology at The University of Aberdeen. Dr. Rasanayagam's works have been published in numerous journals, including the *Journal of the Royal Anthropological Institute* and the *Central Asian Survey.*

CAMBRIDGE UNIVERSITY PRESS
Cambridge, New York, Melbourne, Madrid, Cape Town,
Singapore, São Paulo, Delhi, Mexico City

Cambridge University Press
The Edinburgh Building, Cambridge CB2 8RU, UK

Published in the United States of America by Cambridge University Press, New York

www.cambridge.org
Information on this title: www.cambridge.org/9781107411623

First published 2011
First paperback edition 2012

A catalogue record for this publication is available from the British Library

Library of Congress Cataloguing in Publication Data

Rasanayagam, Johan, 1964–
Islam in post-Soviet Uzbekistan : The morality of experience / Johan Rasanayagam.
p. cm.
Includes bibliographical references and index.
ISBN 978-1-107-00029-2 (hardback)
1. Islam – Uzbekistan – History. 2. Islam and state – Uzbekistan. I. Title.
BP63.U9R37 2010
297.09587–dc22 2010021649

ISBN 978-1-107-00029-2 Hardback
ISBN 978-1-107-41162-3 Paperback

Contents

Illustrations

Acknowledgements

This book is based on research carried out in the course of a postdoctoral fellowship at the Max Planck Institute (MPI) for Social Anthropology. The institute provided the opportunity for the field research and support for the subsequent work of analysis and publication, but what was most special about the MPI was the stimulating and cooperative intellectual environment it made possible. I had the all-too-rare opportunity to be part of a group of colleagues working on similar issues in Central Asia and other postsocialist societies, each of us pursuing our own individual project. I am particularly indebted to my fellow members of the Religion and Civil Society focus group, Irene Hilgers, Krisztina Kehl-Bodrogi, Julie McBrien, and Mathijs Pelkmans, who worked on Central Asia, as well as Juraj Buzalka, László Fosztó, Monica Heintz, and Vlad Naumescu, who worked on Central and Eastern Europe. This book in large part emerged from seminars, workshops, and discussions with these colleagues. I am also indebted to Chris Hann, the director of our department at the institute, who brought us all together and provided invaluable guidance and advice.

A number of colleagues have helped me to identify and formulate the problems addressed in this book. Chris Hann prompted me to think more clearly about my approach to the moral and encouraged me to ground the book more firmly in its ethnographic context. Maria Louw's comments on earlier drafts helped me to think about what was particular

MAP: Uzbekistan and its neighbours

INTRODUCTION

Towards an Anthropology of Moral Reasoning

On 13 May 2005, government security forces massacred hundreds of protesters in the city of Andijan, in Uzbekistan's portion of the Fergana Valley. Accounts are contested, and reliable facts are hard to come by, given the Uzbekistan government's efforts to restrict the flow of information. International human rights and crisis monitoring groups claimed that as many as 750 people were killed, the vast majority of whom were unarmed civilians protesting the economic hardship caused by corruption, government repression, restrictive government regulations on trade, and the arbitrary arrest of individuals on charges of religious extremism.[1] The government, for its part, claims that the demonstrators were armed Islamist extremists and terrorists who had forced civilians into the square as human shields, and that fewer than 200 were killed, most of whom were the gunmen themselves or security service personnel (Human Rights Watch 2005; Kendzior 2007; Khalid 2007, 192; Megoran 2008). The protests were sparked by the trial of a group of local businessmen on charges of religious extremism and involvement in a banned Islamic group named as 'Akromiya' by the state prosecutors. The trial itself attracted large demonstrations by the relatives and supporters of the accused, who protested their innocence and criticised the unfairness of the criminal justice process.[2] At the conclusion of the trial, a group of armed men stormed the prison in Andijan in which the businessmen were being held and freed them, along with hundreds of other prisoners, many of whom were also convicted on charges of religious extremism. The gunmen then took control of the buildings of the local government administration, and a large demonstration of civilians, reportedly numbering in the thousands, assembled in the square outside. The protest was ended when government forces opened fire on the crowd.

The concerns of this book address issues at the heart of this tragic event. They deal with how individuals fashion themselves as Muslim when the government attempts to maintain tight control over religious expression, routinely employing the coercive resources of the state to this end. During the closing years of the Soviet Union, when the reforms introduced by Mikhail Gorbachev allowed for greater religious freedoms, many Muslims in Uzbekistan, as in the other Central Asian republics, began to explore openly the question of what it means to be a Muslim. After the breakup of the Soviet Union, the successor government in Uzbekistan incorporated Islam within its ideology of national independence developed to replace Marxist-Leninism as the legitimating and guiding ideology of the newly independent state. The scope for public religious expression was further expanded, and there was an explosion of interest in Islam. Thousands of mosques were restored or built, and Muslim rituals that had been curtailed during the years of Soviet rule were held openly. For a brief few years just before and after independence in 1991, Muslims throughout Uzbekistan explored and debated the nature of Islam in relative freedom, as theological ideas that had been prevented from being circulated widely within the Soviet Union became available. However, as the government of President Karimov began to view Islam as a potential source of political opposition, restrictions were quickly imposed. Islamic groups independent of the quasi-state Muslim Board of Uzbekistan were banned, and religious expression outside the bounds of what the government considers legitimate began to be ruthlessly suppressed.

This book explores the creativity of moral reasoning as individuals develop understandings of what it means to be a Muslim. Moral reasoning is not just confined to cognitive reflection upon objective values or a conscious striving to develop a virtuous self. It is inherent within experience itself, in an embodied, ongoing engagement in a social and material world. What is distinctive about these processes in Uzbekistan is the constraint on open debate and public expressions of piety. Anthropologists writing about Muslim societies have often described the debates and struggles about the interpretation of sacred texts, the production and transmission of religious knowledge, how different actors accord legitimacy to their positions, and the role of education, literacy, and transnational movement in this process (Abu-Lughod 1993; Bowen 1993a; Eickelman 1992; Gardner 1999; Horvatich 1994; Reeves 1995). Magnus Marsden has written about the importance of debate itself in notions of being Muslim and living a good life more generally in Pakistan and Afghanistan (Marsden 2005, 85–121; 2009).

In Uzbekistan, however, the ruthlessly repressive efforts of the post-independence government to suppress any expression of Islam independent of what it considers legitimate severely restricts the space for open discussion and debate. The government of President Karimov has functionalised the concepts of tradition and cultural authenticity as tools of governance. It constructs legitimate Islam as part of a unique Central Asian cultural and spiritual heritage. State discourse establishes an opposition between an idealised national tradition and an alien, politically motivated religious extremism as the dominant criterion by which citizens must present their practice as Muslims in situations where the coercive organs of the state can be brought to bear. Where open and free debate is effectively stifled, lived experience has become a privileged site for moral reasoning. This book examines the moral quality of experience and the creativity of experiential reasoning. It examines the intelligibility of experience that enables productive communication and interaction among individuals with diverse understandings of moral selfhood.

The businessmen whose trial sparked the protest referred to above are likely to have been involved in nonpolitical charitable activity. They

In recent years, anthropologists working in Muslim societies have increasingly been turning their attention to the formation of subjectivities. If an early question for the subfield of the anthropology of Islam was how to encompass the diversity in the local practice of Muslims within a global object of analysis (Eickelman 1982; el-Zein 1977; Geertz 1968; Gellner 1981; Manger 1999), more recent studies have taken individual experience as their starting point. Questions of power and hegemony, disputes about correct interpretation and practice, and explorations of what it means to be a Muslim have been addressed, for example, through the subjective experience of spirit possession (Masquelier 2001; McIntosh 2004) or in decisions by women to adopt particular forms of head covering (Brenner 1996; Werbner 2005). Saba Mahmood and Charles Hirschkind have described how individual Muslims cultivate pious selves with appropriate desires, dispositions, and emotions through self-conscious work upon the self (Hirschkind 2001; Mahmood 2005), and Gregory Simon has explored the performance of daily prayer as a context in which Indonesian Muslims engage with multiple and contradictory conceptions of moral selfhood (Simon 2009). Writing about post-Soviet Bukhara in Uzbekistan, Maria Louw has described how understandings of Islam emerge from an individual's subjective experience and practical engagement within a lifeworld. She explores the efforts of individuals to reestablish a moral grounding through direct engagement with Muslim 'saints' and sacred space when they find themselves dislocated and alienated as a result of the economic and social upheavals following the end of communist rule (Louw 2007). When anthropologists do address the idea of Islam in global terms, they often ground it in individual experience. Heiko Henkel has written about the subjective experience of the ritual of daily prayer as a practice that unites Muslims from diverse cultural and interpretive settings in a shared Islamic tradition (Henkel 2005).

This book similarly focuses upon subjective experience and moral selfhood. It moves the discussion forward by addressing directly what we mean by the moral quality of experience. Moral reasoning is not only a cognitive process of the mind, a public debate and personal deliberation about objectified values and positions. It is also carried out within an individual's embodied experience. Individuals do not only deliberate over the nature of what it means to be a good Muslim, but they are also continually living out a developing moral self. They are engaged within a field of social relations in which the various discourses and interpretations of Islam circulate. They are immersed within a social and material environment that includes interaction with spirit agents. They suffer illness and healing, and success or failure in projects they hold dear. Individual understandings of Islam are diverse and continually evolving. For many, fulfilling the tenets of Islam as laid down in the Qur'an and Sunna (the exemplary practice of the Prophet Muhammad), visiting the shrines of saints, and fulfilling obligations within their local communities to hold life-cycle rituals in a particular way all contribute to the formation of Muslim selves.

The Usefulness of a Moral Perspective

For Muslims in Uzbekistan, the question of what it means to be a Muslim is in essence a moral one, but what do we mean by 'moral', and how can morality or moral reasoning be studied ethnographically? In Durkheim's conception of society, anything that raises the individual above his or her egoistic concerns and binds a mass of disparate individuals into a unitary society is moral (Durkheim 1964, 1973). Thus, at the extreme, morality is coextensive with the social, so that it might be argued that concern for the moral is diffused throughout the entire project of anthropology. Anthropologists are frequently interested in what might seem explicitly moral questions, such as how individuals in different societies think about the nature of the world around them and the place of humans within it, the relation between human and non-human entities, or how local systems of value respond when they are incorporated within networks of global capitalism. Rather than adopting morality itself as an analytical frame, anthropologists have usually found it more productive to explore these issues through a study of more seemingly concrete concepts and phenomena that can be compared cross-culturally. These have included the differing notions of the person, the phenomena of witchcraft and sorcery, or even the concept of evil (Parkin 1985).

From time to time, some anthropologists have made the attempt to delineate morality itself as a distinct field for study. An early attempt was made by Abraham and May Edel, who adopted the Durkheimian conception of morality as a social phenomenon. Reflecting the dominant trends in theory at the time (the 1950s and 1960s), they viewed morality, or ethics, as they called it, as a social institution embedded in a social structure and performing distinct functions. The field of ethics, in their view, would encompass the rules and norms aimed at instilling particular character traits, goals and ideals, the categories of what constitutes a moral community and a responsible person, and the mechanisms for regulating norms (Edel 1962; Edel & Edel 2000).

In recent years, there has been a renewed interest in developing a distinctly anthropological approach to morality (Heintz 2009; Zigon 2008). Rather than seeking to identify bounded and coherent systems, more recent work has emphasised process and practice, selfhood and subjectivity, and experience. Signe Howell has suggested that the anthropology of morality should consider the dynamic relation between transcendent values and lived practice. Attention would be directed at the effects of relations of power in constituting and regulating moral ideals and practices, processes of moral reasoning, and the multiple, often conflicting moralities that coexist within a single society (Howell 1997). Michael Lambek has drawn inspiration from Aristotle's concept of practical wisdom (*phronesis*) to address the connection between transcendence and lived practice. Aristotle developed an idea of virtue that is not tied to abstract principles alone, but that also incorporates action in relation to contingent circumstance aimed at the good. Virtue is a state of the person rather than a collection of rules. A virtuous person is one who has attained mastery over the self through discipline and training, so that he or she is no longer driven by the demands of bodily senses but has developed the will, the disposition, to act in pursuit of the good. The practically wise person, therefore, is not concerned with a purely intellectual contemplation of virtue but exercises choice within the ongoing and contingent flow of circumstance in the lived world, informed by dispositions that are trained and cultivated (Aristotle 1998). Lambek has drawn on these ideas to locate moral practice in 'situated judgement'. The virtuous subject is a 'virtuoso' who makes practical interventions within the contingent flow of events in terms of shared symbols, myths, and local histories that transcend them (Lambek 2002).

Lambek's approach identifies the self as the location for morality, or at least for the anthropological study of moral reasoning. Morality is a state of the person and exercised in the flow of life. Others have similarly located morality in the self but focus on processes of self-fashioning. James Laidlaw (2002) and James Faubion (2001) have separately built upon Foucault's work on power and subjectivity to locate an anthropology of ethics, following Foucault's use of the term, in a study of the freedom that individuals are able to exercise in fashioning themselves as ethical subjects. For Foucault, morality refers to prescriptive rules and codes for living, whereas ethics encompasses the operations individuals perform upon themselves, the disciplines and technologies of the self that produce a desired state of being (Foucault 1985, 1994a, 1994c).

> Wherever and in so far as people's conduct is shaped by attempts to make of themselves a certain kind of person, because it is as such a person that, on reflection, they think they ought to live, to that extent their conduct is ethical and free. And to the extent that they do so with reference to ideals, values, models, practices, relationships, and institutions that are amenable to ethnographic study, to that extent their conduct becomes the subject matter for an anthropology of ethics. (Laidlaw 2002, 327)

Saba Mahmood's study of women's piety movements in Cairo is an example of this understanding of morality applied in a Muslim context (Mahmood 2005).

Both Laidlaw and Faubion locate ethics in the freedom for reflection, and individuals are free to the extent that they are not utterly subjugated within relations of power. Their choice of the term 'ethics' over 'morality' is intended to foreground the intentional work of self-fashioning over an unreflexive immersion within a preexisting social field. This constructs the moral as essentially a self-conscious activity, even if it is located within a social and cultural context and has the effect of producing embodied dispositions. However, creativity and moral reasoning need not be confined to this sort of self-conscious, cognitive reflection. It is also inherent in an individual's ongoing, embodied experience.

Arthur Kleinman has located morality in just such everyday experience. It is present in the intersubjective relations of kinship and neighbourhood, in religious practices and experiences of illness and healing, and in the entire spectrum of experience and interaction in daily life. This is moral, Kleinman argues, because it involves contestations and compromises through which values are negotiated and reworked (Kleinman 1999). Kleinman's concern is to develop a way to think about standards and values that have universal, translocal relevance, which he defines as ethical, in the context of particular local settings.

Joel Robbins similarly locates morality in experience, but provides a cultural understanding. He takes inspiration from Dumont and Weber to place 'value' at the centre of our understanding of culture, and focuses his attention on situations of culture change. In his ethnographic context, this is conversion to Pentecostal Christianity in a Papua New Guinea society. Morality is located in the everyday living out of the conflicting value systems present in a society, and it is this conflict that provides the space for self-conscious ethical reasoning of the sort that Laidlaw and Faubion have described (Robbins 2004, 2007).

In this book I am not so much concerned with values, how universal values are embedded in the flow of life or how value systems shape experience. Rather, I want to focus more directly on the moral nature of experience itself, and the transcendent quality of experience that enables moral reasoning.

Moral Creativity, Moral Reasoning, and Moral Sources

I have suggested that morality be understood in terms of 'transcendence', but what exactly does this concept signify? As is evident from the foregoing discussion, a common way to think about this has been in terms of 'values'. The philosopher Charles Taylor has linked morality intimately to identity. In his work *Sources of the Self*, he argues that selfhood is developed in relation to the values or commitments that an individual holds:

> To know who I am is a species of knowing where I stand. My identity is defined by the commitments and identifications which provide the frame or horizon within which I can try to determine from case to case what is good, or valuable, or what ought to be done, or what I endorse or oppose. In other words, it is the horizon within which I am capable of taking a stand. (Taylor 1989, 27)

Morality involves what he calls strong evaluation, 'discriminations of right and wrong, better or worse, higher or lower, which are not rendered valid by our own desires, inclinations, or choices, but rather stand independent of these and offer standards by which they can be judged' (Taylor 1989, 4). These independent standards are described as a 'framework', a set of qualitative distinctions in relation to which individuals can assess their own actions and desires and locate themselves in moral space.

I follow Taylor in taking morality to be concerned with standards independent of a contingent life. However, transcendence need not be

during Friday prayers or in the course of communal ritual events, or the interpretations put forward by organisations banned by the government such as Hizb ut-Tahrir. The moral reasoning through which an individual develops a Muslim self also occurs within embodied experiences of illness and healing, through successes and failures in the different projects in which a person might engage, or even in the experience of climatic phenomena such as an unusually violent hailstorm.

Experience is itself moral by being located in what I call moral sources. These are not systems of value, codified in sacred texts, expressed in norms of behaviour, or performed in ritual, but are the transcendent locations in relation to which experience is apprehended. A good place to begin a discussion of what I mean by moral sources is Taylor's own exploration of the development of interiority within the Western philosophical tradition. Taylor begins his account of the development of the modern notion of the Western self with the ancient Greek philosophy of Plato, who locates what might be called 'the Good' in the nature of the cosmos as a preexistent, rational order. Knowledge of this order is accessible through the exercise of reason when freed from the influence of bodily desire. To achieve proper understanding through the exercise of pure reason is to become connected to the order within which we exist. For Plato, it is inconceivable for a person who is ruled by reason to be mistaken about the order of reality, or to be other than virtuous, because to attain self-mastery and exercise pure reason is in itself to achieve a higher moral state. The source of morality is thus the nature of the cosmos itself.

In the Christian philosophy of St. Augustine, Plato's rational order of the cosmos becomes the external expression of God's design. God is not only present in the world but is also an inner light, instilling standards and principles by which the individual should be guided. Similar to the ideas of Plato, what stands in the way of correct understanding is a person's involvement in the sensual world of the body. Whereas the source of the moral continues to be the nature of the cosmos, now created by God, the way that this is apprehended has shifted to incorporate an internal, reflexive stance.

For both Plato and St. Augustine, moral truth is something to be *discovered* either 'out there' in the world or through introspection. Taylor identifies a critical shift in the development of interiority with Descartes' disenchantment of the material universe. The world around us no longer expresses any moral meaning, but is governed by amoral, mechanistic laws. Rationality is defined as the disengagement from an embodied involvement in the world to an 'objective' stance that seeks knowledge and understanding of the material world through standards of evidence. Taylor argues that this introduces the basis for the Western concept of interiority. 'If rational control is a matter of mind dominating a disenchanted world of matter, then the sense of the superiority of the good life, and the inspiration to attain it, must come from the agent's sense of his own dignity as a rational being' (Taylor 1989, 152).

Moral sources are thus directly tied to our understanding of the nature of the universe, of the place of humanity within it, and of the relationship between humanity and the Divine. In the Islamic philosophical tradition, a fundamental moral source is, of course, divine revelation. The universe as God's creation is its material expression. At the same time, there are a number of ways through which divine Truth might be apprehended, not all of which are recognised as equally legitimate by all Muslims. In the earliest period after the death of the Prophet, two paths were recognised, the authoritative given of the Qur'an and Sunna, and also the exercise of human reason in the work of interpretation and extrapolation from basic principle (Ar. *ijtihād*) (Rahman 1966, 101–04). A further principle of consensus among scholars (Ar. *ijmā'*) also became established as a means for authorising knowledge. In the centuries following the death of the Prophet, the Sunna, or the Prophet's exemplary practice, came to be known and transmitted not by a living tradition but by an established body of recorded testimony known as the hadith. By approximately the tenth century, what was and was not true hadith had been finally authenticated through consensus, and the path of independent reasoning, or *ijtihād*, was generally considered closed (Peters 1980, 135; Rahman 1966, 77).[6] The differences in legal thought in the seventh and eighth centuries that had resulted from the free interpretation of the Qur'an in the light of local customary law coalesced into the four legal schools (Ar. *madhhab*) that survive to the contemporary era, of which the Hanafi is dominant in Central Asia. Muslims were henceforth expected to understand the *sharīʿa*, the 'highway of good life', as Fazlur Rahman has described it (Rahman 1966, 100), through the standardised interpretations of one of these schools. Even after consensus was reached, however, some individuals continued to claim the status of independent interpreter (Ar. *mujtahid*), and the practice of *ijtihād* is central to the movements of reform that emerged from the nineteenth century. These, to various degrees, have emphasised the duty of all believers to exercise reason in understanding the Qur'an directly rather than blindly following the interpretations of medieval scholars (Peters 1980).

For both followers of the established legal interpretive schools and for modern reformists, the moral source is God's truth as revealed in the Qur'an and Sunna and materialised in the universe. For some Muslims, this is interpreted to mean that the Qur'an literally encompasses all knowledge, including the scientific knowledge of the empirical world. It was not uncommon during my research in Uzbekistan for individuals to point out how relatively recent scientific and medical discoveries are prefigured in the Qur'an. This view has been developed by the influential contemporary Turkish Islamic scholar and educationalist Fethullah Gülen. Taking inspiration from Sufi philosophy, he argues that the universe is the realm in which God's Names are manifest (Bakar 2005). The Qur'an, issuing from Divine will, is the counterpart of the universe in textual form. There can therefore be no contradiction between empirically derived scientific knowledge and the revealed Truth of the Qur'an. However, while the Truth of the Qur'an is absolute and unchanging, the discoveries of science are relative, transient, and subject to later correction, and the methodology of modern science is not capable of penetrating to the essential, absolute Truth. The Qur'an contains knowledge of the empirically observable world in the form of suggestions or summaries, sometimes only vaguely hinted at. Gülen holds that Qur'anic text is open to interpretation on a number of levels, and what can be derived from it depends upon the knowledge and level of enlightenment of the reader. One of the functions of science, he argues, is to help Muslims to see the Truth contained in the Qur'an and to come closer to God.

Other contemporary Muslim thinkers have taken a less literalist approach to the unity of nature and revelation. Tariq Ramadan, for instance, has sought this unity in the ethical spirit through which scientific knowledge should be pursued, the methodology of which is in itself morally neutral (Ramadan 2004, 55–61). Similarly, Fazlur Rahman has advocated the use of human reason in understanding the essential spirit of the revelation. He argues that the Qur'an is a divine response, through the Prophet's mind, to the moral and social situation of Arabia at a particular historical moment. Qur'anic theology and moral and legal teaching gradually unfolded in that political arena in response to concrete problems. It is possible to deduce general principles by undertaking a historical study of the period of the revelation and by understanding the meaning of the Qur'an as a whole as well as in terms of the tenets that constitute responses to specific situations. From this, general principles can be abstracted. Taken as a whole in this way, there are no 'inner contradictions' in the Qur'an. The second movement, as Rahman calls it, is to undertake a social scientific study of our present situation to understand how the essential message of the Qur'an can be embodied in the present, perhaps changing the present as needed. The task is one of social science and ethical engineering. For Rahman, *ijtihād* is 'the effort to understand the meaning of a relevant text or precedent in the past, containing a rule, and to alter that rule by extending or restricting or otherwise modifying it in such a manner that a new situation can be subsumed under it by a new solution' (Rahman 1982, 8).

Thus, the nature of the divinely created universe, revealed through the Qur'an and Sunna as well as by direct experience and observation of the world around us, is a moral source in relation to which individuals might locate themselves as Muslim. It is not the only source, however, and in Uzbekistan, another, perhaps equally significant source is the sociality within which an individual is immersed. Opportunities for formal study of the Qur'an and its commentaries have become increasingly available in Uzbekistan since independence with the establishment of a number of state-sanctioned madrasas throughout the country. However, most individuals who identify themselves as Muslim do not have any significant religious learning and do not engage with the sacred texts directly. What textually derived knowledge they have might be acquired during the Friday sermon at the mosque (if they are men), in the course of household or communal ritual events at which individuals locally or regionally recognised for their religious learning might be invited to participate or even deliver a sermon, or from everyday interactions within their social networks. They develop Muslim selves in part through celebrating marriages and other life-cycle events within their own households and attending those of their neighbours, and in participating fully within the networks of obligation and reciprocity, in the flow of sociality within their community.

The idea that an individual is obligated to develop a personal and direct understanding of God's will through individual study of the sacred texts is a relatively recent one that has been promoted by reformist movements. Historically in Central Asia and elsewhere in the Muslim world, engagement with Islam is not confined to personal, interior 'belief' but is enacted within the flow of social relations with human and non-human others. The historian Adeeb Khalid has described how, in pre-Soviet Central Asia, education in a lower religious school or madrasa was not only about the transmission of textual knowledge, but also involved the cultivation of appropriate habits of comportment and behaviour through regimes of discipline that students would take with them into the wider social world. The transmission of knowledge was not confined to these specialised institutions but was diffused throughout society, for example, in the master-apprentice relationship within the crafts guilds (Khalid 1998, 19–40). A moral or Muslim sensibility is not solely interior and personal, cultivated through individual study and effort, but is produced and expressed in action and in relations with others.

The social, intersubjective nature of Muslim practice has been explored by a number of anthropologists (Bowen 1993a, 229–50; Tapper & Tapper 1987; Tett 1995), including Lambek, who has commented that Islamic knowledge is acquired and transmitted through the embodied performance of day-to-day living:

> Islam is incorporated not only in the posture of prayers and patterns of ritual intonation, but in the intimacies of daily life. A Muslim follows codes of politeness, food, dress, posture, and cleanliness, along daily, weekly, monthly, and annual rhythms. . . . Not only do Muslims perform ablutions in a highly formalised sequence before each period of prayer, but they eat, urinate, expostulate and make love in an Islamic manner. Islamic knowledge is etched into the forms of spontaneous and regular behaviour. (Lambek 1993, 152)

Whereas a common interpretation by social scientists studying Muslim societies is that everyday interaction is given moral significance through being placed within an Islamic frame, I suggest that it is equally the case that an individual's development of a Muslim self derives moral force through participation within the flow of sociality within which he or she is immersed. This sociality is not in itself 'Islamic', but can be apprehended within diverse conceptions of moral selfhood that may or may not be Muslim.

The final moral source I want to discuss is direct experience of the Divine. In Uzbekistan, dreams and visions in which spirit beings are encountered are an important means through which many individuals develop an understanding of what it means to be a Muslim. The idea that knowledge might be obtained through unmediated contact with the

Divine is well established in the Islamic philosophical tradition, particularly as this has been developed within Sufism. The medieval mystic philosopher Ibn al-ʻArabī (d. 1240), whose ideas have been highly influential in the development of Sufi thought, developed the idea of the unity of God and the cosmos. God is the sole Being, while the universe and the plural phenomena that it contains are manifestations of Being. This unitary Being can be 'found' through pure experience (Rizvi 2005). Ibn al-ʻArabī developed a specific idea of multiple levels of reality based on a concept of the universe as invested, like humans, with the facilities of sense-perception, imagination, and rational thought. The universe is a 'macro-anthropos', while a human being is a 'micro-anthropos'. Human sense perception represents the material world, whereas the human intellect mirrors the intelligible world. The realm of human creative imagination reflects what he called the 'realm of similitudes'. This refers to the dreams and mystic experiences in which humans encounter objects that are neither purely spiritual nor material, but take the quasi-material forms of angels and other visions (Rahman 1966, 123–7). Influenced by the ideas of ancient Greece, Ibn al-ʻArabī viewed philosophy not merely as an intellectual exercise, but also as transformative practice in which, through spiritual practices, an individual comes closer to God. A true understanding of the unity of Being could not be attained through purely rational thought, but had to be approached through inner experience. He considered himself to be a 'realised self' who had become open to divine revelation directly through his soul (Rizvi 2005). The idea of a hierarchy of spiritual enlightenment is well established within Sufi thinking.[7]

Central Asia has a rich historical heritage of Sufism, and a number of important Sufi orders originated in the region, including the Naqshbandi and Yasawi. However, the active practice of Sufism was suppressed during the decades of Soviet rule and continues to be severely restricted by the postindependence government despite the incorporation of prominent figures in Central Asian Sufism in its state-building discourses. A few self-declared Sufi circles continue to exist (Louw 2007, 104–28). In addition, some of the individuals I encountered during my fieldwork, although they did not claim a formal connection with Sufism or practice Sufi spiritual exercises, objectified their own mystical experience in terms that seemed to draw at least some inspiration from Sufi thinking (Chapters 5 and 6). However, in the majority of cases, direct experience of the Divine occurs with no reference to Sufi cosmology or spiritual practice, of which most people, in any case, have little or no knowledge. It occurs in the course of everyday living, in visits to the tombs of Muslim 'saints' in search of their intervention in overcoming illness or material difficulties, during dreams and visions, and in the experience of illness and healing.

This is not to say that the Sufi tradition of thought and practice is irrelevant. On the contrary, it seems to have contributed, for example, to the development of patterns for experience through which individuals become healers in a relationship with spirit beings. Bruce Privratsky has argued that the Sufi spiritual chains of transmission from master to follower evolved in Central Asia into an hereditary lineage. An idea that grace was developed through spiritual exercise and work upon the self under the guidance of an enlightened master became a quality some claimed to embody through descent from saintly ancestors (Privratsky 2001, 156–8; 2004). Among those who heal with the aid of spirits in Uzbekistan, a common element in realising this ability is a dream encounter with an ancestor who was particularly pious or had been a healer, or with saintly figures such as the grandsons of the Prophet. This typically occurs under the guidance of an established healer who identifies the initiate as someone who has his or her own spirits. The understanding of dreams and visions as direct encounters with the Divine is, moreover, not confined to the Sufi tradition but is well established in Qur'anic sources and the tradition of the Prophet (Hoffman 1997). However, I do not intend to trace the distinct cultural origins of local practices of healing, to identify which elements can be attributed to Sufi practices or cosmological ideas and which to other Islamic or pre-Islamic sources. I am more interested in how local cultural models afford possibilities for particular qualities of

Because the dispute was tied to the state discourse of politically motivated Islamic extremism, I refrained from actively exploring the details of these events with those directly involved.

The sensitivity towards certain dimensions of the practice of Islam that I was forced to adopt no doubt directed my research towards 'safe' areas, such as the practice of healing with the aid of spirits or ritual activity that is clearly rooted in the local practice of Islam, such as evening feasts to break the fast during the month of Ramadan, commemorations of the birth of the Prophet, or Qur'an recitations that accrue religious merit for the deceased. In addition, a large part of my research focused on the institution of the *mahalla*, a territorially defined residential subdistrict that has been formalised as an organ of self-government, and its involvement within religious practice.

However, this does not mean that I have provided an unduly incomplete or partial account here. Of course, any account is partial because the anthropologist is always 'situated'. As Renato Rosaldo has observed, the anthropologist occupies a structural location that affords a particular perspective, influenced by such factors as gender, age, and the condition of being an outsider (Rosaldo 1989). Anthropologists in the field are not objective observers who adopt neutral standpoints. They are immersed within social networks, relations of power, and discursive regimes that shape their interactions with others and determine the outcome of their research. However, if this is true for the anthropologist, it is equally true for everyone else. Although I was forced to present myself and my research in a particular light and to steer my inquiries in particular directions, individuals in Uzbekistan live under similar conditions. The focus of this book on experience as a site for moral reasoning, rather than discourse, debate, and contestation, is not an accident or a personal preference on my part. This is how Muslims in Uzbekistan themselves come to understandings of moral selfhood.

ONE

Islam and Sociality in Pakhtabad and Samarkand

Islam hardly featured in my first research project in Uzbekistan between 1998 and 2000 in the city of Andijan in the Fergana Valley and the nearby village of Pakhtabad. At that time, I was not looking specifically at Islam but was interested in the state as it is experienced on a daily basis. I focused my attention on the activities of small-scale entrepreneurs, practices of corruption, household income–generating strategies, and networks of exchange as sites in which the state becomes locally manifested. Even so, looking back on that research, I am surprised by how little attention I devoted to Islam in developing my understanding of the individual, the household, the community, and the state in Uzbekistan.

I was aware while conducting that research that almost all of the people I was working with considered themselves Muslim except, of course, the Russian, Korean, or other non–Central Asian minority populations who mainly resided in the city of Andijan. Life-cycle events for the Central Asian population, such as marriages and funerals, invariably incorporated Islamic rituals, and particularly in the village of Pakhtabad, many of the other occasions of feasting that link households within wider kinship and neighbourhood relations take place within an Islamic frame, such as *iftor* meals to break the fast during the month of Ramadan. In addition, Islamic references are present in much of day-to-day interactions. At the beginning of a meal, people will often say *bismilloh* (in the name of God) and finish with *omin*, accompanied by a gesture of bringing both hands together over the face in a downward motion. Moral judgements were occasionally made with reference to Islam, such as when Tohirjon, one of my hosts in Pakhtabad, complained that in recent years, because of declining incomes, people were not able to live 'fully according to Islam' because they were not able to conduct wedding and other feasts on a large-enough scale by cooking the right amount of food and inviting everyone who should be invited. However, on that first visit, Islam seemed to me more an aspect of local cultural practice than a reflective, spiritual commitment on the part of an individual Muslim or an enactment of a relationship with God. Identifiably Islamic practice seemed to operate no differently than other markers of community belonging, such as offering tea to a guest in a half-filled bowl in an 'Uzbek' manner rather than serving full 'Russian' cups.

The muted presence of Islam in public spaces at the time of my initial fieldwork contributed to this impression. Immediately after independence, a number of mosques were built in the village as they were throughout the country. The oldest one, which served as the Friday mosque where people from throughout the village attended the congregational Friday noontime prayer, had already been reopened in the late 1980s, when more religious freedoms were permitted under Gorbachev, after having been used as a warehouse for most of the Soviet period. Construction on a large new mosque was begun on an adjoining site. The mullah of a *mahalla* (residential neighbourhood) where I lived in Pakhtabad recounted how, in the first years after independence, up to 500 men would attend the Friday midday prayers at this mosque. However, by the time I arrived in the village, all of the mosques had been closed by the state authorities in response to the activities of Islamic opposition groups. As the government increasingly identified Islamist groups as a significant political threat, expressions of Islam outside its control, or those it considered nontraditional, became suspect and were ruthlessly suppressed. An atmosphere of fear was associated with anything that could be interpreted as 'political' and draw the attention of the state security organs, and during my field research I had scrupulously avoided any appearance of interest in such issues. This included Islam as anything but an instance of Central Asian cultural practice. Thus, little space was, and continues to be, allowed for individuals in Uzbekistan openly to discuss and engage with Islam outside the context of what is perceived as clearly 'traditional' practice.

What Lara Deeb, speaking about Shi'i Muslims in Lebanon, has called 'public piety' (Deeb 2006) is muted in Uzbekistan. Deeb describes public piety as the tangible expression of an individual's commitment to, and embodiment of, an 'authenticated Islam' – the sincere and sustained effort on the part of an individual Muslim to come to a correct interpretation of the sacred texts and to enact them in practice. These Lebanese Shi'i Muslims criticise what they see as the nonreflexive stance of 'traditional' Muslims, for whom the practice of Islam is little more than cultural practice with little real effort at true understanding. Public piety indexes correct knowledge, the work of self-improvement, and participation in public life for the betterment of the community. It includes charity work, such as distributing food to the poor or collecting donations for Hizbullah fighters. It is enacted in regular prayer and fasting, adopting distinct forms of veiling, the topics of conversation in which a person chooses to engage, an individual's recourse to the judgements of religious scholars on social issues, forms of greeting, or even the decision of whether to shake a stranger's hand.

In Uzbekistan, not only would public demonstrations of 'excessive' piety risk attracting the unwelcome attentions of the state security apparatuses, but Muslim reformist movements in general also have had limited presence. Such reformist trends first developed in Muslim societies in the nineteenth century in response to European colonial domination. They embraced scientific progress and sought to reestablish a vigorous Muslim society by fashioning Muslims as critical subjects capable of a direct interpretation of the sacred texts. In Central Asia, this took the form of the Jadid movement (Khalid 1998). Dale Eickelman and James

Piscatori have identified the late 1970s and 1980s as a significant watershed in the development of what they have termed the 'objectification of a Muslim consciousness' (Eickelman & Piscatori 1996). The development of mass communications technology enabled the global flow of ideas and theological trends. Interpretation of the sacred texts was no longer the monopoly of a small class of trained experts but was popularised through cheaply available print, audio, and video publications. Islam came to be understood as an abstract system of ideas distinct from other religious systems and disembedded from local practices of interaction and community belonging. Muslims in a particular locality also became aware of other traditions and interpretations within Islam itself. Soviet policies on religion inhibited this process in Central Asia, as Muslims were cut off from formal education in the sacred texts and contact with Muslims outside the Soviet Union. The repressive policies of the post-Soviet government in Uzbekistan have had a similar effect in inhibiting the free expression and circulation of new practices and ideas.

During my fieldwork from 1998 to 2000, it was unusual to find people who, like the entrepreneur in the city of Andijan referred to in the introduction, self-consciously sought to order their lives along Islamic principles. At weddings and other festive occasions, it was common for the hosts to serve alcohol, normally vodka. If they did not, the reason was more often based on a lack of finances than a desire to follow the precepts of Islam. It was a matter of particular note when I came across someone who refused to drink alcohol or eat pork sausages on Islamic grounds, prayed regularly, or when, very rarely, a student wearing an Islamic-style headscarf appeared at the university where I worked for part of my fieldwork. The lack of knowledge about Islam and the failure to adhere to even the most basic ritual prescriptions by most of the self-ascribed Muslim population has led some social scientists and historians to conclude that Islam in Uzbekistan should be understood in cultural rather than religious terms, as an element of secular national identity (Khalid 2003; Ro'i 1995; Shahrani 1995). This was certainly my own implicit understanding when I subsumed the practice of Islamic ritual into norms and patterns of community participation in my early research.

The absence of a public and tangible practice of Islam was not the only reason for the omission of Islam from my initial research. My own preconceptions about what constitutes religious practice also played a part. Nonreflexively, I had carried into my fieldwork an idea of religion as a discrete sphere of human endeavour that concerns an attitude towards the sacred, or at least the supernatural. The problem was not that my implicit understanding of religion was imperfect or inaccurate or that I had not worked out a sufficiently refined definition of religion. Rather, the problem was that I held a notion of religion at all, which created in my mind an opposition between sacred and mundane spheres. This led me to interpret patterns and norms of interaction and notions of moral community in terms of 'culture' in which Islam, as a religion rather than a cultural practice, had little place. Because I did not encounter specifically Islamic discourses or observe many occasions when individuals reflected on their life circumstances or on events occurring around them with reference to Islam, I perceived Islam as subsumed within what were essentially nonreligious, socially constituted ideals of moral community.

For my second research project between summer 2003 and autumn 2004, on which this book is largely based, I was specifically interested in Islam. I was therefore from the start more open to appreciating the different ways and contexts in which individuals come to an understanding of Islam and what it means to be a Muslim, and I actively sought them out. I returned to the village of Pakhtabad and also conducted fieldwork in the city of Samarkand. At first, I paid particular attention to obviously Islamic practice, such as fulfilment of the scripturally founded obligations and prescriptions, or participation in distinctly Islamic rituals such as the *mavlud*, the commemoration of the birth of the Prophet. As my research progressed, however, I increasingly appreciated how nontextually founded practices, such as healing with spirits, an activity frequently condemned by imams as contrary to correct Islamic practice, helps both healers and their patients come to an understanding of what it means to be a Muslim.

Through my altered perspective, Pakhtabad seemed a different place. I came to know a number of individuals in both the village and Samarkand who were self-consciously pursuing Muslim lives, observing ritual prescriptions such as praying five times a day and abstaining from alcohol and pork, studying the sacred texts, and, importantly, willing to talk openly about all of this. During my previous research, I had visited many of the households in the *mahalla* where I lived in Pakhtabad but had been interested in matters such as household composition, agricultural production and income-generating activities, and the patterns of exchange between households. I was completely unaware that some of my neighbours were healers who worked with spirits, including, in a small way, the elderly mother of Tohirjon, my host during both stays in the village. During my first visit, when I arrived at the house after staying for a few days in Andijan, she sometimes told me that she knew I was arriving that day – that she had 'seen' it. I paid little attention, unaware that the source of her prescience was her 'people', the spirits who caused her illness and also enabled her to heal.

During my second period of field research, it was permitted for mosques to function and the call to prayer to be broadcast. In the village of Pakhtabad, in addition to the Friday congregational mosque, each *mahalla* also had its own unregistered mosque that was now in use. When I heard the distant call over a loudspeaker for the first time one evening in Pakhtabad, it took a while for me to realise what it was, as I was so unused to hearing it in Uzbekistan. This made a great difference in my research, particularly in Samarkand, where mosques became an important site for contacting imams and, to a limited extent, congregations of regular prayer goers. For reasons that will become clearer throughout this book, it was never easy to develop contacts with mosque goers – strangers who did not know my background – because of the insecurity associated with the practice of Islam in Uzbekistan.

In his comprehensive study of Islam in the Soviet Union after World War II, Yaacov Ro'i has shown how public participation in Islamic ritual, such as attendance at mosques, fluctuated in response to state campaigns against religious expression or periods of relative tolerance (Ro'i 2000). This pattern has continued since independence, and the period of my second research was one of relative easing of restrictions, at least to the extent that mosques were allowed to open and the call to prayer was permitted to be broadcast. That villagers, the local police, and government officials in Pakhtabad already knew me was also important. I was returning to a place where I had already developed enduring social relationships and where my past research was known, and this likely made it easier for me to broach potentially sensitive topics. My experience in rural districts outside Samarkand, where I had no personal history or contacts, was very different. There I was unsuccessful in attempts to develop a rural research site to complement my work in the city. The local police viewed me with suspicion, and even when they granted me permission to remain in the area, most people I encountered were unwilling to discuss anything related to Islam or any other potentially sensitive subject.

Apart from mosque attendance, it seemed to me that some of the public piety Deeb describes was also a little more in evidence in 2003–04, although still to a limited extent. Some of the young men I came to know who regularly attended a mosque near where I lived in Samarkand wore Muslim-style plain, circular, black velvet skullcaps rather than the Uzbek-style *do'ppi*, which is square in shape, stiff, and black with white embroidered patterns. It was also more common to see men with long beards that indexed their commitment to Islam. However, this 'freedom' is tightly circumscribed. Individuals are safe as long as their practice falls within what is accepted as Central Asian tradition, or else they risk being labelled as extremists. The young men who wore self-consciously Islamic headgear were pushing against dangerous boundaries.

Most significantly, I came to see that religion is an inadequate framework for understanding Islam as it is lived. With a concept of religion as a countable noun, Islam is one religion among others, such as Christianity or Hinduism. It is an object distinct from other religions in terms of particular texts, beliefs, rituals, practices, and histories. Any practice, idea, or discourse is Islamic to the extent that it contains or refers to these. However, many of the actual practices of Muslims often are not, or are only very loosely, founded on a universally recognised Islamic core of knowledge and practice. In Uzbekistan, many of the practices and experiences through which individuals come to an understanding of Muslim selfhood, such as encounters with spirit agents, are considered by other Muslims, as well as by some social scientists and historians who study ritual practice in Central Asia, as pre-Islamic survivals or shamanic practices (Basilov 1992; Snezarev 2003). This has given rise to discussions among anthropologists of Islam about how to encompass local diversity within a conception of Islam as a single category of study. The pragmatic approach has been to include anything a self-ascribed Muslim considers to be Islamic. Rather than defining what is or is not genuinely Islamic, the social scientist studies the understandings and debates of Muslims themselves. However, it then becomes difficult to sustain the idea that Islam, as it is enacted in the lived practice of Muslims, constitutes a distinct and coherent religion, and its boundaries become impossible to fix.

Religion as an uncountable noun, meaning the concept of 'the religious' that refers to a specific dimension of human endeavour and experience, is equally not helpful. As I have already argued, it sets up distinctions between sacred and mundane spheres. Culture is constituted as a category separate from religion, but the material world is also understood as separate. Distinctions of this sort do not reflect how individuals come to an understanding of Muslim selfhood through participation within their households and communities in ways that are not identifiably Islamic from such an objective perspective or through experience of natural phenomena or illness. By understanding Islam in terms of morality rather than religion, the question is not whether practices or processes of reasoning are objectively Islamic or can be understood as concerned with the sacred, but whether they contribute to the development of a moral self that is understood by the individual as a Muslim self.

This chapter describes the practices of sociality in Pakhtabad and Samarkand. Although they may not qualify for inclusion into a concept of Islam as a religion or as distinctively religious practice, they nevertheless contribute to the development of Muslim selves. I also give an overview of how Islam is lived within everyday sociality. I use the term 'sociality' to refer to the material as well as affective interchange among members of a community. It is intended to encompass the idea that what we might think of as the social – the mutually shared norms and expectations, the ideals of moral personhood and community, the production and reproduction of persons – takes place through the flow of daily interaction. Sociality is opposed to the notion of society seen as a thing abstracted from the individuals who inhabit it.[1]

Muslimness

During both of my stays in Pakhtabad, I lived mostly with the family of Tohirjon, an English teacher in one of the schools in the village who became both a vital facilitator for my research in Pakhtabad and an invaluable companion with whom I could reflect on my experiences. Tohirjon, who is head of his household, was in his late thirties at the time of my second period of research in 2004. He lives with his mother, wife, and four daughters and has about a quarter of a hectare of land in a number of small plots. His teaching salary (about U.S.$20 a month) is only a small part of his household income, which, as is typical in Pakhtabad, is generated through a number of different activities. In his case, this is private English tuition to help students pass university entrance exams, agricultural production on his plots of land, and rearing one or two bull calves at any one time for sale. During my research in 2000, I conducted a survey of the incomes of twenty households in the village. This was not a random sample but was targeted at specific households to give an idea of the range of income levels and occupations. In this survey, combined household monthly incomes, including official salaries, pensions, and other transfer payments from the state as well as income from agricultural activity, other businesses, and trade, ranged from the equivalent of U.S.$26 to U.S.$170.

A dispute that arose during my first period of research in 2000 provides an idea of how Muslim selves are developed and enacted within ongoing sociality. One of our neighbouring households is one of the wealthiest in the village, operating the largest private livestock farm with several hundred head of cattle and 120 hectares of land. In the agricultural reforms that took place after independence, much of the collective farm's land was broken up into privately operated farms, although these are still subject to state production plans for wheat and sometimes cotton.[2] This family has been the main beneficiary of the process in the village. They had bought the cattle from the collective farm, and the land was allocated on the basis of a long-term lease along with the cattle. The retired grandfather in this household had been the chief veterinarian in the collective farm during the Soviet period, and by the time of independence he had retired. One of his three sons manages the cattle and land they had acquired. Soon after independence, the grandfather made the hajj pilgrimage to Mecca, which became more feasible after independence, especially in the 1990s, when it was cheaper. Since then, he has been attempting to play an active and leading role in the social life of his *mahalla*, but feelings of other residents towards him are ambivalent.

The dispute was over how to organise the surfacing of a road running through our *mahalla*. Previously, this sort of work would have been the responsibility of the local government or the collective farm, but now neither has the resources. The retired vet had taken the initiative himself, using his extensive contacts to secure cheap supplies of gravel and asphalt and persuading the collective farm to supply tractor support.

He wanted money that had been collected from *mahalla* residents for the renovation of the *mahalla* mosque, a sum equivalent to about U.S.$100 at the time, to be used for this, because the mosque, along with all the others in the village, was closed down by the state authorities in response to concerns about the threat posed by Islamic political groups. The leader of the *mahalla*, known as the *oqsoqol* (literally, 'whitebeard') refused to release the money. In the end, the vet organised a collection from households located along the road. Tohirjon told me that the *oqsoqol* and the retired vet did not get on. It would normally have been the *oqsoqol*'s role to organise such a project, and I was told that he criticised the vet for taking too much upon himself and not consulting other residents. The vet, for his part, criticised the *oqsoqol* for being too slow in taking the initiative. Some of the *mahalla* residents with whom I talked about this affair criticised the vet for only lately, since his retirement and pilgrimage, becoming interested in contributing to *mahalla* projects. Some downplayed his efforts, saying it was not his own money he was using on the road and that it was easy for him to organise tractors through his son. They remembered that before his retirement, he had only looked out for his own interests and had not participated in village life.

Tohirjon himself expressed a similarly ambivalent attitude about some of the other residents of our *mahalla* who had held prominent positions within the collective farm in the Soviet period but who were now retired. He would sometimes complain about the routine practices of corruption, both in the present and during the Soviet period, of appropriating resources he felt should be used for the benefit of all.

In our society people work in different posts. They might benefit from their position, and when they do this they harm other people in pursuit of their own benefit. They abuse their positions, and even though this might not be discovered, God will punish them. In the past managers in the collective farm in the Soviet period, including the chairman, the accountant, the brigadiers in charge of *qora ekin*,[3] the manager of the vineyards, the livestock section manager. . . . From all these sections, the collective farm didn't get

> any profit, they all made a loss. But these people made use of their position to hide the profits. They made it look as if there was a loss and the money all went into their own pockets. Almost all of these people have died [prematurely].... God punished them.

On one occasion he pointed out two of his retired neighbours who suffered from a skin condition that causes white patches to develop from a loss of pigmentation. One had been the leader of a construction brigade and another had been in charge of grape production, and both had appropriated for their own use produce and materials entrusted to them. This skin condition marked them as being punished by God for past misconduct, for which they were ashamed, he said. He interpreted the recent contribution of both men to projects of communal benefit as attempts to atone for their past misdeeds. The former construction brigadier had, for example, erected, free of charge, a shelter in a graveyard in the village with material provided by the *mahalla*. By contrast, Tohirjon regarded much more positively another wealthy resident of the village, a successful businessmen who owns a lorry and trades agricultural and consumer goods between Uzbekistan and Russia. Although he is considered *oros*, meaning that he counts every penny in his business relations, he is generally respected in the village for his constant readiness to support community projects with financial contributions.

In previous publications, I have described what I termed 'spheres of communal participation' (Rasanayagam 2002a, 2002b). With this somewhat cumbersome phrase, I sought to describe a social ethic, an ideal of interaction and participation within a moral community. It is enacted in an ideal of household relations in which the labour, production, and the monetary income of individual members are treated as a common resource and ordered according to needs and priorities identified by the household head. In virilocal marriage, in which the bride comes to reside in her husband's home, a single compound at the peak of the domestic cycle might comprise a husband and wife with their unmarried daughters and sons, their married sons with their wives (*kelin*), and, perhaps, surviving parents of the father. In Pakhtabad the expectation is that parents are responsible for eventually settling their married sons in independent households of their own. This typically means initially building an extension of one or two rooms to the existing house and ideally procuring a land plot from the collective farm for building a new compound, or buying an existing one. However, even after a couple leaves with their children to reside in a separate location, the main house (*katta eshik* – literally, 'main door') might continue to maintain control over their labour, land, and incomes to finance the marriages and settlement of the remaining sons and daughters. In this way, households can extend in space to take the form of networks or satellites living as *bir kassa, bir qozon* (one budget, one cooking cauldron). Married sons become independent only when the main house no longer depends on them to fulfil its obligations, while the youngest son and his wife are expected to stay with the parents, looking after them into old age and inheriting the main family compound.[4]

In practice, this pattern is not universally followed, but at its core is an ideal of interaction within a moral community that is invoked in diverse contexts. Individuals are enmeshed within webs of exchange and mutual support in a multitude of more or less institutionalised situations beyond the household. The practice of *hashar* is one such instance. This is the contribution of labour to community projects or the production efforts of a household without financial reward. Who takes part in *hashar* depends on the project. The road surfacing project is an instance of *hashar*, and in this case only those households along the road were involved, incorporating households from neighbouring *mahalla* though which the road ran as well as the collective farm that supplied tractors for transporting materials. An entire *mahalla* as a unit might contribute to building a mosque (in Pakhtabad, each *mahalla* is associated with a mosque), but the collective farm and local government are also involved, as they allocate the land. In the city of Samarkand, a *mahalla* committee in the old city organised the renovation of the mosque in the *mahalla* centre, where its offices were located, using labour from residents and materials partly supplied by the city government. *Hashar* can also be employed by individual households for agricultural work. In this case, those who take part are typically in close and regular social and exchange relations with the organiser. Contributions to *hashar* organised by individuals and households are not immediately calculated but form part of the general flow of goods, services, and support among those involved. In the case of projects of communal benefit, participation is not expected to be on equal terms, but an individual or household contributes labour, materials, or money depending on their abilities, with the wealthier expected to contribute more in financial terms.

Contributions to communal projects, including the greater contributions of the wealthy, are thought of in terms of *savob*, merit from God, and this is so if the object is building a mosque or repairing an electricity transformer, neglected by the local government because of lack of resources. However, it is not only participation in discrete projects of this sort that can be thought of as a meritorious act (*ehson*). Neighbours and kin in Pakhtabad routinely exchange foodstuffs, the produce of each other's household plots, labour, and services without immediate calculation or reciprocation.[5] In the case of close kin, this may not even be considered an exchange – for example, when villagers gather fruit or vegetables from the plots of close relatives. During my second period of research in 2004, Tohirjon planted carrots on part of his agricultural land. The harvest was good and he distributed some of it to about ten households in his immediate vicinity, including to the wealthy cattle farming household. He described it as *ushr*, the Islamic obligation to donate one tenth of agricultural produce as assistance for the poor, as *ehson* and *musulmonchilik* (Muslimness). His harvest of tomatoes, on the other hand, had been poor, and he expected to be able to obtain any extra he needed from his neighbours.

I found it interesting that on this occasion, he chose to use Islamic references to describe his actions, as this was not typical for him. Only four days before, we had been discussing the topic of *ushr* in his home with Qori-aka, a villager known for his knowledge of the Qur'an. A *qori* is a person who has memorised at least part of the Qur'an and recites it at ritual occasions. Tohirjon's understanding of what it means to be a Muslim and live in a Muslim community seemed to be developing alongside my own research, which he played an important role in facilitating. When I commented that I had noticed some older villagers using the term *masjid qaum* (mosque community) to refer to the *mahalla*, he, too, started to use it on occasion.

In addition to instances of *hashar* directed at a particular project or the ongoing, diffuse exchanges of goods, services, and labour that take place day to day, sociality is also enacted in more institutionalised settings. Rotating feasting circles are a common forum for exchange and sociality. An instance of this is the *gap*, an occasion when a group of work colleagues, relatives, or classmates from university or school regularly meet over a meal, taking turns as host or gathering in a restaurant. They are usually single-sex gatherings but may be mixed, especially if they consist of work colleagues or ex-classmates from the university. In some groups, money may be collected from participants and given to the host. This may be just enough to pay for the food or may provide a little extra for the host, in which case the *gap* also serves as a form of rotating credit group; this is particularly true for women's *gap*.[6] Although capital may be raised in this way, the *gap* is primarily an occasion of communal consumption and sociability.

Rotating feasting can also provide a template for explicitly Islamic ritual. My field research in Pakhtabad in 2004 coincided with the four lunar months when the *mavlud*, the celebration of the birth of the Prophet, is held.[7] A *mavlud* typically involves a feast, and men and women attend separately. At men's *mavlud*, specialist chanters (*qori*) will recite the Qur'an, while at women's *mavlud* it is more common for female specialists, known as *otincha* in Pakhtabad and *bibikhalfa* in Samarkand, to recite poetry in praise of the Prophet. In the *mahalla* where I resided

FIGURE 1. A women's *mavlud* in Pakhtabad

in the village of Pakhtabad, about thirty women formed a group who took turns hosting a *mavlud* each week during the four months of the season. A significant aspect of this *mavlud* circle is the extended time spent socialising over the meal. In addition to the food, salt, water, and *issrik*, an aromatic plant burnt for its medicinal properties, were placed at the centre of the *dasturkhon*, the cloth on which the food is placed and around which the participants sit. The idea was that the power of the recited verses is absorbed by the food and other objects on the *dasturkhon*, bestowing blessing and healing properties upon them, which are conferred to those who consume them. At the end of the *mavlud*, all of the participants took sips of the water. The *issrik* and leftover food was wrapped with pieces of cloth into small bundles, which the women took home to their families.

The *mavlud* gatherings of this circle also incorporated a *zikr*, a prolonged chanting of the profession of faith and the name of God. This was dedicated to the deceased relatives of those present and was intended to compensate for their lapses in ritual observance during life. A common belief in Pakhtabad is that a Muslim is obligated to utter the profession of faith a certain number of times during his or her lifetime (the mullah of my *mahalla* stated that the number is 72,000). Others in the community are expected to pay the debt for the number the deceased failed to complete. At the women's *mavlud* in my *mahalla*, the women counted out small stones during the *zikr* that later would be placed on the graves of relatives. These stones absorbed the chanted words of praise and remembrance of God and transferred them to the deceased.

This interpretation of events is not shared by everyone in the village or perhaps even by all who participate in the same ritual event. Imams and others with a scriptural knowledge of Islam, who criticise many local practices, including the idea that one person can make up for the sins and omissions of another, routinely participate in *mavlud* celebrations and other ritual gatherings where they might recite verses from the Qur'an. The same is true for the imams who say prayers for visitors at the tombs of prominent *avliyo* (those thought to have been particularly close to God). They might acknowledge that God hears the prayers of Muslims and might grant them but do not share the perceptions of other participants that they are making up for the sins and omissions of the deceased, that appeals can be made to *avliyo* directly, or that the water collected from the shrines or the tea and other objects on the *dasturkhon* have any inherent healing power. Healing comes from God alone. However, this does not prevent their participation within the common sociality enacted on these ritual occasions.

What I am trying to convey with this account is that it makes little sense to treat Islam as a distinct category of 'religion' and to separate it from a category of cultural practice or social relations. Uttering Islamic phrases such as *bismilloh* (in the name of God) before a meal, greeting with the formula *salomalaykum* (peace be upon you), or considering contributions to communal projects as *savob* do not just provide an Islamic frame and moral legitimacy to 'mundane' social interaction. This sort of interpretation would view Islam as essentially an object separate from sociality, as something that can be added to sociality to give it a certain quality. Rather, the flow of sociality within which individuals participate becomes Muslim within the individual's development of a moral self. Individuals do not necessarily make distinctions between Islamic and non-Islamic enactments of sociality, or Islamic and non-Islamic elements of a particular occasion. These distinctions are sometimes made, as I will discuss in later chapters (particularly Chapters 4 and 5) when I describe how some criticise much of the practice of Central Asian Muslims as un-Islamic, originating in local pre-Islamic traditions rather than being founded upon a correct reading of the sacred texts. Separate categories of culture, tradition, and Islam emerge from ongoing debates among Muslims about the nature of 'true' Islam, and interpretations are not shared equally by all. They are less helpful as absolute, analytical distinctions for social scientists seeking to understand how Islam is lived or how Muslims come to an understanding of what it means to be a Muslim.

A discussion of marriage provides a good illustration of this. By state law, a marriage is constituted by a civil registration, but almost all marriages among Muslims in Uzbekistan also incorporate the *nikoh* (Muslim marriage ceremony). The ceremony needs to be presided over by an individual authorised by the Muslim Board of Uzbekistan and is usually the officially appointed imam of the nearest registered mosque. Typically, this will have been preceded at some point by a *fotiha to'y*, a feast to mark the agreement between the two families to the marriage, named after the *fotiha*, the opening sura of the Qur'an, which is recited on this occasion. For most, the state registration is just a formality, but it would be misleading to interpret the 'religious' ritual elements as constituting the real marriage. It would be more accurate to see the actual wedding ceremony as an event within the reproduction of a household both in terms of its immediate members and its place within a larger moral community, and it is participation in this project as a whole that makes an individual a Muslim.

I attended a wedding *to'y* in Pakhtabad in the autumn of 1999 of a relative of the household where I was staying at that time (I was not living with Tohirjon's family). It was for the son of the brother (then deceased) of the head of my host household, who lived in a compound adjacent to ours. Preparations began in earnest on the day before the actual feast, when relatives and neighbours visited the household, most giving small gifts of money to the groom's mother, the head of that household. Benches, tables, pots, bowls, teapots, and other items were brought from the *mahalla* mosque and laid out in readiness. A group of men, mainly from my host household and their friends, cut up onions, carrots, and meat in preparation for cooking the *osh* (a rice pilau) the next day. My host, the groom's uncle, had provided a sheep and rice, and 'our' household also baked much of the *non* bread (flat round loaves baked in a *tandir* oven), some of which was mixed with meat or onions.

On the day of the *to'y*, we arrived at 7:00 A.M., at which time the guests were mainly relatives of the groom's family and some neighbours. A hired cook made the *osh* at about 11.30 A.M., after which a convoy of cars and a lorry full of people set off for the bride's home. There, the actual marriage ceremony (the *nikoh*) took place before an imam, while the groom's party waited in the street outside. After the brief ceremony, the couple emerged, the groom dressed in a suit and the bride in a white Western-style wedding dress, to be greeted by musicians playing large, elongated trumpets (*karnay*). During my field research in the village of Pakhtabad, their call became a familiar part of my mornings in the summer and autumn months. The couple then got into a car, and the whole convoy, amid much hooting of horns, went to a local beauty spot at one of the main irrigation canals, where everyone got out and walked up and down, taking photographs and videos.

FIGURE 2. Musicians at a wedding in Pakhtabad

After this, everyone returned to the groom's house, and the couple was again greeted by the musicians. By about 3:00 P.M., there was a different group of musicians, with amplifiers, traditional and modern instruments, and a singer, at one end of the house plot in front of a large area for dancing surrounded by a rectangle of tables and benches. After arriving at the groom's house, the bride and the female relatives of both families sat inside the house, where the bride's dowry (*sep*) was displayed. The groom sat at the head of the rectangle of tables in the dancing area with his friends and male members of his family. At this point, many more people were present, including those from the groom's *mahalla* and others. Bread, tea, and fruit were laid out on the tables, though much less than had been served earlier in the day. A friend of the groom acted as the master of ceremonies, inviting people to wish the couple well and to dance, and people came forward to give the dancers money. This money was then given to the musicians. The groom was the most forward in giving money, and those in a closer relationship to the dancer gave more. The whole affair ended at about 6:00 P.M.

In addition to the events on the day of a wedding, there may be numerous other feasting occasions connected with marriage, such as the *chaqirdi* or *charlar*, when the groom, his family, and friends are invited to the bride's parents' home. This takes place about three days after the *nikoh* but can be put off for six months or a year. Wedding feasts are not simply household events but are organised, particularly in Pakhtabad and in the older sections of the city of Samarkand, with the close involvement of the *mahalla* leadership. The *mahalla* communally owns tables, chairs, and large cauldrons for use on such occasions. The *oqsoqol* is involved in advising the families on whom to invite and how much food to cook, as well as in coordinating the timing of wedding feasts. In the *mahalla* in which I lived in Pakhtabad, there was a *mahalla* cook who was employed at most feasting events.

Marriage is an event within the ongoing sociality that ties individuals and households within an encompassing community. In 2000, Tohirjon organised an *iftor*, the first meal after sunset to break the fast during Ramadan. He invited the *mahalla oqsoqol*, the mullah, and other older men from the two neighbouring streets, and the reason he gave for organising the meal was to show respect to those attending, to repay the times his deceased father had attended similar gatherings in his old age, and because he had not held a feasting celebration (*to'y*) in the previous five years since his youngest sister's marriage. Households sometimes host feasts for their neighbours in the absence of a recent marriage or circumcision *to'y* as a way of 'paying back' for the celebrations they have attended and to participate in the social life of the *mahalla*. My own research was carried out through this sociality, as I taught English in a school in the village and helped Tohirjon with his private courses. Towards the conclusion of my stay in the village, I organised a *mavlud*, inviting those with whom I had worked most closely as a way of saying thank you, and I donated a carpet to the *mahalla* mosque.

Marriages entail an extended series of feasts, dowries for the bride and gifts to the groom that represent a very substantial expense. Few households are able to cover this from their own resources, and they depend on contributions and financial support from kin and neighbours. I calculated the expenditure on a wedding in 2000 that was described as 'above average' in Pakhtabad. The bride's side spent more than 1,076,000 *sum* (U.S.$ 1,537) on the dowry, furniture, and wedding feast, and the groom's family spent 735,000 *sum* (U.S.$ 1,050) on gifts to the *kelin*'s family, clothes for the groom, and the wedding feast itself. Organising and financing a wedding therefore binds a household within networks of exchange and participation within a community.

A marriage is not a discrete event within the life of a household but needs to be understood within the ongoing life projects of its members. Tohirjon has four daughters, the oldest of whom was ten years old in 2000, but he was already accumulating items for their dowries and was continuously acting upon a long-term income-generating strategy to pay for their marriages. Earlier in the chapter, I discussed how the main household, the *katta eshik*, is responsible for finding spouses for sons and daughters and for settling them in their own households, and how this determines exchange relations and settlement patterns. It is therefore less enlightening to ask what makes a marriage a Muslim one by identifying particular Islamic rituals than to ask how individuals understand themselves to be Muslim through engaging within a project to marry and settle their children and participate fully within their community. This makes Tohirjon's earlier comment quoted at the beginning of this chapter – that villagers were not able to live 'fully according to Islam' – more understandable. He had been referring to the fact that because of declining incomes, many villagers were no longer able to organise wedding feasts in a proper manner, participating in the feasts of others and allowing neighbours and relatives to fully participate in their own. Living according to Islam is not just about fulfilling Islamic ritual commitments but also about fully participating in a sociality that contributes to an understanding of Muslim self and community.

The *Mahalla*

The ideal of moral community is expressed within the *mahalla* both as an ideal of interaction and as an institution of social organisation. Various locally constituted institutions of social organisation have long existed throughout the territory of what is now Uzbekistan (Geiss 2001). Many of these were related to the maintenance and regulation of the region-wide irrigation infrastructure that tied local water management communities to a government administrative hierarchy (Murray Matley 1967, 280; O'Hara 2000, 371–3; Pierce 1960, 144–5). In the area around Samarkand in the nineteenth century, a collection of villages irrigated from a single main canal formed a water-managing unit. They elected a representative to supervise the watering of fields, buying and selling of land, maintenance of the main canal, and rotation of crops. The villages making up such a unit were known as *qozonsherik* (sharers of one cooking pot), reflecting the fact that they formed a social unit as well, jointly owning large cooking pots for communal feasts and attending each other's celebrations of life cycle rituals (Rassudova 1969).

With the collectivisation of agricultural production in the Soviet era, state institutions and collective farms took over the regulation and maintenance of the irrigation infrastructure and the distribution of land. Locally organised institutions continued to exist in an altered form, however. Drawing on research conducted in the area around Khiva in eastern Uzbekistan in the 1950s, the Soviet ethnographer Lobacheva describes the role of what she calls an *elod*.[8] These varied in size, some being subunits of a village and others constituting a village on their own. She notes that various forms of mutual aid, especially in agricultural work, were carried out within the *elod* in prerevolutionary times, and that this tradition

FIGURE 3. *Osh* being prepared in a large *qozon* at a feast

continued into the 1950s in the communal building of houses, sewing of clothes, and preparations for marriage and circumcision feasts. Members of an *elod* elected a group of officers, including an *oqsoqol* (elder) who acted as community leader and officiated at ritual feasts, and other community celebrations. The *khodim* was a woman who acted as an intermediary among women in negotiations about marriages, notified women of upcoming celebrations, organised the preparation of food at the feasts, and generally acted as a mistress of ceremonies. The male equivalent of the *khodim* was the *peikal*. Alongside the *oqsoqol*, the mullah and a group of older residents supervised the arrangements for marriages and negotiations about dowries and *qalin* (bride-price), intervened in disputes between and within households, and in general concerned themselves with the moral conduct of *elod* members. The *kaivona*,[9] a female religious authority, was responsible for the moral upbringing of girls and their preparation for adult life (Lobacheva 1989).[10]

During the 1930s, the Soviet authorities partially formalised some of these local social forms by instituting the *mahalla* committee, utilising them as a channel for ideological education (Arifkhanova 2000; Koroteyeva & Makarova 1998a; Moryakova 1998), but the present government has gone much further and has instituted a comprehensive network of *mahalla* committees as local organs of self-government encompassing all residential districts in the country. They are nominally independent of the government administrative structure (although in Chapter 3 I will describe how they are co-opted as an extension of executive government), and each is headed by a chairman who receives a small state salary. Other salaried personnel are the secretary and a *posbon*, a community policeman who is part of the *mahalla* committee but who works closely with state law enforcement agencies. It also contains a number of commissions dealing with issues such as women's affairs, domestic conflict resolution, and household events (such as weddings, circumcisions, and funerals), the members of which are not paid.[11]

We need to make a distinction between this state-formalised institution and the informal *mahalla*, which is a local social institution but has no legal status. Informal *mahalla* do not exist in the city of Samarkand, but they are an important institution in Pakhtabad. In order to avoid confusion, I will always refer to the institution of the official *mahalla* as the *mahalla* committee. In relation to Pakhtabad, I will talk mainly about the informal *mahalla*. This is a territorial subdistrict within the village, centred on a mosque and with a number of roles attached to it, including an *oqsoqol* (the leader of the *mahalla*) and a mullah. I follow local usage in using the term 'mullah' to refer to individuals locally recognised for their knowledge of Islam and the conduct of ritual, who are called upon to officiate on ritual occasions and who lead the prayers at unregistered *mahalla* mosques. The term 'imam' is reserved for the official appointed by the Muslim Board to officiate at a registered mosque. Whereas imams have generally completed at least a madrasa education, mullahs do not necessarily have any formal religious training.

a *duo*, a free prayer in Uzbek. Thus, the *oqsoqol* needs to be an expert, or at least have proficiency, in the conduct of ritual occasions. The new, younger *oqsoqol* of the *mahalla* where I lived was still heavily reliant on the advice of his predecessor and other senior residents for this.

Administratively, too, there are a number of ways in which *mahalla* and mosque merge in Pakhtabad. The mosque is a general meeting place for discussing *mahalla* issues, such as organising the annual spring feast to which representatives of other *mahalla* are invited, and which is financed by donations from households in accordance with their levels of wealth. Another issue that was discussed during my field research was the local government plan to resupply the village with gas, demanding a payment of 3,000 *sum* (about U.S.$2 at the time; a teacher's salary is around U.S.$20) from each household. The gas had been cut off for a number of years because of general shortages and also nonpayment by villagers.[13] The meeting discussed how to allocate this charge among the households in the *mahalla* so that some would pay more and others less, again depending upon relative levels of wealth. In addition, mosque and *mahalla* finances are integrated. A fund managed by the *mahalla* leadership is raised from sources such as individual donations from residents, the income from agricultural production on land attached to the mosque (usually managed by the mullah), or the money the mullah or *oqsoqol* receives from households for reciting the Qur'an on ritual occasions, although there are no hard and fast rules about what counts as collective *mahalla* income. The newly chosen *oqsoqol* in my *mahalla* considered the income from mosque land to belong to his predecessor, the mullah, although the mullah himself stated that he intended for the trees he was growing on that land to be used for maintenance of the mosque. This fund is referred to interchangeably as the mosque or *mahalla* fund, and the money is used to pay for the expenses of operating the mosque, projects of general benefit, or to assist households in need, as the leaders of the *mahalla* see fit. This is the fund that the former vet wanted to use for repairing the road in the dispute I described.

In Pakhtabad, the informal *mahalla* is an extension of the daily flow of sociality. A villager in Pakhtabad described his household as a mini-*mahalla*, expressing the way that the main house (*katta eshik*) and the families of married sons who occupied separate compounds operate as a single unit of production and consumption, where income is pooled and distributed in accordance with the collective good (Rasanayagam 2002b). The official *mahalla* committee, by contrast, is seen as an organ of the state, and its chairman made use of the *oqsoqol* of the informal *mahalla* to implement directives from local and national government, such as organising work parties to maintain the roads and irrigation channels or to identify which households were eligible for state benefits. The formalisation of the *mahalla* is part of the postindependence government's attempt to utilise tradition as a tactic of governance, which will be discussed in Chapter 3.

In Samarkand, there are no informal *mahalla*, only the official *mahalla* committee with duties and posts defined by the state. The *mahalla* committee there is much less an extension of an ongoing sociality than in Pakhtabad, and its social significance for residents of different neighbourhoods varies greatly. Abdumajid-aka, the founder of the association of *mahalla* committee leaders and a person to whom I will return in later chapters, estimated that of the 190 or so *mahalla* committees in the city, only one-third played a meaningful role in the social lives of their residents, these being mainly situated in the older residential districts in the historical centre and some surrounding areas. Of the rest, he judged that about half had merely a formal administrative existence, relevant to residents only when they needed official documentation such as proof of residence. I lived in one of these for part of my stay in the city, a relatively modern *mahalla* founded in the 1950s and made up of individual household compounds with internal courtyards. Residents had very little interaction with the *mahalla* committee, and many people even viewed the *mahalla* leadership as corrupt, interested only in exploiting their positions for personal gain, such as extorting illegal charges for providing essential documentation. I was told that the previous chairman of this *mahalla* had borrowed a large sum of money from a bank and then fled the country. The social distance of the *mahalla* committee is a reflection of the fact that in Samarkand, as might be expected of a large, urban context with an ethnically and linguistically diverse population, an individual's social relations, networks of support, and means of livelihood are less closely bound up with those living in his or her immediate neighbourhood.

Because of the more formalised and regulated nature of both the *mahalla* committee and registered mosques, mosque and *mahalla* do not overlap in the urban context as they do in Pakhtabad. Unregistered mosques do exist in Samarkand but as a rule only in the older sections of the city, often located within the complex of *mahalla* committee offices, which sometimes also include a general meeting area called the *choykhona* (teahouse). Some have been renovated after independence through the collective work and financial contributions of *mahalla* residents coordinated by the *mahalla* committee. However, they are much less active than the local *mahalla* mosques in Pakhtabad, usually only operating with official dispensation at particular times of high demand, such as during Ramadan. Those who attend prayers daily do so at one of the twenty or so officially registered mosques in the city. Registered mosques and *mahalla* committees are administratively and financially separate, with official imams reporting within the structure of the Muslim Board and *mahalla* committees reporting to residents and to the structures of local government.

Nonetheless, the *mahalla* committee can play a role in the ritual life of residents, especially in areas where it is socially significant. Committee memberships often include individuals who are locally recognised for their religious learning and invited to recite the Qur'an at household ritual events, as well as the imams of nearby registered mosques. In addition, registered mosques with large congregations, which are able to collect substantial sums in donations, regularly distribute part of this money to needy families through neighbouring *mahalla* committees. In a number of *mahalla* I visited, the *jensovet* (Rus. head of the women's affairs commission) also acted as a *bibikhalfa*, officiating at women's ritual occasions in the same way that a mullah does at men's rituals. Some of these women regularly organised pilgrimages (*ziyorat*) for women to the tombs of *avliyo* (saints) in Samarkand and beyond. Moreover, minor tombs or other sites that attract visitors are often controlled by the *mahalla* committee in whose territory they are located. In one such *mahalla* neighbouring the one where I lived in the old city of Samarkand, the committee appointed a mullah to recite prayers for pilgrims and installed collection boxes, taking control of the income generated.

The involvement of the *mahalla* committee in the old, central districts of the city is also important in the organisation of life-cycle rituals. These committees have a subcommission for *to'y* that coordinates the celebration of marriages and a stock of crockery that can be used. A relatively wealthy household might hold its own celebrations in a restaurant or other location without the involvement of the *mahalla* committee; however, particularly in the older districts of Samarkand, they will typically also hold some sort of affair in the neighbourhood as well with the cooperation of the *mahalla* committee, even if just for the sake of maintaining neighbourly relations. The *mahalla* committee is more important in the case of funerals, when its officials are involved in organising the burial and the *janoza*, the funeral prayers; in calling residents to attend the burial; and in engaging a mullah to recite prayers at the mourning and commemoration events in the days and weeks following the funeral. Even in the relatively modern neighbourhood where I lived, where the *mahalla* committee is mostly ignored, when a family held a circumcision feast (*sunnat to'y*), my hosts and I were called to the event by the *mahalla* committee's *peikal* (an individual who informs residents of an event). As well as distributing state-funded poverty relief and child-benefit payments, *mahalla* committees in the older sections of the city tend to be active in raising money and donations in kind from wealthier residents, enterprises, and businesses located in their territory and may use this for communal projects or to aid poorer residents. They are also actively involved in the resolution of domestic conflicts, although this is a topic I do not have space to expand upon here.

In Samarkand, the *mahalla* committee in practical terms may not be an expression of everyday sociality to the extent that the informal *mahalla* is in Pakhtabad, but it remains an ideal of interaction within a moral community. An important way in which individuals understand themselves as good Muslims is by participating fully within their communities as good parents, spouses, or neighbours, and this is reflected in the way the mosque and life-cycle ritual is integral to the practical operation of the *mahalla*. The present government attempts to co-opt these ideals of sociality within its legitimising discourses by presenting the Uzbekistan state as a *mahalla* writ large and local ideals of mutual cooperation as duty to the nation and its president. Chapter 3 will develop this further in a discussion of state discourses on cultural authenticity and how the concepts of 'good' and 'bad' Islam are constructed within it.

Developing Understandings of Islam

An important development since independence has been the spread of formal knowledge of the sacred texts and interpretations of what constitutes correct Muslim practice based upon them. The expansion of the number of madrasas has meant that more young men, and to a more limited extent young women, are able to obtain a formal Islamic education. Popularised interpretations and advice on how to lead a Muslim life have also become readily available. Affordable, locally printed texts in Uzbek are on sale in many bookshops, on street and market stalls, and at many of the larger mosques. All literature published and publicly available in Uzbekistan is, of course, regulated by the state. To give an idea of the nature of these texts, one that I picked up was titled *Morality and Correct Behaviour in Islam*[14] by Hoji Ahmadjon Bobomurod, which gives

FIGURE 5. The end of Friday prayers at Kho'ja Abdu Darun mosque in Samarkand

guidance on, among other things, how to pray and behave in a mosque; how to conduct rituals such as circumcision, marriages, and funerals; relations between newlyweds; how to conduct oneself in a public street; and personal hygiene and clothing, among other things. Others had titles such as *The Responsibilities of Muslim Women to Their Husbands.*[15] Expositions on the Qur'an are available in Uzbek for more serious students, such as the *tafsir* (Qur'anic commentary) and sermons of Muhammad Sadiq Muhammad Yusuf, a former chief Mufti in Uzbekistan who was forced out of office in the early 1990s.

In addition to the official madrasas under the control of the Muslim Board, a number of young men in Pakhtabad have attended unofficial, unregistered schools where they learnt to recite the Qur'an and become a *qori*, someone proficient in the chanted recitation of the Qur'an. The services of a *qori* are in demand at rituals such as *mavlud* commemorations or the *khatmi qur'on*, a ceremony at which the Qur'an is recited for the benefit of the deceased. I was told that these schools had closed after the bombings in Tashkent in 1999 that were aimed at assassinating President Karimov, which were attributed to Islamist opposition groups by the government. One of these *qorikhona* had been attached to a mosque in the city of Andijan. A young man in Pakhtabad recounted how he had attended it for five years in the early 1990s and had memorised the Qur'an. There were about 200 students there during his time, ranging from young boys of six years to married men, and some of the boys would board there. When the *qorikhona* was closed, the lessons were moved into private houses. Organising unregistered religious gatherings can be dangerous in Uzbekistan, as the government seeks to regulate the expression of Islam within the limits of what it deems acceptable. Individuals who step over this boundary are vulnerable to be labelled as religious extremists. A group of young men who meet regularly to study the Qur'an are likely to be viewed with suspicion by the law enforcement and security organs of the state. However, the private teaching of Qur'anic recitation of the type that occurs in a *qorikhona*, even if it does not take place in formally registered premises, is less threatening to the government because it can be seen as falling within the category of 'tradition'. In any case, what is an unregistered, illegal, and therefore politically suspect gathering, and what is a 'traditional' event that happens outside the premises of a registered religious establishment is not always clear.

Formal study is not the only means through which Muslims in Uzbekistan gain an awareness of scripturally grounded Islamic knowledge. Although mosque attendance was reported to have been much higher immediately after independence, a significant number of men attended mosques during my fieldwork, where they heard the Friday sermon. At the time of my field research in 2004, attendance at Friday prayers at the twenty or so official mosques in Samarkand ranged from 30 or 40 men of all ages at smaller mosques, to between 800 and 1,000 at one of the main mosques in the city (women do not commonly attend mosque prayers, except on feast days). At the mosque in the *mahalla* where I lived in the old city in Samarkand, more than 100 men attended on Fridays, and about 20 or 30 gathered daily for the early-morning prayers. In the village of Pakhtabad, which has a population of 4,000, about 2,000 men attended Friday prayers at the registered mosque, and although most appeared to be older than fifty, about a quarter were younger men and boys. About 10 men prayed on a daily basis at the small unregistered mosque in my *mahalla*. No sermon is delivered at the unregistered *mahalla* mosques. This can only be given by the imam at the registered Friday mosque. The mullah stated that in the winter, when people have more free time, there are usually about 35 men in the congregation of his informal mosque and that it is full during the month of Ramadan. I was told that attendance at all of these mosques had been much higher prior to the government's crackdown on religious extremism following the 1999 bombings in Tashkent.

The spread of textually based interpretations of Islam and a Muslim life is increasing awareness amongst Central Asians of being part of a global community of Muslims, which transcends territorial and cultural boundaries. The increasing numbers of people undertaking the pilgrimage to Mecca is contributing to this awareness. The pilgrimage is organised through the state, and in 2003 I was told that it cost about U.S.$ 1,000 for the air ticket and accommodation. In the past it had been much cheaper, because pilgrims were able to exchange Uzbek currency for U.S. dollars at an artificially low official exchange rate. Villagers in Pakhtabad told me that until 2001, it had also been possible to undertake the pilgrimage privately through Kyrgyzstan and that it had been cheaper, between U.S.$300 and U.S.$500, because the journey could be made by bus. According to the Muslim Board of Uzbekistan, about 4,000 Muslims from Uzbekistan make the hajj pilgrimage each year.[16] In the *mahalla* where I lived in Pakhtabad, more than twenty individuals of the approximately 100 households had performed the hajj. These individuals have a wider impact in the village. They are respected for having performed the pilgrimage and are addressed as 'Hoji-bobo' if they are older men. Those who return from the hajj are expected to conduct themselves in a morally upright manner, refrain from drinking, and perform the prayers regularly. The former vet had altered the way he participated within his immediate community after his pilgrimage, becoming more oriented to working for the common good rather than for his own gain or that of his immediate household.

Those who have performed the hajj are local embodiments of the universal, transcendent nature of Islam. The inverse of this is that the morality that the *hoji* (person who has performed the hajj) should ideally embody is often at odds with perceived reality. It is, of course, costly to undertake the pilgrimage, and in a society where most people struggle to get by, it is predominantly the wealthy who are able to finance it. In addition, because of pervasive corruption, low salaries, and the difficulty of operating a business in Uzbekistan without either personal connections within the government administrative structures or bribery, the wealthy are often assumed to have obtained their money by illegitimate means. This is particularly the case in urban contexts. In Samarkand, I commonly heard expressed the cynical attitude that people who had made their money by exploiting their position as, for example, a shop manager or public prosecutor in the Soviet era were suddenly, after completing the hajj, dressing in white, pretending to be pious Muslims and insisting that everyone address them as Hoji-bobo. This cynicism is much less present in the village of Pakhtabad, although the ambivalent attitudes towards the former vet I have described result from this sort of feeling. There is an ideal that the money used to go on the pilgrimage should be 'clean'. The former *oqsoqol* of my *mahalla*, now the mullah and himself a *hoji*, advised Tohirjon that the money he receives from his private tuition could not be used for the hajj because some of it might have been given by people resentful or unwilling to pay. He advised him to invest the money in buying and fattening a bull calf (a common savings and investment strategy in the village), and then the money from the sale would be pure.

These developments might be characterised as an objectification of Islam, to use the terminology developed by Eickelman and Piscatori.

However, this term is misleading if we take objectification to imply a disjuncture between a reflexive stance that constructs Islam as a distinct object or sphere of life in opposition to a previous unreflexive immersion within 'tradition' or 'culture'. Many Muslims in Uzbekistan do in fact define a true or correct Islam in contrast with what they consider to be traditional practice, innovation that has no foundation in the sacred texts, and in doing so they echo debates among Muslims throughout the world. For many, however, an understanding of what it means to be a Muslim is developed through participation within the moral community of household, neighbourhood, and village *as well as* with reference to the sacred texts. Later chapters will discuss how it is also developed through direct encounters with the Divine and spirit agents in the context of visiting shrines, in dreams, and in the course of illness and healing. A clear and absolute categorical distinction between culture and religion is not useful. Although Islam may be objectified within an individual's developing understanding of what it means to be a Muslim, moral reasoning is not bounded by a self-conscious, deliberative stance of 'belief' but also occurs within ongoing experience and participation within the flow of sociality.

I do not want to suggest that the sociality of Muslims in Uzbekistan is itself Islamic. The sociality within which an individual is immersed contributes to the development of moral selfhood, which may or may not be a Muslim self. I came across many individuals during my research, particularly in the city of Samarkand, who participated in a sociality of friends, relatives, and neighbours that includes distinctively Islamic ritual such as Muslim marriage ceremonies and circumcisions, but who understood these as expressions of a Central Asian culture. As Khalid, among others, has observed, being a Muslim for these individuals might be seen as an expression of an ethnic or cultural identity (Khalid 2003). What I have sought to do in this chapter is not to collapse the distinction between culture and religion but to recognise that they are contingent constructions rather than absolute analytical categories. Islam as an object is best approached not as a religion defined by distinct beliefs, practices, and histories, or as a religious stance defined in terms of the sacred or the spiritual. This book argues that Islam as an object emerges within the development of a Muslim self through a process of moral reasoning that takes place, in part, through the flow of sociality.

TWO

The New Soviet (Central Asian) Person and the Colonisation of Consciousness

Olimjon, whom I met in 2004, is a lecturer in philosophy at a higher educational institute in Samarkand. He described himself as having been a committed communist in the Soviet period, but since independence, he has become an actively engaged Muslim who regularly attends the Friday prayers at a registered mosque near his university. The mosque was built in the years after independence by staff at his institute, and he was one of the original hundred signatories needed for its registration in 1996. He was born in 1942 and graduated from the history faculty at Samarkand State University. For his military service, he was posted to a district near Moscow, where he rose to a leading position within the branch of Komsomol (the youth organisation of the Communist Party) in his unit. He was proud that he had held this leadership position in a Union-wide context, despite the fact that he was from Central Asia. Olimjon described how, as a youth, he had internalised a communist consciousness during his school and university education. At the same time, from his present perspective as a practicing Muslim after the collapse of the Soviet Union, he maintains his former self at arm's length, explaining his previous consciousness as something he automatically, unreflexively developed in response to the pervasive propaganda to which he had been exposed at school and university, a 'child's consciousness', as he described it. Being a communist was part of being a 'correct person' (Rus. *pravil'nyi chelovek*), a necessary part of his career path as a university lecturer at a time when things were clear and straightforward, unlike the present. After returning from military service, he reenrolled in the history faculty at Samarkand as a postgraduate student and was eventually awarded a *kandidat* degree (the equivalent of a Ph.D.) with a dissertation on the religiosity of believers in southern Uzbekistan. He went on to teach the subjects of atheism and philosophy.

Reflecting on how he had arrived at his present active engagement with Islam, Olimjon described this as an almost unconscious process during which he was influenced, even during the Soviet period, by his family and social environment as well as his professional research and teaching. His father had been killed in Germany during the Second World War, and his mother had remarried a religiously observant man who performed the five daily prayers regularly. To show respect for them, he had arranged for his sons to be circumcised, but because of his position as a university lecturer – in particular, one whose specialty was atheism – he had to do so discreetly. He organised the operation in a clinic far from his home so that state officials would not notice, holding only a small celebration feast (*to'y*) for a few close relatives and friends. 'On the one hand there was the idea of communism, and on the other our parents', he explained. 'We had to listen to communist ideology and do the rituals according to Islam'. In that period, the spiritual or theological significance of such rituals had not been important to Olimjon. This did not mean that his participation in them was empty formality. By including the Muslim *nikoh* within wedding ceremonies; holding the *janoza*, the funeral prayers for deceased relatives; or circumcising sons, a person was doing good (Rus. *dobro*), he stated. These were enactments of a shared sociality and full participation within a community, as discussed in Chapter 1. Had he not arranged for the circumcisions, it is likely that his sons would have been rejected as suitable marriage partners by other Uzbek or Tajik families.

From his present location as an actively practicing Muslim, Olimjon interprets his immersion within this sociality as having influenced him without his being aware of it, preparing him for a swift transition

(Rus. *perekhod*) from being a communist to a Muslim after the strict insistence upon the formal adherence to communist ideological norms began to slacken during Gorbachev's perestroika period and after independence when communism was abandoned altogether as state ideology. Interestingly, in retrospect, Olimjon sees his study of scientific atheism in the Soviet period as having had a similar influence:

> In the course of researching Islam I came across religious literature. As a future specialist I had to know about communist ideology and Islam, and as a young man I was interested in both. I criticised Islam but subconsciously knowledge of Islam entered my soul. To criticise Islam you had to know the sources. My family circumstances also influenced me, my relatives and others close to me. That's why I quickly went over (to becoming a believing Muslim).

Olimjon describes himself as a modern or contemporary believer (Rus. *sovremennyi veruyushchii*) with a multifaceted (Rus. *raznostoronnii*) relation to Islam, and he has not completely abandoned his previous outlook. He does not perform all of the prescribed five daily prayers, only the early morning prayers (*bomdod*) daily and the Friday noon prayer at the congregational mosque. This is not because he does not have the time, but because it is the habit of the 'contemporary intelligentsia'. He reasons that it is possible to find a number of references in the Qur'an and hadith stating that God has promised to be with a person who performs the *bomdod* and that the Prophet has said that a Muslim can make up for the prayers he has omitted to perform – that God would forgive the omission. He also admits to drinking alcohol occasionally in company. He looks to Islam for inspiration in answering his questions about virtuous conduct in society and to address the existential questions for which science has no answer. He puts Islam in a comparative context, pointing out that core values of humanism and tolerance are central to all religions, and he regards the Baha'i faith as a particular instance of this. This is no doubt influenced by his professional study and teaching of religion. He has not simply rejected communism but feels that communist ideology also promoted these core values – ideals of equality and social justice. Where communism went wrong was in its class analysis and denial of God, but its moral message had much in common with religions such as Islam and Christianity.

Olimjon's account is similar to the narratives of others I encountered during field research, particularly university lecturers and other members of the former Soviet intelligentsia, who described themselves as committed communists in their youth but have become active Muslims since independence. An alternative, commonly repeated account by observant Muslims was that they had always performed the Islamic ritual prescriptions, such as prayer and fasting, even during the Soviet period, but they had done so discreetly, at home rather than in public space such as a mosque, and that they had learnt about Islam informally, usually from relatives. Most of the people who gave this sort of account had close relatives who had been imams or mullahs, people known for their knowledge of Islam who had been called upon by their local communities to perform ritual services such as Qur'an recitations or to lead the congregational prayer, during the Soviet period and before. Most commonly, men who at the time of my research described themselves as active Muslims, who at least regularly performed the congregational Friday prayers, and who had reached adulthood during the Soviet period recounted how they had not observed Islamic ritual prescriptions in the past, although they did not characterise themselves as committed communists either, as Olimjon had done. They considered themselves to have been Muslim but had not prayed except perhaps at major Islamic festivals, had drunk alcohol, and had eaten pork. Typically, they blamed their former laxity on the antireligious atmosphere of the period, which made it difficult to hold a formal salaried job in the social sector and at the same time to be seen as an observant Muslim. It must be noted that a large number people in Uzbekistan continue to ascribe to being Muslim in these terms. Although they participate in a sociality that includes Muslim ritual, they do not pray regularly or observe Islamic prescriptions, and being a Muslim is not necessarily a central reference for their own understandings of moral selfhood. I will return to a discussion of what some have called a 'cultural' or 'secular' Muslim identity at the end of this chapter.

This chapter provides an account of Soviet policy on religion as it was practiced in Central Asia. It describes the Soviet discursive regime; the attempt, particularly in the early years of Soviet rule, to fashion the New Soviet Person in Central Asia; its efforts to classify social space and the category of religion within it; and the state regulatory infrastructure. The state-building project and tactics of governance of the postindependence government owe much to the Soviet legacy, and this chapter provides an historical context for later discussions.

The chapter also discusses how best to understand Olimjon's swift 'conversion' from communist to Muslim. Analysis in terms of the success of a discursive regime in fashioning individual subjectivities and how domination is negotiated or resisted does not capture the ways Soviet citizens in Uzbekistan developed moral selves that were Muslim, communist, or neither, or how we might understand their engagement with Islam since independence. We are directed to interpret Olimjon's self-representations and actions in the Soviet period in terms of sincerity and dissimulation. He was either acting out a performance as a communist while really being a believing Muslim, or his participation in Muslim ritual was the performance behind which he concealed his true communist and atheist beliefs. This dichotomy is implicit in those accounts of Islam in Soviet Central Asia that oppose an officially state-sanctioned Islam, promoted by the Spiritual Directorates that regulated and monitored the practice of Islam, to a 'parallel' or 'underground' Islam that existed outside state regulation. Islam and religion in general, in this view, are treated as ideologies, beliefs, or worldviews that exist in competition with other ideologies or beliefs, such as communism or alternative interpretations of Islam. However, Olimjon's account complicates any straightforward dichotomy. He recognises the tensions between the expectations of the

Party and his state employers, on the one hand, and his family, on the other. However, both his self-representation as a communist and his participation within the sociality of his family and community were sincere. He sees his participation within this sociality during the Soviet period and even his professional work as a lecturer on atheism as significant in the development of his present Muslim self.

The Hegemony of State Discourse

John and Jean Comaroff have written about the 'colonisation of consciousness' in nineteenth-century colonial southern Africa (Comaroff & Comaroff 1992). Colonial domination was not only a matter of establishing political and economic supremacy. They argue that an essential part of this process was an attempt by the European colonisers to shape the subjectivities of colonised peoples, to gain control over the symbolic categories through which the colonised interpreted and acted within their lifeworlds, and to refashion them as individualised subjects in the colonisers' own idealised image of European capitalism. The Protestant evangelical missionaries who were the vanguard of the ideological colonisation in Africa described by the Comaroffs saw themselves as engaged in a civilising mission to liberate the native from traditional modes of thinking and superstition that mystified the objectively true relation between human effort and production. In their place, they sought to instil a consciousness founded on empirical reason and individual responsibility where an individual's labour was recognised as the source of creativity and value and the means by which nature was dominated and made productive. The Comaroffs describe how these European norms could be recast in local terms, but they nevertheless played an important part in the eventual subordination of the black population within a capitalist economy as dependent wage labourers and domestic servants.

The Bolshevik reformers in Central Asia in the early years of the Soviet Union shared with these Protestant evangelical missionaries a vision of a civilising mission in which they set out to remake the Central Asian person. Both saw themselves as liberating the savage from the bonds of superstition and tradition, replacing these with rational argument and empirical reason. In achieving their goals, Christian missionaries and Bolshevik reformers alike focused their efforts on transforming the practices of day-to-day living in what the Comaroffs have called a 'mastery of the mundane'. In the early years of Soviet rule, the Bolshevik authorities turned their attention to reforming the family, particularly targeting women, in an attempt to transform everyday lifeworlds. However, the New Soviet Man or Woman was not to be the individualist subject of modern European capitalism. Rather, he or she was to be a loyal citizen working for collective rather than individual goals, embodying communist ideals and committed to building socialism.

Following the 1917 October revolution, one of the most urgent tasks facing the Bolshevik authorities was the 're-classing' of society, not only in Turkestan but also throughout the territory of the former Tsarist empire.[1] They needed to reshape Soviet society in line with Marxist class analysis, a process that culminated in Stalin's tripartite categorisation of workers, collectivised peasants, and intelligentsia as the only legitimate groups in the Soviet Union. In the immediate aftermath of the revolution the occupational structure of the population was far from this ideal. Groups that could most readily be classified as proletariat, namely wage workers in industry and landless peasants, made up only a small proportion of the population. The Bolshevik revolutionary leadership needed to identify 'class enemies' as well as those whose interests were perceived to coincide with their revolutionary aims and who might more easily be moulded into a proletariat class (Fitzpatrick 2000).[2]

Gender relations were identified early on as an important site for an attack upon the prerevolutionary foundations of society in order to replace them with a socialist consciousness (Ashwin 2000; Lapidus 1979). This was nowhere more the case than in Central Asia, where Gregory Massell (1974) has argued that women were regarded as a 'surrogate proletariat'.[3] Because of low levels of industrial development, the problem of identifying and allying with a marginalised and alienated class was particularly acute. Those sections of the population who were underprivileged had not developed a class consciousness, in Marxist terms, which made them aware of their condition of oppression. The targeting of women served a dual role. Because they were perceived by the Soviet leadership as the victims of a patriarchal society, the lowest of the low, segregated, exploited, and degraded, it was assumed that they would readily ally themselves with the Communist Party, which offered them greater freedoms, dignity, and independence. Moreover, Party activists believed that the position of women within the family and in broader society expressed and sustained the prerevolutionary social and religious order. The liberation of women was viewed by the Bolsheviks as one of the key strategies for replacing this order with a new revolutionary consciousness.

Massell identifies three elements in the Bolshevik effort to reshape Central Asian society in the early years of Soviet rule: revolutionary law, administrative assault, and systemic work. Judicial reform included the gradual replacement of religious courts, presided over by a *qozi* (Muslim judge) who administered *sharīʿa* law, with civil judges and courts. The family was targeted for reform by laws granting equal rights to women within marriage in matters of inheritance and divorce. The payment of bride-price (*qalin*), polygamy, and forced marriage were outlawed, and the minimum legal age of marriage for girls was set at sixteen. These offences were included in the newly created category of 'crimes of daily life' (Rus. *bytovoye prestuplenie*). They were characterised as dangerous survivals of religion and tradition that were antithetical to the new revolutionary order.

In parallel with legislative reform, the Soviet authorities engaged in direct action, or administrative assault. In an attempt to challenge directly and sweep away the preexisting social system, thousands of mosques and religious schools were closed and religious endowments were nationalised. Muslim religious practitioners, such as mullahs or *eshon*,[4] were condemned as the agents of oppressive classes and were subject to arrest and exile (Keller 2001). These direct measures culminated in the *hujum*, the campaign for the mass desegregation and unveiling of women that was launched in 1927, during which women publicly burned their veils in mass rallies. Communist Party activists sent to Central Asia to support this policy saw themselves as engaged in a modernising project, introducing enlightened social relations to a Muslim population mired in oppressive tradition. The 'missionary imagination' (Massell 1974, 69) of these activists resonates strongly with the Comaroffs' account of Protestant missionaries in southern Africa, and they similarly targeted everyday lifeworlds, the intimate sphere of relations within the family, in an attempt to instil a socialist consciousness.

However, the historian Douglas Northrop has observed that Communist Party rule in Central Asia was relatively weak in the early years of the Soviet Union, and the Party leadership could not rely on its local representatives to implement central policies. Although a number of Central Asians became committed communists (Kamp 2002), the antireligion campaigns seem to have had the effect of strengthening a local Muslim identity. During the *hujum*, thousands of women activists and those who removed their veils in public were attacked or murdered. In fact, the practice of veiling became more widespread in response to the *hujum* and was adopted even by the wives and daughters of Communist Party members (Northrop 2004). Laws banning the payment of bride-price, polygamy, and early marriage were commonly ignored or circumvented. Fathers colluded with doctors and local officials to obtain certificates falsely attesting to their daughters' age, or an older woman would be sent to the state registry office in place of the real underaged bride (Massell 1974; Northrop 2004, 264–74). The measures taken against Islam were perceived by the local population as an attack on their moral ideals and way of life and Soviet rule was interpreted by many as God's punishment on Muslims for straying from the path of Islam in the same way that many understood natural disasters such as earthquakes (Massell 1974, 275; Northrop 2004, 165). Veiling, bride-price payments, and polygamy, which were characterised within Soviet discourse as means of oppression and a block to enlightened progress, were instead adopted as markers of piety and community belonging.

By 1929, the Soviet authorities came to the conclusion that a direct assault on religious and cultural practices was not having the desired effect. Instead, they refocused their attention to 'systemic work', a long-term strategy of gradual social reconstruction through education, industrialisation, and socialist modernisation (Massell 1974). It was assumed that religion, as well as 'feudal' family relations and other elements of the prerevolutionary social order, would naturally wither away as they became irrelevant within a changed social and economic environment. Indeed, the use of the veil quickly disappeared after the Second World War, and in the postwar years, women gradually began to participate in all sectors of employment and public life (Lubin 1981). By the 1960s, many Islamic norms were no longer regularly adhered to by the majority of the population in Central Asia. Only a tiny percentage regularly attended prayers at the very few mosques permitted to function legally, and Islamic prohibitions against the consumption of pork and alcohol were commonly ignored.

Much of the historical and anthropological analyses of this early period of Soviet history have been framed in terms of power. They have addressed the efforts of the Party and state organs to fashion a socialist society and consciousness and how individuals negotiated or resisted these efforts. The works of Massell and Northrop referred to in this chapter are examples. Writing about other parts of the Soviet Union, Stephen Kotkin (1995) and Oleg Kharkhordin (1999) have similarly examined efforts to shape the consciousness of citizens. Both have taken inspiration from Foucault's work on subjectification – the processes by which individuals are fashioned, and also fashion themselves, into subjects with particular habits, orientations, and interpretive frames within technologies and disciplines of power. Kotkin describes how workers in an industrial new town in the Stalinist period were individuated within the regime of the factory through the public honouring of model workers and shaming of slackers. Material incentives such as access to better food, clothing, housing, medical care, and holidays were tied in the Soviet Union to work performance. This was a powerful tool in an economy of shortage that fixed a worker's material well-being to centrally defined performance standards and ideological orientations.

Kharkhordin, for his part, analyses the nature of the Soviet collective as an institution designed to produce a communist consciousness. The Soviet collective would tie the everyday activities of the individual to the collective goal of building socialism within the Soviet Union and beyond. This consciousness was to be instilled through techniques of mutual surveillance and admonishment and also through the practice of *oblichenie* – self-examination and self-fashioning. The latter practice became routinised in institutional settings such as the school classroom, where classmates would discuss each other's positive and negative features, offering up the character traits of the individual to group judgement.

Central to the analyses of these authors is the manner in which individuating practices were resisted, partly through the manipulation of partial and hidden transcripts (Scott 1985). Kotkin develops Foucault's notion of capillary power, which sees power as a relation, dispersed throughout society rather than located in particular institutions such as the state (Foucault 1990, 1994). He locates both resistance and the formation of subjectivities in the 'politics of everyday life', the 'little tactics of the habitat'. People did not openly reject the individuating pressure from above, but alternately submitted to, circumvented, or resisted state efforts, 'working the system' to their own ends. In public, they 'spoke Bolshevik', mastering a language of ideological compliance, taking part in official demonstrations and 'voluntary' activities outside working hours, whereas in private, they violated the rules and engaged in the black economy of goods and services. Kharkhordin similarly describes the dissimulation that became commonplace as workers and officials simply stopped practicing suspect behaviour in pubic and maintained a private self hidden from public gaze.

The perspective of power, domination, and resistance is a useful one for understanding the early period of Soviet rule in Central Asia, when the state and Party engaged in a concerted effort to reshape society and fashion socialist subjects. However, it is less helpful when we turn to late socialism, particularly after the 1970s and the Brezhnev era, the period during which Olimjon and many others I encountered during field research reached adulthood. Alexei Yurchak (2006) has identified a critical shift during the late socialist period in the quality of state ideological representations, reproduced in daily life in documents, speeches, slogans, posters, architecture, and monuments. With the death of Stalin, he argues, the editorial voice external to the discursive regime of the state disappeared. Stalin had been a charismatic personality, capable of occupying a position outside state discourse from which he evaluated the soundness of cultural, political, and scientific expression against the standard of Marxist ideology. When this voice disappeared after Stalin's death, Yurchak identified what he calls a 'performative shift'. Ideological representations increasingly became a matter of reproducing a standardised structural form from one context to another, with little attention to literal, referential meaning, as this was seen as fixed. When delivering or listening to an address, voting in an election, or participating in a parade, the literal meaning of the act, the stating of an opinion or belief, became less important than the performance of reproducing oneself as a 'normal' Soviet person.

Yurchak's perspective moves away from seeing these performances as being either true representations of an individual's interior beliefs or dissimulation. The fact that Soviet citizens routinely transgressed officially proclaimed norms did not necessarily mean that they were not committed to the fundamental values of socialism as they understood them. Some individuals in effect reinterpreted communism in their own terms, making a distinction between 'mere formality' and meaningful discourse and action. They were able to perceive themselves as committed communists, genuinely engaging in efforts to build a socialist society, while rejecting what they saw as unimportant (Yurchak 2003). Others occupied what Yurchak calls 'deterritorialised' milieus, which simultaneously were inside and outside the system. These were circles of friends, networks of scientists, literary clubs, and other circles whose members did not see themselves as either in opposition to or in support of the state's authoritative discourse, but simply separate from it or deterritorialised in relation to it (Yurchak 2006, 126–57). The state's discursive and regulatory structures themselves made these milieus possible, providing the employment opportunities and institutional settings in which clubs and associations were able to exist. Members could maintain a position within the system by performatively reproducing themselves as Soviet persons while ascribing to alternative meanings and forms of sociality.

Echoes of this relation to authoritative discourse, which developed in the late Soviet context, were evident during my field research. While working as a lecturer in the Foreign Languages Institute in Andijan, I sat through a number of general meetings that the entire faculty was obliged to attend. The rector or vice rector addressed the audience, but no one paid any attention as they chatted with their neighbours and moved about the room, so that sometimes the person making the address could not even be heard. People seemed to be attending merely for form's sake, and what was said at these meetings was irrelevant. During the period of the cotton harvest in autumn, the production achievements of the different provinces in the country were regularly aired on national television, showing how plans were being met or exceeded. These broadcasts were sometimes playing on televisions in the background in living rooms, with no one paying much attention. Everyone knew that the official figures bore little relation to real production. Particularly productive workers were interviewed for the cameras and given prizes of carpets. On one such occasion, a woman interviewed for the television talked about how well and regularly she was paid – a patent falsehood obvious to everyone, because collective farm workers are rarely paid for their efforts (Rasanayagam 2003). I was forced to adopt this stance myself on occasion. As a foreigner in Pakhtabad, peripherally involved in teaching at one of the village schools through Tohirjon, my host in the village, I was asked to address the pupils at the national Independence Day celebrations. I was given a 'script' by Tohirjon, who told me to talk about how well the country was developing and how bright the students' futures were. Whether my audience or I (which included an inspector from the district police), believed what the other speakers or I actually said was not the point. Everyone knew that there was only one script available and that what mattered was reproducing it. In my case, in doing so I was ensuring that I represented Tohirjon, my host in the village and at the school, in the way he wished. In part, I was also reassuring the teachers, pupils, and their parents, whose support was a necessary condition for my research, that I could play the game and that my project was not 'political', that I would not bring them to the attention of the security services. To the police representative, I was reproducing myself as a harmless researcher interested only in Uzbek 'culture' and not in any political or sensitive issues.

Yurchak's analysis provides a useful perspective for interpreting Olimjon's self-representation as a committed communist and his participation in the everyday sociality of his family and neighbours. The performance of Muslim ritual outside state regulation need not be seen, as it has so often been presented, as 'underground Islam', oppositional in some way to the official Islam of the Spiritual Directorate or to state socialist ideology. The everyday sociality, of which Muslim ritual was a part, was simply separate from these state discourses, deterritorialised in relation to them, to use Yurchak's term. Tamara Dragadze has described what she calls the 'domestication' of religion in Soviet Georgia. As a result of the state suppression of public, institutionalised forms of religious practice, religious expression migrated to the private space of the household and came more under the control of ordinary people, particularly women, rather than dominated and regulated by expert practitioners (Dragadze 1993). Gillian Tett has described a similar dynamic in her account of Islam in rural Tajikistan during the period of perestroika in the late 1980s. Whereas men were constrained by their greater public visibility through their employment in state and social institutions, women's location in domestic space made them less visible. Their performance of religious duties, albeit less prestigious activities of shrine visitation and domestic propitiatory rituals and adherence to local ideals of proper female behaviour, helped to maintain the community's sense of Tajik and Muslim identity, not only for themselves but for men as well (Tett 1995).[5]

The enactment of Muslim ritual in 'private' or domestic space need not be opposed to 'public' performance in terms of dissimulation or resistance to state discursive regimes. It is best understood as standing outside it, so that for Olimjon, participation in this sociality did not contradict his conception of himself as a communist. He just had to be careful that his participation in Muslim ritual did not interfere with his performance of authoritative discourse that reproduced him as a 'correct person'.

The Soviet State Regulation of Islam

Following the active repression of Islam before the Second World War, state policy became more accommodating when popular support was needed for the war effort. The Muslim Spiritual Directorate for Central Asia and Kazakhstan (SADUM) was established in 1943, with two more regional Muslim directorates for Transcaucasia and the North Caucasus set up the following year. A further Muslim regulatory body in Ufa founded by Catherine the Great in 1788 was already in existence. This now became responsible for Muslims in Inner Russia and Siberia (Ro'i 2000, 100f.; Saroyan 1997b). These directorates administered the registration of mosques and the training and registration of imams and decided on matters of religious dogma within their jurisdictions. SADUM also administered the only two officially recognised institutions for Islamic education within the Soviet Union: the Mir-i Arab Madrasa in Bukhara, which was opened soon after the war, and the Imom al-Bukhoriy Institute, founded in Tashkent in 1971. Although the Muslim Spiritual Directorates were formally independent, self-governing organizations, they were, in effect, subordinate to state policies on religion, although I will discuss later in this chapter the extent to which religious personnel within these bodies were able to express independent views.

The directorates were not the only organs responsible for the administration of Muslim religious affairs in the Soviet Union. The Council for the Affairs of Religious Cults (CARC) was formed in 1944 as a link between central government and religious communities in the Soviet Union, with the exception of the Russian Orthodox Church, which was assigned its own council. Both councils were amalgamated in 1965 into a single Council for Religious Affairs. The CARC and its successor were responsible for drafting laws relating to religious communities for consideration by government, supervising their implementation, and compiling statistics on religious practice (Ro'i 2000, 12). The actual implementation of laws and the direct supervision of religious activities, however, were the responsibility of organs of local government, and a large measure of effective control was exercised by these officials. Thus, there were multiple organs and officials with overlapping responsibilities involved in the administration of Muslim religious affairs in Central Asia.

Yaacov Ro'i has shown in his detailed study of Islam in the decades following the Second World War that the different regulatory bodies frequently diverged in their approaches. The CARC generally favoured the registration of sufficient religious associations and their mosques to address the needs of the bulk of the Muslim population. In line with

Communist Party policy, the leadership of the CARC aimed at the eradication of religious belief in the long term, but felt that this could best be achieved by incorporating all Islamic practice under state registration, where it could be more easily monitored and regulated. This policy regularly put them in conflict with the organs of local government, who shared the responsibility for registering religious associations. On the one hand, CARC reports accused local officials of turning a blind eye to unregistered religious activity and accused the imams appointed to registered mosques of cooperating with the unregistered mullahs. On the other hand, at times they argued in favour of the oversight by officially appointed imams of unregistered mullahs as a means of bringing this activity under official scrutiny, and SADUM itself issued instructions to this effect. CARC was also critical of local government officials for not registering religious associations, even where there was a clear lack of registered places of worship in the area, forcing local Muslims to resort to unregistered mosques and prayer houses (Ro'i 2000, 550–606).

Additionally, the local officials who actually implemented policy on the ground interpreted it in the light of their own shifting priorities. On the one hand, their actions, along with those of others in positions of public authority such as teachers or the managers of state enterprises, were evaluated in accordance with conformity to state policies and discourses. On the other hand, like Olimjon, they were immersed within an alternative sociality of families, kinship, and neighbourhood networks. As a result, their implementation of state policies and laws was inconsistent. At times, local government officials ignored unregistered religious practice and even participated in Muslim rituals themselves (Rorlich 1991). In fulfilling their own obligations to their superiors and ensuring that state production targets were met, they sometimes worked with unregistered mullahs and other community leaders to mobilise workers (Rasanayagam 2002a, 91–92; Ro'i 2000, 434). At other times, they closed unregistered mosques, withdrew registration from existing associations, and refused approval for the formation of new ones, sometimes opposing the CARC representatives in doing so (Ro'i 2000, 607f.). Their attitude tended to mirror the campaigns of repression and periods of relative tolerance towards religion expressed in the pronouncements of the Communist Party's central leadership. During periods when the central leadership was particularly critical of religion, such as during Khrushchev's anti-religious campaign in the late 1950s and early 1960s, local officials needed to demonstrate their loyalty to the government by taking a harder line. Attendance at registered mosques likewise mirrored the fluctuations in central policy, falling off during periods of repression (Ro'i 2000, 218).

The religious personnel of the Muslim Spiritual Directorates were generally loyal to the Soviet state in that they did not challenge communism within the Soviet Union and were willing to cooperate in its foreign policy in relation to Muslim states. Through their instructions and guidance to the imams appointed to administer the few officially registered mosques allowed to operate, and through their administration of the two institutions of Islamic learning, they promoted their own vision of theologically correct Islam. In general, this followed the interpretation of the Hanafi legal school, dominant among Sunni Muslims in Central Asia. However, in his analysis of fatwas issued by the board, their letters to the republican structures of the CARC, and their guidance to imams, Bakhtiyar Babadjanov has shown how the official clerical establishment could be flexible in their theological interpretation to make it fit in with Party and state priorities (Babadjanov 2001).

Babadjanov focuses particularly on pronouncements regarding what was considered to be 'superstition' and 'pre-Islamic survivals' within the practice of local Muslims. These included pilgrimage to holy shrines, what the Directorate termed 'ishanism' (the ability to channel blessing and healing attributed to members of certain lineages, such as the descendents of prominent Sufi scholars), the extended series of feasts held to commemorate the deceased, and Qur'an readings to make up for people's sins and omissions. This is an area where the interests of the Party and the ulama of the Muslim Spiritual Directorate coincided to some extent. As noted above, such practices were considered by Party ideologues as reactionary and harmful practices that inhibited the socialist enlightenment of the population. Many of these practices were also considered innovation (*bid'at*) by the scripturally trained scholars of the Muslim Spiritual Directorate, practices not derived from a correct reading of the Qur'an and hadith, which they criticised as un-Islamic (Saroyan 1997b, 50). Babadjanov has shown that in criticising these practices, the theological interpretations of establishment ulama went well beyond Hanafi orthodoxy. Some of their fatwas criticised as innovation anything not present within the practice of the Prophet himself and the first four Caliphs. This excludes many practices that have for centuries been regarded as legitimate by scholars within the Hanafi school, such as the Sufi pursuit of mystical, experiential knowledge. Moreover, although scholars working within the Hanafi tradition have condemned the visiting of the tombs of individuals regarded as being particularly close to God (*ziyorat*) when this crossed the border into idolatry or polytheism, they have recognised the legitimacy of praying to *God* at such tombs (Babadjanov 2001). Babadjanov has shown how the hard line has softened since independence, when fatwas were issued that condemned practices of 'ishanism' but recognised the legitimacy of Sufi practice. The change follows the new Idea of National Independence set out by the postindependence government, which presents the great Sufi scholars of the past who lived in the region as bearers of the 'Golden Heritage' to which the nation is returning. This will be discussed further in Chapter 3, and the different interpretations of officially appointed imams will be discussed in Chapter 4.

The scholars of the Muslim Spiritual Directorate were not mere mouthpieces for the central Party leadership, however. In promoting their own vision of theologically correct Islam, they were also offering an alternative to the socialist secularism of the Communist Party. Mark Saroyan has argued that the Muslim leadership in these directorates attempted to demonstrate that the values of Islam were compatible with

after he became a pensioner he first of all started to visit the *choykhona* (teahouse), then started going to *khatmi qur'on* with the old people. Gradually he started going to the mosque on occasion. He didn't pray, but went and talked to people there. If he had lived a little longer he would probably have started praying as well. People who weren't fervent communists, who were just workers like [my wife's] father – he was a driver – when they become pensioners, some of them start praying. That's natural.

For many, seeking divine intercession in overcoming illness or other life crises through the medium of saints or spirits was a significant element of Muslim practice. Healers who worked with spirits or by using the power of the Qur'an were active in the Soviet period, and some people visited the tombs of Muslim 'saints' (Basilov 1992; Snezarev 2003). A Russian language teacher in one of the schools in Pakhtabad described how his mother and grandmother had served as representatives of a female descendant of the Prophet.[10] This particular woman was considered a *pir*, a blessed and honoured person (*tabarruk*). The man's grandmother had been 'given the hand' (*qo'l bergan*) by the *pir*, which meant that she acted as an intermediary between the *pir* and those seeking her blessings.[11] People would bring offerings of food and money to the teacher's grandmother, who would then pass them on to the *pir*. This is the sort of practice the official ulama of the Muslim Spiritual Directorate criticised as 'ishanism'. When his grandmother died, this duty passed to his mother. However, she soon asked the *pir* for permission to give it up because it was making her ill, and afterwards she quickly recovered. The teacher interpreted his mother's illness as evidence of the power of the *pir*, and it contributed to the development of his understanding of Islam.

Throughout the Soviet period, practice understood as Muslim never ceased to be an important dimension of the flow of sociality, but Soviet policy and regulatory practice significantly influenced the way Muslims in Uzbekistan were able to express themselves as Muslim. In most Muslim societies, there are active debates and sometimes conflicts about what constitutes 'real' or 'genuine' Islam. In the Soviet Union, such debates were stifled. The official ulama within SADUM attempted to establish their own orthodoxy, criticizing much of local Muslim practice from the pulpits of the registered mosques. However, because most Muslims were effectively barred from attending mosques, they were deprived of their audience. Until the perestroika reforms, education in the core Islamic texts was largely confined to the few who studied in the two official Islamic educational institutions in Uzbekistan or who were sent abroad. For the majority of the population, those who received knowledge of Islam did so through the informal teaching of *mahalla* mullahs or female religious specialists, known as *otincha* in Pakhtabad or *bibikhalfa* in Samarkand.[12] As a result, during the Soviet period, Muslim practice was diverse and decentred. Most people developed their sense of themselves as Muslim through engagement in life-cycle rituals that created and confirmed them as members of their community. They did this through fulfilling their obligation to perform the prayers, fast during Ramadan, and participate in communal gatherings and rituals when they reached a certain age or position within the life cycle of their household. Some also expressed themselves as Muslim through engagement in what John Bowen has described as transactional relationships with spirits, where the intercession of spirits is invoked to address material concerns in exchange for sacrifice or prayer (Bowen 1993a, 229–50). Some experienced direct encounters with divine power in the course of illness and healing or in dreams and visions. However, there was no open and active debate about the nature of Islam and no coherent, scripturally based theological positions that reached the mass of the Soviet Union's Muslim citizens.

Cultural Muslims

How should we understand what Olimjon described as his swift 'crossing over' (Rus. *perekhod*) to Islam? Should this be seen as a radical conversion or transformation of belief and worldview, a return to a cultural and spiritual heritage suppressed during the Soviet period, or a transformation of Islam from a cultural identity to a spiritual commitment? All of these characterisations convey an aspect of what is taking place, but none is fully adequate. They imply that 'culture' and 'religion' are discrete categories, the former being an unreflexive immersion in tradition, whereas the latter is a matter of self-conscious, considered belief. The relation of Muslims in the Soviet Union towards Islam should not be seen as a belief in opposition to the ideology of Marxism, or as culture in opposition to true religion.

The concept of religion as belief or worldview is implied in the dichotomy that has often been proposed between official and 'underground' or 'parallel' Islam. Some analysts have interpreted the continued practice of Muslim life-cycle rites, such as circumcision and Islamic marriage ceremonies, as evidence that Central Asian society remained firmly 'traditional' despite Soviet efforts to produce a secular, socialist worldview (Poliakov 1992; Vaisman 1995; Vishnevskii 1996). They have emphasised the ubiquitous, 'clandestine' practice of Islam at 'underground' mosques and the activities of unregistered mullahs who presided at household rituals. Alternatively, a contrast has often been drawn between official and 'parallel' Islam (Bennigsen & Wimbush 1985; Ro'i 2000; Rorlich 1991). The former refers to the imams and mosques operating under the auspices of one of the four Muslim Spiritual Directorates. The latter is characterised as an underground movement operating outside state control and even in opposition to it.

Such analyses have already been thoroughly critiqued (DeWeese 2002; Rasanayagam 2006b; Saroyan 1997a, 1997c). As the recollections of villagers in Pakhtabad show, there was no simple dichotomy in the practice of Islam in Soviet Central Asia between a public, official domain and clandestine or underground practice. Villagers did not make a distinction between worship at officially registered mosques, unregistered mosques, or ritual outside mosque space, all of which constituted Muslim practice. Even in terms of administrative classification, it is impossible to make a clear distinction between registered and unregistered activities, as registered mosques were often the site of officially condemned practices such as shrine visitation (Saroyan 1997a). Moreover, the imams appointed to the registered mosques frequently worked closely with unregistered mullahs who officiated at household and community ritual occasions. The latter were routinely given authorisation to conduct ritual in private households and returned to the mosque a proportion of the payments they received (Ro'i 2000, 135–6, 267; Roy 2000, 151).

The dichotomy between official and underground Islam is produced within the Soviet regulatory framework itself rather than being an expression of differing theological interpretations or beliefs. This system assumed religion to be a matter of individual belief and ignored the intersubjective and performative nature of Muslim practice. Within the state regulatory framework, a religious association consisted of a defined membership with a prayer house, a group of twenty original signatories to the application for registration, an executive organ, an auditing committee, and a religious functionary appointed, in the case of Islam in Central Asia, by The Muslim Spiritual Directorate for Central Asia and Kazakhstan (Ro'i 2000, 20–1). No religious activity was permitted to take place outside these associations and their prayer houses. However, for much of the Muslim population of Central Asia, as elsewhere, Muslim practice is not solely a matter of interior belief, but is carried out within and is constitutive of sociality. Most of this takes place in household spaces or sacred sites rather than in mosques or other premises recognised by the Soviet regulatory structures as specifically devoted to religious worship. This clearly does not conform to the Soviet model of discrete religious associations and individual belief, abstracted from the social context within which individuals develop a sense of Muslim selfhood. As a result, a large proportion of Muslim practice in the Soviet Union was placed outside the state regulatory framework in that it took place outside formally registered places of religious worship and was therefore criminalised.

Another common interpretation has been that the suppression of religious expression during the Soviet period transformed Islam from a genuine spiritual commitment to an element of cultural or ethnic identity for the majority of the self-ascribed Muslim population. This understanding stems from a concept of religion as concerned ultimately with belief and the sacred, distinguished in these terms from culture – an understanding that is implicit in much social scientific and historical analysis of the region. Low levels of mosque attendance, greater participation of women in public employment, and the general decline in ritual observance is interpreted as evidence that Central Asian society became 'secularised' and Sovietised in the decades following the Second World War. It is sometimes argued that socialisation within Soviet schools, the experience of military service in the Red Army, and the transformation of work and production through the collectivisation of agriculture and employment in state industries succeeded in large measure in achieving the transformation of consciousness that the Soviet leadership desired (Medlin & Cave 1964; Medlin et al. 1971; Northrop 2004, 347–57). It is argued that the isolation of the region from the rest of the Islamic world and the severe restrictions on the availability of religious education diminished not only theological knowledge but also engagement with Islam as a system of belief, as an intellectual and spiritual relationship with God. Instead, Islam was reduced to an element of secular national identity (Khalid 2003, 2007; Ro'i 1995; Shahrani 1995). Some have suggested that Islam became mere superstition and an expression of communal belonging enacted in life-cycle celebrations, the wearing of protective amulets, and the visitation of the shrines of Muslim saints in search of miraculous cures for illness and misfortune (Akiner 1996).

These are not necessarily inaccurate accounts. The idea of a 'cultural' or 'secular' Muslim, a person for whom participation in Muslim ritual and identity as Muslim is part of the sociality of family and community but who has no engagement with Islam as a theological system, is one that Olimjon himself would probably understand. This is how he described his orientation during the Soviet period. It could similarly be used to describe many individuals I encountered during my field research who continue to have a similar orientation, some of whom would consider themselves to be atheist. 'Cultural Muslim' in this sense was an ascription used consciously by many I encountered during my time in Uzbekistan. These were often people from indigenous populations who had joined one of the evangelical Protestant Christian groups that have appeared since independence. They used the term to describe their own former selves and the orientation of the majority of people who call themselves Muslim in Uzbekistan. They commonly asserted that they had not 'converted' as such, in the sense of switching from one belief to another, because in the past they had not had any genuine faith at all, but had only occasionally participated in Muslim ritual as a form of cultural expression.

In the context of post-Soviet Kyrgyzstan, Mathijs Pelkmans and Julie McBrien have described how the category of culture is manipulated in interesting ways. They agree with authors who argue that Soviet nationalities policies had the effect of making religion a marker of ethnonational identity, so that Christianity became seen as a 'Russian' religion, and the concept of a secular atheist Muslim became a comprehensible category for many Kyrgyz. They describe how evangelical Christian missionaries who have entered the country since independence, as well as some Muslims, have attempted to redefine the concept of culture in different ways and to break the identity between the categories 'Islam' and 'Kyrgyz'. For evangelical Christian missionaries, this is done to show that, in fact, Christianity is more in tune with Kyrgyz identity than Islam, so that a Kyrgyz can become a Christian without forgoing his or her identity as Kyrgyz. The concern of Muslim missionaries, for their part, is to rid the local practice of Muslims of non-Islamic 'tradition'. For 'secular' Muslims, the emphasis on pure or genuine Islam is seen as extremism (Pelkmans 2007; Pelkmans & McBrien 2008).

The concepts of tradition and culture employed by Protestant missionaries and the new members of Protestant groups are produced within their own constructions of the proper relation between God and an individual human being and what constitutes an authentic Christian person, which they understand in terms of a stance of interior belief. Their construction is different from the way the concept of tradition, as *urf-odat*, is employed by scripturally trained Muslim scholars in their criticism of un-Islamic innovation in the practice of local Muslims, and it is different still from the postindependent government's construction of authentic tradition and the national 'Golden Heritage'. These different constructions will be examined in later chapters. Here I want to distinguish the operation of these *located* discursive constructions from the use of culture and religion as *universal*, analytical categories. Although the idea of a cultural or a secular Muslim is perfectly intelligible within local understandings, I am arguing that for the purpose of understanding Islam as it is lived in Uzbekistan or elsewhere, we should be wary of adopting the categories of religion and culture as meta-analytical tools, abstracted from the local processes that give them specific significance.

In Chapter 1, I argue that much of what many individuals in Uzbekistan consider to be Muslim practice would not fit into an idea of Islam as a discrete, bounded phenomenon, and that participation within an everyday sociality, which is by no means always explicitly 'Islamic', can nevertheless contribute to the development of Muslim selfhood. This is not to say that the sociality within which an individual in Uzbekistan is immersed is in itself Muslim. It was not so for Olimjon during the Soviet period, nor is it so for many of those I encountered, particularly in the city of Samarkand. Many might recognise a ritual or life-cycle event as Muslim without developing a specifically Muslim self through participation within it. Rather, they see the event and their own involvement as an expression of 'tradition' and may readily ascribe to being 'cultural Muslims'. An argument I am making in this book is that for the purpose of understanding Islam in Uzbekistan, it is not useful to take Islam itself, independent of how it is enacted within a Muslim life, as the object of study. Rather, Islam becomes an object within the development of a moral self when this is understood as a Muslim self. What we have is a multitude of objectifications of Islam within diverse individual moral narratives of self that develop though ongoing experience. I am arguing that everyday sociality is a moral source that gives experience the quality of transcendence and enables moral reasoning. For Olimjon, participation in everyday sociality of family and neighbourhood during the Soviet period is retrospectively reevaluated from the standpoint of his current Muslim self. Analytical frames that set up religion, culture, and the social as discrete categories are not helpful for understanding how sociality itself can provide the quality of transcendence typically reserved for the 'religious'.

THREE

Good and Bad Islam after the Soviet Union

The Instrumentalisation of Tradition

Since independence, the government of President Islam Karimov has instrumentalised Islam as part of its nation-building strategies. Islam has been incorporated within the ideology of National Independence that the government has developed to replace the Marxist Leninism of the Soviet era. Religious expression continues to be closely monitored, and like the governments of many Muslim majority states, the government in Uzbekistan attempts to shape the way Islam is interpreted and expressed by citizens. This chapter extends the previous discussion of the efforts of the Soviet state to shape the consciousness of citizens and explores the nature of the citizen-subject and of Islam that is constructed within post-Soviet state discourse. In this discourse, Islam is not treated as a universal Truth that transcends cultural and national boundaries but is localised within the government's conception of an authentic, indigenous culture. It is constructed as an element of a Central Asian 'Golden Heritage' (*oltin meros*) to which the nation is returning after decades of Soviet rule. 'Good' Islam is portrayed as culturally authentic, tolerant of other religious traditions in the region, and nonpolitical. 'Bad' Islam is characterised as alien in origin, antithetical to Central Asian spiritual values, intolerant in that it espouses a narrow version of Islam that excludes many Central Asian practices, and politically motivated. Interpretations of Islam not endorsed within state discourse are labelled as extremist and 'Wahhabi', with links to international networks of terror. Any religious practice not conforming to the preferred version of Islam is actively suppressed, and the Soviet structures for monitoring and regulating religious activities have been retained and modified for this purpose.

The chapter goes on to discuss how the postindependence government uses the idea of an authentic, national tradition as a tactic of governance. In their efforts to shape the subjectivities of citizens, Soviet political elites and ideologues at the centre had at their disposal the state provision of jobs, housing, and social welfare. However, with the withdrawal of the state after independence from comprehensive provision, these tools are no longer available. Instead, the government has made use of the concepts of tradition and cultural authenticity. Chapter 4 explores the practical workings of the state structures for the regulation of religion. In this chapter, I describe the government's functionalisation of tradition through a discussion of the *mahalla*.

Secularism and the State Construction of Religion

In official ideological pronouncements, Uzbekistan is presented as a secular state.[1] Article 31 of the constitution guarantees the freedom of the individual to profess any religious faith, while article 61 underlines the separation of religious organisations from the state and prohibits state interference in their affairs. Although, in light of actual state intervention, these guarantees remain 'on paper', they are not meaningless or merely intended to present an acceptable face of liberal democratic governance to foreign observers. Nor is the discourse of good and bad Islam solely a defensive reaction to the political challenge posed by Islamist groups. These are no doubt important considerations, but this chapter argues that state discourses on Islam and secularism extend beyond immediate tactical concerns. They are part of a broader project to shape society and the subjectivities of citizens in a particular way – a project that in many respects has been influenced by Soviet attempts at social reconstruction discussed in Chapter 2.

A useful frame for understanding this project is secularism itself. Following a number of recent studies on secularism that use Muslim societies as a reference (Asad 2003; Mahmood 2005, 2006; Navaro-Yashin 2002), I approach this as a practice through which the state seeks to classify and regulate all aspects of society, including what constitutes the religious. As such, it is not sufficient simply to speak of the government's using Islam to legitimate its rule, or of its co-opting or functionalising Islam for its own purposes. The ambition is no less than to shape the conditions of possibility within which citizens in Uzbekistan are able to relate to Islam and fashion their own Muslim selves. This secularist project, as I describe it here, is in fact shared by all modern nation-states, whether in the context of Muslim majority societies or otherwise, which everywhere seek to define the boundaries of the religious and the political, public and private spheres, and which entail particular visions of citizen subjectivities. I do not claim that authoritative state discourse in Uzbekistan succeeds in determining the subjectivities of citizens. In Chapter 2, I argue that this is not a productive way to understand its operation in the Soviet context. Its actual effects – the practical hegemony of state discourse – are discussed in Chapter 4.

Secularism is not simply the exclusion of religion from the conduct of government or the confinement of religion to a 'private' sphere separate from the 'public' political and economic spheres. A number of commentators have argued that this conception of the secular is an historically rooted construction, a normative ideology that is the product of the European enlightenment critique of religion (Casanova 1994; Nandy 1998). It is tied up with teleological assumptions about the progress of rational scientific thought and modernity, whereby religion is assumed either to decline or to become marginalised within a sphere of private belief and morality. However, it is difficult to ignore the fact that religion has continued to thrive in the modern world. The high levels of religious affiliation in the United States cannot be viewed as a perplexing exception to a general decline in religious faith in the modern West

(Casanova 1994). In addition, a number of studies have pointed to the popularity of religious movements, such as charismatic Pentecostalism, in societies that are fully part of the 'modern world', bound up within networks of global capitalism (Maxwell 2005; Meyer 2004; Robbins 2004).

Talal Asad (2003) has argued that religion, and by extension the secular, are not natural, objective categories. Rather, they are produced within discourses and technologies of power that act upon the subject to make certain kinds of knowledge, action, and desire possible and others not. He traces the emergence of separate secular and religious spaces in colonial Egypt, where a new legal code based on a European model was introduced. These reforms established a distinction between private morality and public law, which previously had not existed. Asad argues that the medieval Islamic conception of *fiqh* (Ar. jurisprudence) did not separate private virtue from correct public conduct as defined within the *sharīʿa*. An individual's ability to judge what is right or good did not depend on an inner conscience, or even on formal learning alone. Correct discernment depended upon the acquisition of desired habits of thought and behaviour through disciplined practice. This was not acquired autonomously by individual effort but was a social process in which the actions of the individual were subject to comment and intervention by relatives, friends, and authoritative figures within the community. Thus, in many precolonial or premodern Muslim societies (including Central Asia before the Russian conquest), training at religious schools and madrasas aimed as much at inculcating appropriate habits of comportment, behaviour, and practical judgement as in transmitting scriptural knowledge (Eickelman 1978; Khalid 1998, 19–44). The authority of judges who arbitrated disputes on the basis of the *sharīʿa* depended more upon their personal reputations for piety and integrity than upon any official position they may have occupied within the state bureaucracy (Khalid 1998, 38; Lindholm 1996, 159–60). When, in the course of legal reform in colonial Egypt, the *sharīʿa* was transformed from a socially embedded guide for conduct into a disembodied and formalised legal code authorised and regulated by the state, a separation was established between personal morality and public law. The *sharīʿa* was confined to the sphere of personal status and a newly defined category of the family, governing issues of marriage, inheritance, and divorce. This, Asad argues, created the conditions whereby it became possible to conceive of a distinct religious sphere, confined to the private space of personal morality and separate from a public ethic codified in law and regulated by the state.

The key feature of secularism, therefore, is not simply a separation of the religious and the political. This is only one form that secularism might take. Rather, secularism refers to the claim of the modern state to classify and regulate the entirety of social space, part of which entails defining what constitutes the religious. As such, the efforts of many European states to establish a clear boundary between religious and political spheres, the Soviet project of social reconstruction in Central Asia, as well as the efforts of some states in the Muslim world to regulate Islam directly and incorporate religion within the state bureaucracy are equally secular endeavours. Secularism as a state project of classification need not be modelled upon a Western European separation of a public sphere from an internal space of private morality. This is not the type of society and person that either the Soviet state or the post-Soviet government in Uzbekistan has sought to produce.

A comparison of Ataturk's secularist reforms in Turkey with the early Soviet reconstruction of Central Asia, which was largely contemporaneous, is illustrative. Kemalist secularism in Turkey both parallels and diverges in important ways from the Soviet project. The Kemalist project was one of modernist development modelled on a conception of Western European 'civilisation'. It attempted to fashion a new Turkish subject whose consciousness was rooted in rational reasoning and empirical science. In a manner that recalls the Soviet policies in Central Asia in the 1920s and 1930s discussed in Chapter 2, Ataturk's reforms were directed at liberating the individual from the regressive, communitarian constraints of religion and tradition, embodied in Islamic institutions such as the Caliphate, Sufi brotherhoods, the Arabic language and script, and social institutions such as the *mahalle* (Mardin 2004; Shankland 1999).[2] Religion ideally was to be a matter of private conscience, excluded from the public conduct of political life. However, the type of subjects envisioned by the Kemalist and Soviet states were radically different. The Turkish subject whom Ataturk attempted to fashion was modelled on the European concept of the autonomous, morally responsible individual, free from the collective constraints of 'traditional' community-oriented life. By contrast, the new Soviet citizen was conceived not as an autonomous individual but as part of a larger collective that ultimately extended to encompass the entire socialist state. The individual was not so much subordinated to the collective, as collective values and goals were intended to be embodied within and constitutive of individual subjectivities. Within official ideology, there was no distinction between private and public, an important point to which I will return later in this chapter.

Despite these radically different conceptions of the citizen, both the Soviet and Kemalist states conceived of their projects as modernist and progressive. Islam and tradition, insofar as they posed a threat to this project, had to be circumscribed, and both states dealt with this in a similar manner by subordinating religion within a state or quasi-state administrative structure. In Turkey, Islam was institutionally incorporated through the Directorate of Religious Affairs, which reports to the Prime Ministry, and through other relevant ministries. The state controls the education and the assignment of religious professionals, approves the content of Friday sermons, controls education at religious schools, and enforces laws regulating religious attire in certain public spaces (Shankland 1999; White 2002). This is a tactic of governance that has been adopted by a number of governments of Muslim majority states in their attempts to shape religious subjectivities,[3] and Chapter 4 discusses the present Karimov government's attempt to control Islamic expression through the quasi-state Muslim Board of Uzbekistan.

also adopt the dichotomy between good and bad Islam (Abu-Lughod 2005, 163–91). Cultural authenticity is an important reference for this indigenous construction, and in the case of Muslim states, the 'Other' is not so much an external, alien force as it is constructed in Western discourses, but an inauthentic or misguided version of the self.[4]

The distinction between good and bad Islam made by the postindependence government in Uzbekistan largely takes this form. Tradition and cultural authenticity are important references in its discourse. However, bad Islam is not portrayed as an inauthentic self, but as a completely alien 'Other', opposed to Uzbek national character and tradition. At the same time, although good Islam is constructed as tolerant and moderate, it is not located in a private morality, outside the sphere of public governance as the dominant Western model of secularity would have it. Within state discourse, no claim is made to Islam as a divine revelation applicable to all of humanity. Instead, a distinctly Central Asian form of Islam is constructed as an element within a uniquely Uzbek cultural and historical heritage. This heritage is portrayed as providing norms and values, which all Uzbeks are expected to share. Non-Central Asian nationalities, such as Russians, Koreans, and others who make up approximately 10 percent of the population, are incorporated in terms of the tolerance and secularism inherent to the spiritual heritage. Central Asia is presented as a region in which historically different religious and ethnic groups coexisted peacefully,[5] and values of tolerance and hospitality are portrayed as inherent to the Uzbek character. Thus, morality and religion are not matters for the private belief of autonomous, morally responsible individuals. Instead, like the Soviet concept of citizen-subject discussed in Chapter 2, citizens are expected to share collective values and orientations that now are defined in terms of an authentic national tradition.

The postindependence government's concept of culture and historical heritage, its ideas about the nature of the citizenship and society, and the practical strategies it pursues owe much to Soviet ideological constructions and tactics of governance (Adams 1999). The independent state that emerged in 1991 was itself a Soviet creation. In the 1920s and 1930s, the Soviet authorities categorised the local populations of Central Asia into distinct ethnonational entities and drew up the borders of the five Central Asian republics largely as they exist today. There is now an established body of good historical analysis of this process, examining the extent to which the national delineations were the product of a divide-and-rule policy on the part of central authorities in Moscow or a result of the efforts of local Central Asian elites who were following their own varied interests (Haugen 2004; Hirsch 2005; Roy 2000). What is relevant here is the ideological conception of ethnicity and nation within Soviet nationalities policy and its enactment in practice.

As finalised by Stalin, this policy was based on a primordialist conception of ethnonational development, within which each 'people' (Rus. *narod*) constituted a stable community characterised by shared language, culture, and territory. Each was thought to follow an evolutionary path of development from kin-based or clan groups, through tribes and tribal federations, and finally reaching the stage of the nation-state. Soviet ethnographers were employed to categorise in these terms the vast diversity of peoples within the Soviet Union, which then were ascribed a nationality and granted an administrative status commensurate with their assessed stage of development.[6] Uzbeks, Georgians, Armenians, and Ukrainians, for example, were considered to merit an 'independent' republic. Peoples at a lower stage of national development were given the administrative status of an autonomous region or national territory within one or another of the republics. The paraphernalia of statehood were set up in every republic, including a national flag and anthem, a head of state, and ministries. Moreover, each nationality was supposed to have its own 'Great Tradition', and by the end of the 1930s, all of the Union Republics had their writers' unions, theatres, opera companies, and academies that specialised in national history, literature, and language (Abashin 1999; Slezkine 2000; Smith 1996).

The Karimov government has inherited the Soviet concept of the ethnonational state, whereby the existence of the state as a political and territorial entity depends upon, and is legitimated by, association with a culturally and linguistically defined group. Within Soviet nationalities policy, the separate national republics were to be a temporary stage on the road to eventual merger into a supranational socialist collectivity. In the famous formula worked out by Lenin and Stalin, they were to be national in form and socialist in content. Since independence, the Uzbekistan government has discarded the Marxist-Leninist ideology and filled the Soviet-created form of the nation with a new Uzbek nationalist content. Soviet historiography has been retained, but the previous negative valuation of historical figures and events has been reversed (Roy 2000, 161). Amir Timur (Tamerlane), for example, has been adopted as the founding father of the Uzbek state, and his statues have replaced monuments to Lenin in prominent locations throughout the country.

Central to the government's nationalist project is its construction of 'Uzbekness' (*O'zbekchilik*) as an historically developed complex of distinctly Uzbek spiritual values and national personality traits, which are promoted as the basis for economic, political, and social life in the country. Islam forms an important element within the new ideology the Karimov government is promoting. However, Islam in Uzbekistan is not treated as a transcendent or codified system of belief and practice that exists independent of Uzbek culture. Rather, the Islam constructed within state discourses is subordinated to the national spiritual heritage. The territory of Uzbekistan is portrayed as having played host to a number of religious traditions, including Buddhism, Hinduism, Christianity, and Zoroastrianism, and Central Asian society is characterised as one in which historically multiple faiths and places of worship peacefully coexisted (*Milliy istiqlol g'oyasi*, 60–1). Emphasis is placed upon the 'spiritual originality' of Central Asian Islam, which incorporates many elements of pre-Islamic culture and religion (Karimov 1997, 124). It is just

FIGURE 7. The Imom al-Bukhoriy mosque and mausoleum complex near Samarkand

such nonscripturally founded practices that are criticised by 'reformist' Muslims in diverse Muslim societies as illegitimate, un-Islamic innovation, and particularly in Chapters 4 and 7 I will discuss how such debates are played out in contemporary Uzbekistan.

In state discourse, Central Asian Islam is evidence of the uniqueness of Uzbek culture and of its tolerance and openness. The word 'secular' (*dunyoviy*) is interpreted within the context of this tolerance. It is used to reference political pluralism, the coexistence and recognition of multiple religious viewpoints, and interethnic harmony. Central Asian Islam is associated with this idea of tolerant secularism through the assertion that it was the combination of secular science and religious ideas in the region that produced great medieval Islamic philosophers, theologians, and scientists such as Ibn Sino (Avisenna), Imom al-Bukhoriy, and al-Beruniy (*Milliy istiqlol g'oyasi*, 17–18). All of these 'great ancestors' have contributed to the unique national heritage.

Key themes within the Karimov government's construction of Uzbekness are thus uniqueness and tolerance, and much is made of the 'Uzbek model' – the distinctly Uzbek path of development (*o'zimizga khos va o'zimizga mos taraqqiyot yo'li*). The rationale of the Uzbek model is used to justify the government's continued direct control over many sectors of the economy, as well as the limited extent of democratic reforms. The experiences of other parts of the world are declared irrelevant and unsuitable for Uzbekistan. It is in these terms that alternative interpretations of Islam are condemned. They are characterised as alien, intolerant because they espouse a narrow version of Islam that excludes many Central Asian practices, dangerous to interethnic harmony, politically motivated, and opposed to 'true' religion. Interpretations of Islam not endorsed by the Karimov government are labelled as extremist and 'Wahhabi', with links to international networks of terror. Echoing the Soviet construction of religion as socially regressive, foreign forms of Islam are characterised within state discourse as preserving backwardness and inhibiting the civilised development of society. Neighbouring Afghanistan is held up as an example of the civil conflict and social and economic devastation wrought by alien forms of Islam (Karimov 1997, 39–40).[7]

By contrast, the Karimov government celebrates Uzbekistan's own national Islam, exemplified by the region's Sufi tradition (Kehl-Bodrogi 2006; Louw 2007; Schubel 1999). The government has renovated and monumentalised the mausoleums of past Sufi masters such as Baha' al-Din Naqshband (d. 1389), founder of the Naqshbandi Sufi order, as well as those of other prominent figures. It has supported the publication of numerous books and newspaper articles and the broadcast of programmes in the media about the lives of prominent figures in the history of Central Asian Sufism. The official endorsement of these *avliyo*,[8] and the public state recognition awarded to their shrines, has granted implicit endorsement to the practice of shrine visitation whereby Muslims seek the intercession of *avliyo* in overcoming illness or worldly difficulties (Schubel 1999). During the Soviet period, shrine visitation was criticised by state authorities as a practice that preserved prerevolutionary attitudes and inhibited the development of a progressive, socialist consciousness. It is also condemned by some Muslims who subscribe to a strictly scripturalist interpretation of Islam. As such, the practice of visiting shrines has become an important focus for debates about what constitutes 'authentic' Islam.

The postindependence government has inherited not only the primordial concept of ethnicity and the form of the ethnonational state from the Soviet Union, but also the Soviet concept of citizenship. As noted earlier in this chapter, this was not founded upon the rights of the sovereign individual and the concomitant existence of an inviolable space of private morality. No private space was recognised, because individuals were expected to internalise collective goals and values. Whereas in the Soviet period, these were defined in terms of building a socialist society, in state discourses in independent Uzbekistan, they are phrased in terms of the unique cultural and spiritual heritage, the *oltin meros* (Golden Heritage), of the Uzbek people. To formalise and disseminate the official construction of this heritage, the Karimov government has developed what it calls the 'Idea of National Independence' (*Milliy istiqlol g'oyasi*).[9] The main ideas of this ideology are published in a booklet of this title (henceforth referred to as MIG), and the themes it contains are developed in numerous other publications, many penned in the name of Karimov himself. Thus, tradition and cultural authenticity are intensely political fields in Uzbekistan.

State discourses stress the need to avoid an ideological and spiritual vacuum that would allow space for the influx of alien and dangerous ideas and to provide an 'ideological immunisation' (*mafkuraviy immunitet*) in the form of an indigenous national idea, particularly for the younger generation (MIG, 41–2).[10] The Idea of National Independence contains a passage titled 'The Perfect Person' (*komil inson* – MIG, 56–7), an ideal described as an organic element of Uzbekistan's spiritual heritage, fed by Islamic philosophy and developed by great thinkers in Uzbek history. The 'perfect person' is a morally complete, harmoniously developed individual who is master of an independent worldview. This clearly echoes language used in Soviet discourses on the need to cultivate harmonious and complete persons who embodied a modernist, socialist ethic (Hoffmann 2003, 35–6), and perhaps also Sufi ideas of individual self-perfection. Of course, 'independent' in this context refers to the uniqueness of the Uzbek model rather than to an individual moral autonomy.

The postindependence Karimov government does not have at its disposal many of the tools that were available to the Soviet state. The Communist Party attempted to develop a collectivist, socialist subjectivity through direct control over all aspects of a person's life. Work, housing, leisure, and the provision of the necessities of daily life, as well as the media and the system of education, were all intended to be encompassed within the social sphere controlled by the state. Since independence, the state in Uzbekistan no longer directly provides employment and housing to all and has left individuals and households to obtain the necessities of daily life for themselves. The government therefore can no longer use social and material provision as a tool for shaping subjectivities. Instead, it utilises its control over the security apparatus, the media, and education and has made the concept of cultural authenticity into a tool of social control.

The *Mahalla*: Tradition as a Tool of Governance

In Chapter 1, I describe the institution of the *mahalla*, a residential neighbourhood in both urban and rural settlements. Despite the fact that the present form of the *mahalla* is relatively recent, it is presented in government discourse as a repository of centuries-old traditions and as embodying authentic 'Uzbekness'. In its construction of the *mahalla*, the Karimov government is attempting to use tradition as an instrument for social control, and even refers to the *mahalla* as a 'lever' it can manipulate to achieve desired ends.[11] It attempts to use the *mahalla* as a medium for extending the presence of central government into the intimate spaces of the family. Relations within the *mahalla* are presented as founded upon an ethos of mutual respect, support, and cooperation, guided by elders known as *oqsoqol* (literally translated as 'white beard'). The *mahalla*, along with an idealised image of the Uzbek family, is put forth as a model for national rule, in which citizens are expected to perform their duties to the nation, mutually supporting each other and the state leadership, with the president, as the head of the national family, making decisions for the common good. Under the slogan 'from a strong state to a strong society' (*kuchli davlatdan, kuchli jamiyat sari*), an all-powerful executive presidency is legitimated with reference to the timeless traditional values of the Uzbek people.

The *mahalla* plays a dual role for the Karimov government. It uses the ideal of the *mahalla* to naturalise the authoritarian rule of President Karimov. The state is presented as the family or community writ large, where all members perform their allotted duties and look out for each other's well-being. The following extract from one of the many publications produced by the government is typical of the way in which the *mahalla* is functionalised.

> Our choice of the road of transition to a market economy to a decisive extent stems from a comprehensive consideration of national and historical factors, i.e. traditional way of life of the people, their outlook, thinking, customs and rituals. The people of Uzbekistan are historically characterised by their communal form of social self-organisation, which is rooted in the traditional lifestyle of the people. This is displayed in the priority given to the interests of a family, the commitment to the community in daily activities, careful preservation and consolidation of the institution of the mahalla, but has had a deep impact on the entire social structure of the society. . . . The republic itself may be considered as a kind of community, as a big family where no one can live a prosperous and decent life without mutual respect and lasting order, without strict commitment to their obligations and mutual concern, i.e. as a system of informal social relations imbued with the spirit of ethnic group solidarity. (Karimov 1993, 27–8)

At the same time, on a more immediately practical level, the institution of the *mahalla* is used as an instrument of surveillance and control over the population (Massicard & Trevisani 2003). Although the *mahalla* committee is by law a self-governing institution with a locally elected leadership and is outside the government administrative hierarchy, in practice it is treated by centrally appointed local governors (*hokim*) as an extension of their own personal authority.[12] Indeed, the local governor must approve the list of candidates for election as *mahalla* committee chairman. A number of benefits and services that previously had been provided by state organs have been devolved to *mahalla* committees. These include the identification of which households qualify for state welfare payments, the distribution of child support, and the maintenance of registers of those eligible for military conscription. This structure exists partly to relieve the state from the responsibility for directly providing these services, but the Karimov government also intends to use local networks of social interaction and sociality to extend the reach of central government (Noori 2006). For example, local government uses the *mahalla* to collect payments for utilities such as gas and electricity, to collect taxes, and even to aid in the fulfilment of production targets for industries. *Mahalla* committees are expected to promote government propaganda through the work of their various subcommittees. They are expected to organise state-sponsored festivals, such as Independence Day and *navro'z* (a festival in early spring celebrating the New Year). In addition, the educational programmes undertaken by the *mahalla* committees mirror government priorities, and each year the committee is obliged to present its programme of activities to the office of the district or city governor for approval.

Mahalla committee leaderships are expected to act as the eyes and ears of the government and to be on the lookout for antigovernment sentiments among their residents. They keep a record of all residents who are working abroad and report this information to the district government. Residents and local organisations must approach the *mahalla* committee for proof of residence or references to obtain a number of official documents, such as passports or exit visas for foreign travel. After a series of bomb attacks in the capital in 1999, the president called on *mahalla* leaderships to monitor the populations and mosques in their territories for indications of what the government considers 'extremist' tendencies.[13] During the period of my field research in the spring of 2004, there was a further spate of bombings and shootings directed against the police, after which *mahalla* chairmen were asked by the state security forces to inform them of any residents who expressed dissatisfaction with the government.[14]

Central government has functionalised the *mahalla* as an element within its legitimating ideology and as a practical extension of its authority and control. This is possible because the concept of the *mahalla* as a model for virtuous living resonates powerfully with much of the population. In Chapter 1, I argue that immersion within a shared sociality can contribute to an individual's understanding of moral selfhood and discuss how the institution and ideal of the *mahalla* is a part of this sociality. The *mahalla*, like Islam, has resonance outside its construction within state discourse. Individuals come to their own understanding of the *mahalla* that emerges from their ongoing experience, but this is shaped in important ways by government discourses and practice. I explore this dynamic through an account of Abdumajid-aka, whom I met on my first day in Samarkand in 2003 and who cooperated with me in much of my fieldwork in that city.

Abdumajid-aka was in his late fifties when I met him. He is a lecturer in mathematics at the University of Samarkand and director of a secondary school. In 2003, he was elected chairman of his *mahalla* committee. Abdumajid-aka is someone who could be called a social activist: He takes seriously the official legal status of the *mahalla* as a self-governing institution and believes that the *mahalla* can form the basis for a genuine democratic society in Uzbekistan. He is active in promoting the interests of *mahalla* residents. He does not see himself or his residents as opposed to the state. On the contrary, he believes in cooperative relations with residents, the *mahalla* leadership, and city officials working towards a common goal. Of course, many local government officials do not share this idealistic view.

Much of his work as *mahalla* chairman involves cooperation with the city government officials or supporting central government policies. For example, he has taken the initiative in working with the public utility providers and local government to find a means to ensure that the gas and electricity bills are paid on time. Abdumajid-aka is not simply concerned that his residents are guaranteed supply. In fact, the gas supply to an individual household is rarely cut off because of nonpayment. Instead, shortages of gas result in an overall reduction in provision. In the case of electricity, it is common for people to connect their houses directly to overhead power lines, avoiding payment altogether. Abdumajid-aka has a larger vision of the equitable distribution of resources in the nation as a whole and in the contribution of individuals to the collective good. In the case of natural gas, he expressed the view that it is the property of the people (Rus. *narodnie dostoyanie*), as it is extracted from the ground. He does not accept the view that the gas-supplying organisation is in financial crisis, arguing that the cost for gas has increased much faster than salaries and that those who pay are in fact making up for those who do not. As evidence, he points to the relatively high salaries of its employees, with their leather coats and mobile phones. The solution he has suggested is to cancel past debts and for the *mahalla* leadership to work in cooperation with local government in collecting payments. In return, the *mahalla* would be allowed to keep a percentage of the revenue to aid poorer families.[15]

Abdumajid-aka is widely travelled, having visited Iceland and Israel for academic conferences and courses, and he has visited the United States to participate in a project promoting the creation of civil society sponsored by the U.S. government. On his return, he founded an association of heads of *mahalla* committees with the aim of supporting their members and increasing awareness of their legal rights and status. To this end, his association runs seminars to educate *mahalla* chairmen of their rights vis-à-vis the local state representatives. This is something unprecedented in Uzbekistan and, in the political context in which any hint of activism independent of central government control is regarded as suspect, it is not a little dangerous. What protects Abdumajid-aka and his association is the state discourse itself. It provides space for such initiatives, as long as they can be presented as fitting within official discourses about the *mahalla* and as being supportive of the Karimov government, or at least not in conflict with it.

This democratic vision of the *mahalla* is exceptional among the committee chairmen I encountered. Most described the *mahalla* as the lowest layer in the state governing hierarchy, directly under the control of the city or district governors. Some described themselves as 'little *hokim*', mapping the national structure of executive government onto the *mahalla*. In this structure, state power is largely concentrated in the hands of the president, who appoints the provincial governors (*hokim*), who have similar executive authority in their regions. These governors, in turn, appoint the lower-level district and city *hokim*. Although the *mahalla* leadership is not appointed directly by governors but elected by residents, their appointment must be approved by the district governor.

Even where *mahalla* leaders see themselves as primarily acting in the interests of their residents rather than as mere extensions of the state, they do not perceive this in terms of representative democracy. They tend to view themselves in paternalistic terms, as acting in the best interests of their communities, upholding and enforcing correct conduct, looking after the economically vulnerable, and protecting residents from the excesses of state authorities. To support their authority over residents, they use their control over the resources and functions that have been devolved to them, such as the issuing of documentation people need to obtain exit visas for travel or work abroad, the allocation of state-provided relief for poor families, and the issuing of character references for jobs and court cases. The state judicial system often refers back to the *mahalla* domestic disputes and other cases that judges consider of minor importance. *Mahalla* chairmen might also organise social boycotts of those they consider are ignoring their authority. Their vision of the *mahalla* and the role of the *oqsoqol* as an authoritarian but benevolent leader mirrors central government discourses. However, because they are not outsiders cynically attempting to instrumentalise the *mahalla* for their own ends, but are seeking to protect residents from interference from the outside, their self-representations are perhaps more convincing to *mahalla* residents.

Abdumajid-aka's activities have led him into direct confrontation with the city government and the leadership of law enforcement agencies on a number of occasions. One such conflict concerned their efforts to force the *mahalla* chairmen to collect fees from prospective army conscripts for a reduced term of military service. During the time of my field research, military service was no longer compulsory. However, a requirement for entry into the police force, the National Security Service (successor of the Soviet KGB), and the public prosecution service (all highly desirable careers, not least because of the opportunities for earning money through bribes), is a certificate of completed military service. People can either serve for a full year or can pay the equivalent of approximately U.S.$140 to serve for one month. This has led to the unusual situation in which people actually pay a bribe or use personal connections to enter military service for the full one-year term, as such positions are now limited. A large number of people who did not manage to get a place and were signed up for the one-month service had failed to pay, and the local government was forcing the *mahalla* chairmen to collect this money.

At a meeting organised by the city district authorities to which the *mahalla* chairmen were summoned, the assistant district public prosecutor tried to bully the chairmen into compliance. He referred ominously to certain chairmen who were refusing to collect this money and thus opposing the president. When some of the *mahalla* chairmen objected, the prosecutor rudely dismissed them. Abdumajid-aka and the press secretary of his association decided to publish an article in a national newspaper dedicated to *mahalla* matters about how the assistant public prosecutor was exceeding his authority and failing to treat the *mahalla* chairmen with respect. In a meeting with the head of the provincial branch of the national Mahalla Foundation (a body set up by the government to develop the *mahalla* as an institution), it was decided that the assistant public prosecutor would be asked for an apology. However, the Mahalla Foundation official refused to allow the article to be published. He did not want to portray Samarkand in a bad light to central government authorities and just wanted to smooth over the whole affair. Determined to publish the article in any case, Abdumajid-aka and his press secretary did so through the Uzbek language newsletter of The Institute for War and Peace Reporting, a British nongovernmental organisation (NGO) supporting journalism. As a result of the embarrassment this article caused to the local government officials, portraying them as opposing an institution the president was publicly supporting in his official pronouncements, the assistant public prosecutor was transferred to a position in the provincial administration.

This conflict reveals something about the nature of governance in Uzbekistan, which, to a large extent, is a legacy of the Soviet period. Formal adherence to the law is not as important as displaying loyalty to the Karimov government. In this situation, state officials themselves can be just as vulnerable to the application of the coercive capacities of the state as citizens within their jurisdictions. It is not simply a matter of state officials having access to state power and directing it at others. Both state officials and nonstate actors manipulate presidential pronouncements and publicly stated goals to portray themselves as in accordance with them and their opponents as violating them.

Abdumajid-aka is aware that he is treading a dangerous line. He is safe only as long as his actions cannot be portrayed as being in opposition to the Karimov government, and his only protection against such an interpretation is his prominent position within Samarkand society, his reputation for integrity and disinterested public service, and his close relationship with local government authorities in forwarding their own work in a number of areas. He does not openly confront the government but directs his protests at the actions of individual officials, drawing attention to how their actions are in contravention of presidential pronouncements and the law. He stresses that he is not opposed to payment for the shortened period of military service and supports the law, as the money that previously had gone into someone's pocket in the form of a bribe to avoid service now goes to the government. In his view, it is the implementation of the law that is the problem. He was not even opposed to being asked to help in the collection of payments and considered it the duty of the *mahalla* chairmen to cooperate with state authorities wherever possible. His objection was to the dictatorial manner of government officials. After the public prosecutor changed his attitude in the face of open opposition from the *mahalla* chairmen and asked politely, Abdumajid-aka decided to cooperate and visit the residents who had not paid:

> I fulfilled his request, but if he hadn't asked politely, I wouldn't have gone. But I know that the army needs money, needs to protect the borders, fight terrorism. I understand. An educated person should understand, but you have to understand at the level of the subconscious, and not on the level of insult or pressure.

Abdumajid-aka and the state officials he is criticising are, in fact, all operating within the same discourse of the *mahalla* and its presentation within the official pronouncements of the Karimov government, but the meanings they attach to it and the ends to which they direct their actions are very different. State discourse on the *mahalla* emphasises its importance in providing support for residents, socialising and educating young people, and instilling traditional Uzbek spiritual values. It is even described as a school for democracy (MIG, 67). The Karimov government's aim is to instrumentalise the *mahalla* within its construction of an Uzbek cultural heritage as a tactic of governance. For local governors, the *mahalla* is an extension of their own authority, a tool for monitoring and controlling the population and for fulfilling the directives handed down to them from the central government. Abdumajid-aka has a different view: He shares the conception of the *mahalla* as an embodiment of traditional modes of sociality and morality, but he understands the ideals and practice of social solidarity and equality within the *mahalla* as a genuine basis for democracy in the context of the modern nation-state. He takes seriously the government's own discourse, reversing the president's slogan 'from a strong state to a strong society' to argue instead that in order to have a strong government, you need a strong society. In day-to-day interaction, he encounters local government officials who have very different ideas of this institution, and in struggles, negotiations, and cooperation with these officials, Abdumajid-aka is attempting to realise his own vision of a moral community.

Abdumajid-aka's freedom to interpret tradition and the *mahalla* as the practical enactment of a moral community is shaped by the way it has been constructed within state discourse and practice. I describe in Chapter 1 how the institution of the *mahalla* has been standardised as a residential subdistrict with a leadership and a set of personnel with defined duties. It has been imposed in areas where it had no history before, and variations in local forms of social organisation have been regularised through the now-official structures. Moreover, the relationship of the *mahalla* leadership both with state authorities and residents is, to a large extent, a product of the official duties and practical power bestowed by the government. Were Abdumajid-aka to exceed the bounds of expression considered politically acceptable by the government, he would be forced into the position of political opposition activist, with all of the dangers and restrictions on personal freedoms that would entail. He would no longer be able to retain a self-representation as someone trying to improve the lot of his residents through cooperative engagement with the state.

The post-Soviet government needed to find an alternative to Marxist-Leninism as an ideological basis for the newly independent state and for its authoritarian vision of governance. Lacking the resources to ensure that the state remained the dominant provider of livelihoods and welfare, it also needed to find alternative means to ensure the hegemony of its ideological vision. It attempts to answer both problems with the concept of cultural authenticity and tradition. It has made its own construction of 'Uzbekness' and cultural authenticity the standard to judge what is acceptable and what is not and has attempted to mould existing patterns of sociality embedded within local patterns of interaction and social organisation into a practical tool of governance. Citizens in Uzbekistan must present themselves in terms of the government's constructions of good and bad Islam, tolerant tradition and extremist Wahhabism. The practical hegemony of this discourse in the practice of individual Muslims is discussed in Chapter 4.

FOUR

The Practical Hegemony of State Discourse

This chapter addresses how citizens in Uzbekistan are able to express themselves as Muslim while being subject to an authoritarian regime that narrowly defines what is acceptable Islamic practice and is prepared to punish ruthlessly anything it sees as deviating from it. Previous chapters have argued that hegemony should not be understood as the capacity of a dominant discursive regime simply to determine subjectivities. Rather, the discourses of the postindependence government in Uzbekistan are hegemonic in the sense that, to a significant degree, they fix the terms in which citizens are able to present themselves and others as Muslim and develop their own understandings of Muslim selfhood. The government's construction of good and bad Islam, of cultural authenticity, and of a national spiritual heritage at the heart of its state-building ideologies has made the notion of tradition intensely political. Practices that can be placed within its narrative of a historically developed national tradition are permitted and celebrated by the government, whereas anything that falls outside this narrative or is simply unfamiliar is open to being perceived as alien and potentially dangerous.

The government is prepared to employ the coercive capacities of the state, the organs of law enforcement, and the judiciary to ensure that citizens adopt appropriate attitudes and practices. It encourages an atmosphere of mutual surveillance and fear. Through frequent exhortations in the president's speeches, in the media, and from the pulpits of mosques it calls on the public to be constantly on the alert for deviant activities and attitudes. Compounded by the often arbitrary exercise of state coercion by local functionaries, this has engendered an atmosphere of existential vulnerability associated with religious practice. In situations where state power can be invoked, citizens in Uzbekistan must present themselves as Muslim in terms of the government's constructions of good and bad Islam; of tolerant, local tradition and alien, extremist Wahhabism. The actual nature of an individual's belief or practice is less important than whether it might be perceived, or be made to seem, contrary to state-approved forms.

The chapter begins with a broad outline of government policy towards Islam since independence. It goes on to outline the structure of directly regulated Islam, the registered mosques incorporated within the oversight of the Muslim Board of Uzbekistan, and the efforts of the government to extend its control to unregulated religious practice through the establishment ulama. The practice of Islam, which is unregulated but nevertheless institutionalised within the framework of the *mahalla*, is also described. The dilemma of establishment ulama is discussed. Official imams are expected to promote and enforce the government's construction of a culturally authentic Central Asian Islam, but this conflicts in fundamental ways with their own understandings. In the final section, I describe how the practical efforts of the government to control and regulate religious expression and its instrumentalisation of the concept of tradition influence the way individuals are able to present themselves and others as Muslim.

Throughout this book, I use the term 'imam' to refer to the officially appointed head of a registered mosque, formally known as *imom khatib*. The title reflects the duties of this individual both to lead the prayers (*imom*) and to deliver the sermon (*khatib*). The sermon can only be delivered by the *imom khatib* appointed by the Muslim Board at a registered Friday mosque. Following local usage, I use the term 'mullah' to refer to men recognised locally for their knowledge of Islam who are invited by individuals and households to recite the Qur'an and deliver prayers on ritual occasions. These individuals may have extensive religious education, or their knowledge may be limited to appropriate prayers and Qur'anic verses. Female religious practitioners who perform this function for women are known as *otincha* in the Fergana Valley and *bibikhalfa* in Samarkand. Again, their levels of religious knowledge and education vary greatly, as does the extent to which they combine recitation of the Qur'an at ritual occasions with healing practices, often with the aid of spirit agents.[1]

Divergent Discourses

The government's construction of good and bad Islam is not the only discourse that has been available to Muslims in Uzbekistan. Ideas of Islamic reformism were present in Central Asia in the Jadid movement at the beginning of the twentieth century. Like reformist trends in other Muslim societies during this period, the Jadids arose largely in response to European colonial domination. The best account of Jadidism in Central Asia is provided by Adeeb Khalid (1998).[2] The Jadids identified the root cause of Muslim weakness in the face of Tsarist Russian domination as a moral decay caused by the outmoded pedagogy, the approach to the sacred texts, and the corrupt personal conduct of the established ulama. They sought to move away from the rote learning of sacred texts through the mediation of a master to the cultivation of a critical, reflective stance. They advocated the spread of functional literacy, with an emphasis on the meaning of the text rather than solely on its accurate reproduction. The Jadids criticised much of local customary practice as not truly Islamic and condemned the wealthy for waste and immorality. The solution was not the Russification of Central Asian society but an Islamically informed modernisation.

After the Jadid movement was suppressed in the early years of Soviet rule, reformist ideas once more began to enter Central Asia beginning in

societies, both non-Muslim and Muslim, as being in a state of unenlightened ignorance or *jāhilīya* (Ar.). Significantly, he declared that to be a Muslim, one had to live in complete accordance with the *sharīʿa*, in effect declaring the majority of Muslims and all Muslim governments to be un-Islamic. He called on Muslims to remove themselves from the *jāhilī* environment and to work to overthrow *jāhilī* governments, replacing them with a truly Islamic society (Qutb 1990). The final trend identified by Ramadan is 'liberal reformism', which follows a Western-style secularism in which religion becomes a private affair of the individual.

In Uzbekistan, disputes about the nature of Islam in the late Soviet period and the early years of independence involved a number of these trends. The establishment ulama of the Muslim Spiritual Directorates generally advocated a Hanafi interpretation of Islam and were critical of many of the practices of local Muslims they considered heterodox. However, the restrictions placed on religious practice in the Soviet Union limited their influence among the mass of the population. A limited number of nonestablishment, independent scholars provided Islamic education to small circles of students discreetly in their own homes. These individuals were distinct from the mullahs and *otincha* who provided informal training in most village contexts because they had obtained an advanced Islamic education either in the pre-Soviet period or outside the Soviet Union. Many, such as Muhammadjan Hindustani (1892–1989), who has received a fair amount of recent scholarly attention (Babadjanov & Kamilov 2001; Naumkin 2005, 43–51; Whitlock 2002), could also be described as Hanafi traditionalist scholars.

In the 1970s, however, a younger group of scholars, some of them former students of Hindustani and other independent scholars like him, began to adopt interpretations of Islam divergent from the Hanafi tradition. Some of these referred to themselves as Mujaddidiya, or movement of renewal (Babadjanov 2004, 49). They could be categorized as salafi to the extent that they criticized a blind adherence to the local Hanafi interpretation of Islam and advocated a direct reading of the Qur'an and

Sunna. On a practical level, they performed the daily prayers (*namoz*) in a manner that was not the established practice in Central Asia, and they focused their attacks upon the incorporation within the practice of local Muslims of what they considered non-Islamic customs and traditions (*urf-odat*). The Hanafi traditionalists also acknowledged that such practices had no basis in the Qur'an or Sunna, but, according to Babadjanov, they were more open to incorporating and regulating them within an officially sanctioned Islam (Babadjanov 2004; Khalid 2007, 144–7). However, those who follow salafi-inspired ideas cannot be distinguished from traditionalists on the basis of their opposition to local customary practice alone. Most of the officially appointed imams I came to know during my own research do not adopt the salafi literalist position that all interpretation is illegitimate, but they acknowledge that there is both good and bad *bid'at*. However, they also criticise what they consider to be heterodox practice in equally strong terms, including the extended series of commemoration feasts associated with a death or physically touching the structure of the tombs of *avliyo*, placing the 'saint' as an intermediary or companion alongside God rather than praying directly to God at the site.

More significant is the opposition of followers of salafi trends to the local Hanafi tradition of Islam and their willingness to engage in political activism. During the perestroika years in the late 1980s, there was a resurgence in popular interest in Islam and a great diversity of interpretation. After a brief period of intensified repression of Islam that lasted until 1988 (Hanks 2001), obstacles to the building of mosques were eased, and their number increased rapidly.[3] By the end of the decade, Qur'anic clubs and study groups were being organised outside the parameters of the official religious administration (Malashenko 1994a). A number of organised Islamic groups with an explicitly political agenda sought to create an Islamic society (Babadjanov & Kamilov 2001, 205). Two significant groups that emerged in the Fergana Valley at the beginning of the 1990s were Islam Lashkarlari (Warriors of Islam) and Adolat (Justice). The latter initially addressed deteriorating standards of living, declaring its aims to be maintaining public order, combating corruption, and promoting social justice. It organised patrols of young men to police bazaar traders to prevent them from increasing their prices and to maintain order in residential areas. The movement quickly took on an Islamic character and worked with local imams, holding meetings in mosques. In the city of Namangan, they demanded that the president establish a public centre for studying the Qur'an in the former Communist Party building (Malashenko 1994b, 133–4; Naumkin 2005, 58–60). These groups began to be referred to collectively by their Hanafi traditionalist opponents and by state authorities as 'Wahhabi' after the politically engaged and puritan movement in Saudi Arabia, although they did not necessarily have any concrete connection with that movement. As I discuss in the final section of this chapter, the term 'Wahhabi' has come to denote any form of religious (and sometimes clearly nonreligious) practice that falls outside what the government considers part of its definition of national-heritage Islam (Khalid 2007, 172–3).

The response of the government of Islam Karimov has been to ban these groups and to arrest anyone suspected of involvement in any independent Islamic organisation. In 1992, the government clamped down on Adolat and ordered the arrest of its leaders. Foreign Muslims suspected of missionary activity were expelled, and members of opposition groups, whether Islamic or otherwise, were arrested or fled the country (Naumkin 2005, 70). Muslim religious groups independent of state control are not tolerated, and those who are suspected of overstepping these limits are defined by state authorities as 'extremist' regardless of their actual ideological or spiritual orientations (Khalid 2007, 168–91). People who have been labelled in this way range from Muslims who merely pray regularly and strictly observe the tenets of Islam to those who actually advocate the establishment of an Islamic state and *sharīʿa* law.[4] People who openly proselytise, encouraging others to observe the Islamic duties of prayer, abstinence from alcohol, and other prescriptions have also been labelled 'Wahhabis' by law enforcement agencies, whether or not they have any links to political or militant Islamic movements (Human Rights Watch 2004, 20–4). After police officers were murdered and a local government official was beheaded in the city of Namangan in 1997, arrests of suspected Islamists increased. Measures against independent Islamic activity reached a peak in the aftermath of the bombings in Tashkent in 1999 that were attributed to Islamic groups, after which thousands of suspected 'extremists' were arrested.

By the late 1990s, organised independent groups had only a limited presence in the country, although an Islamic political opposition continued in the form of the Afghanistan-based Islamic Movement of Uzbekistan. This group was critically damaged in the U.S.-led invasion of that country following the attacks on New York City in 2001.[5] Within the country, the most prominent organised group is Hizb ut-Tahrir al-Islami, a transnational organisation that seeks to transform Muslim societies in line with the *sharīʿa*. It professes to achieve this through nonviolent, bottom-up change, transforming the consciousness of individual Muslims through education. It seems to have become active in Uzbekistan from the mid-1990s onward, but little can be said with certainty about its activities or the extent of its following because of the clandestine manner in which any independent group is forced to operate in Uzbekistan. It is viewed by the government as extremist and politically motivated. Commentators on Islam in Central Asia have claimed that Hizb ut-Tahrir is organised in small cells or circles (Khalid 2007, 163; Naumkin 2005, 143), and it is estimated to have approximately 10,000 followers in Uzbekistan (Naumkin 2005, 158). However, this figure remains largely guesswork, and it is unclear how one could precisely identify who is a member or follower of the organisation.

In her research on *otincha* (female religious practitioners) in the Fergana Valley in 2001–02, Svetlana Peshkova recounts how some of the women she interviewed described a theological divide among the teaching of *otincha* between 'traditionalist' and 'Hizb' approaches (Peshkova

2006, 227–8). The latter were critical of non-Islamic customary practice in the manner of the salafi reformists mentioned earlier in this chapter, whereas other *otincha* supported these practices as part of a local tradition. She also records encounters with study groups of women who acknowledged that they followed Hizb ut-Tahrir teachings (Peshkova 2006, 311). However, most *otincha* distanced themselves from Hizb ut-Tahrir, even those who followed a scripturalist interpretation of Islam and criticised much of local practice as un-Islamic. Peshkova describes how some *otincha* used the accusation of belonging to Hizb ut-Tahrir as a tactic to discredit the teachings of rivals. Thus, whatever the actual extent of Hizb ut-Tahrir's activity in Uzbekistan, its presence in the consciousness of local Muslims is shaped by the government's opposition between good and bad Islam. Those who promote a version of Islam that may be viewed as attacking local tradition are open to being characterised as extremist and Wahhabi, regardless of their actual orientation.

State Regulation and the Category of Religion

The Karimov government has sought to maintain tight control of religious expression. The Soviet-era Spiritual Directorate for the Muslims of Central Asia and Kazakhstan has been transformed into a nominally nongovernment, national body and renamed the Muslim Board of Uzbekistan,[6] and religious affairs within the republic more generally are overseen by the Committee for Religious Affairs of the Cabinet of Ministers. In May 1998, the Law on Freedom of Conscience and Religious Organizations, which codifies the government's position on religious expression, was passed. This law reiterates the secular character of the state; however, as discussed in Chapter 3, secularism here is not conceived as the separation of religion from a public political sphere, whereby religion is the private affair of the individual. The law explicitly places the state in the position of arbiter, deciding what religious expression is permissible; guaranteeing the observance of what it considers good, tolerant practice; and excluding 'fanaticism' and 'extremism' (article 5). The interests of stability and interconfessional harmony, as these are interpreted by central government, are placed firmly ahead of individual freedom of religious expression. The wearing of religious clothing in public, except by officially recognised functionaries, is banned, as is the private teaching of religion outside officially registered institutions, proselytism, and any kind of missionary activity. Anything interpreted by the government as antistate propaganda or destabilising ideas, as well as the storage or distribution of what it considers extremist literature and other material, is also banned.

Through the process of registration, the government retains the right to define what counts as genuine religion, politically motivated extremism, or merely foreign ideas with no place in Uzbekistan. The Soviet model, which treated religious expression as contained within discrete organisations, has been retained, most likely because of the control this gives to state bodies through the process of registration. Every mosque or church is legally an independent religious organisation that must apply for registration to the Ministry of Justice, and applications must also be approved by the Committee for Religious Affairs. The application must be signed by 100 citizens older than eighteen years who are permanent residents in the country and must include a list of the managerial committee, information about its sources of funding, and a charter detailing, among other information, its goals, activities, and management structure.[7] Central religious administrations, such as the Muslim Board of Uzbekistan, may be established by the representatives of religious organisations from at least eight provincial regions (*viloyat*) of the country. Registration of these administrations is similar to that for individual religious organisations, and like the latter, they have the status of a legal entity. Central administrations are able to set up religious educational institutions to train clergy (open to those leaving state secondary school); these also have to pass through the registration process of the Ministry of Justice.

FIGURE 8. A registered mosque in the old section of Samarkand

Nonregistered religious organisations are banned, but unlike the Soviet authorities, the postindependence government recognises that religious activity takes place outside the physical premises of the formal religious organisations. The 1998 law allows for worship and religious rites at the premises of religious organisations (mosques and churches), but also at pilgrimage sites and cemeteries; within prisons, hospitals, and other residential institutions; and within the home. However, in light of the government's aggressive pursuit of cultural authenticity, the overall effect is not an increase in freedom but an ambiguity that further heightens the atmosphere of existential vulnerability associated with religious expression and practice. On the one hand, gatherings in a domestic context – for example, a Muslim or Christian prayer group – could be considered an illegal gathering of an unregistered organisation, and participants would be prosecuted accordingly. On the other hand, a wide range of ritual gatherings are regularly held in households, such as *mavlud* ceremonies, which celebrate the birth of the Prophet, or *khatmi qur'on*, at which the Qur'an is recited for a deceased individual. Visiting the shrines of *avliyo* is widespread. Whether or not these gatherings are permissible depends upon how the local law enforcement functionaries choose to view them. In making such interventions, the frame of cultural authenticity is critical, leaving individuals in a condition of uncertainty when their practice does not fall unambiguously within the category of 'national tradition'.

Establishment Islam: Control by Proxy

Within Sunni Islam, there is no 'clergy' in the sense of an institutionalised hierarchy of religious specialists located within a centralised administrative structure. There is no recognition of an intermediary between an individual Muslim and God. In Muslim communities, anyone who is acknowledged to possess adequate religious learning and an appropriate character can lead communal prayers or fulfil other ritual functions. However, in Uzbekistan, the state system of regulation has created what might be described as an official or quasi-state hierarchy of religious personnel. Registered organisations and the central religious administrations, such as the Muslim Board, are formally independent, self-financing entities, but in effect they are subordinated to the state and expected to promote the government's policies on religion. The territorial administrative structure of the Muslim Board mirrors that of executive government. The board is headed by the Mufti based in Tashkent, and there are offices at the provincial (*viloyat*), district (*tuman*), and city levels. Although the management committees of individual mosques are chosen by the founders of the religious organisation, the Muslim Board appoints the *imom khatib*. The 1998 law stipulates that the leaders of religious organisations must have an appropriate religious education, and *imom khatib* without official qualifications are steadily being replaced by those who have graduated from one of the ten madrasas or the Imom al-Bukhoriy Islamic Institute in Tashkent, which are run by the

Muslim Board, or from the Tashkent Islamic University, which is under the jurisdiction of the Ministry of Education.

A registered mosque is a legally discrete entity, an organisation headed by the *imom khatib* with a management committee and a number of salaried personnel who usually include an accountant, a *muazzin* (a person who performs the call to pray), and perhaps a night guard. Although the Muslim Board pays salaries to its representatives at the provincial level, it gives no financial assistance to individual mosques, which are expected to be self-financing from the donations of their congregations. Indeed, they are expected to send a proportion of these donations to the Board, and according to interviews with a number of *imom khatib*, this amount seems to be anything between 15 and 50 percent of the regular monthly income and 80 and 90 percent of donations given at festivals such as *qurbon hayit* (the festival of sacrifice) and the festival to mark the end of the fast of Ramadan. A mosque's income may come from donations given directly to the mosque, donations in connection with cemeteries they control, or the payments to mullahs who carry out rituals on behalf of the mosque. It is used to pay for utilities bills, such as gas and electricity, as well as salaries, the level of which is decided by the management committee.

The incomes of mosques, and thus the salaries of the *imom khatib*, can vary enormously. Large mosques associated with the tombs of particularly prominent historical figures and with extensive attached cemeteries attract large congregations and a steady flow of pilgrims and therefore can raise significant levels of income. By contrast, newer mosques with smaller congregations raise barely enough to cover running costs. The *imom khatib* of the mosque located in the *mahalla* where I lived in the old city of Samarkand received the insignificant monthly salary of 5,000 *sum* (about U.S.$5), and claimed to live off the voluntary donations of the congregation. The *imom khatib* of a village neighbouring my research site of Pakhtabad in the Fergana Valley received no salary at all. He made his living by working in a textile factory in a nearby town and only attended the mosque on Fridays to lead the prayers and deliver the sermon. In fact, he had not applied for the post but had been asked to fill it by the Muslim Board, as no one else with a madrasa education was available. He was scornful of those who made a living from religion. Being an imam, he said, should not be seen as a profession:

> People don't go to mosques to earn money, but to pray. The old imams from before independence used to live from *ehson* (charitable giving), 1000 *sum* today, 2000 *sum* the next. This idea has sunk in, but it really shouldn't be like this. People should earn money from their own work.... I could do the same, sit in the mosque and wait for people to come for [weddings, funerals and other ceremonies], but I don't want to do this. Why should they give me money for doing nothing?... Ordinary people do their own work and then pray. I'll also have another job. *Imomlik* (being an imam) is not a profession for a person. This is something which should only be done for God, as a service to the people.

During my field research in 2004, the Muslim Board was introducing a hierarchy of grades or ranks of *imom khatib* depending on knowledge and experience, which was to be reflected in salary levels. However, because the incomes of mosques are so varied, it is hard to see how this can have any meaningful impact.

Through the sermons and teaching that take place in the mosque, the government seeks to shape the religious subjectivities of citizens in line with its own version of good Islam. The Department for Fatwas at the Muslim Board issues an outline for the sermon that all *imom khatib* must deliver at the Friday congregational prayers. This contains the themes to be covered and suggests references to Qur'anic passages or hadith, but imams are expected to flesh this out on their own initiative so that an identical sermon will not be delivered from every mosque in the country.[8]

Just as significant as fatwas and sermons is the indirect control the government exercises through the quasi-state religious structures over religious expression that takes place outside the sphere of official

FIGURE 9. The chief imam of Samarkand province delivering a sermon

regulation. This constitutes the bulk of Muslim practice and occurs at the tombs of Muslim saints and in life-cycle celebrations and other ritual occasions that are conducted within households and local communities. In a manner that recalls the strategy of the Soviet-era Council for the Affairs of Religious Cults (see Chapter 1), *imom khatib* appointed by the Muslim Board see it as part of their duty to monitor and supervise the activities of the unofficial mullahs. In the village of Pakhtabad, there is only one officially registered mosque, but there are a number of unregistered mosques that cater to particular *mahalla*. Villagers who pray regularly typically will attend their local *mahalla* mosque on a daily basis and go to the main mosque for the Friday noontime prayers that can be held only at a registered mosque. These *mahalla* mosques and their mullahs, though unregistered, are under the effective supervision of the officially appointed *imom khatib*, although there is no legal or formal relation between them. Certain religious rituals, such as the *nikoh* (marriage) or the *janoza* (funeral prayers), by law can be performed only by those with appropriate religious education, usually the *imom khatib* of an official mosque or his assistant (although imams might give official authorisation to mullahs). For most other ritual occasions, households in principle invite anyone they think appropriate. In the village of Pakhtabad, this is usually the mullah who is chosen by the inhabitants of a *mahalla* to look after its mosque and lead the prayers there.

The *imom khatib* of the official Friday mosque in Pakhtabad described these mullahs as his apprentices (*shogird*), whom he appoints on the recommendation of the *mahalla* residents. The mullahs themselves see things differently. Although they acknowledge that they are subordinate in terms of religious knowledge to the *imom khatib*, they see themselves as appointed by the leaders of their own *mahalla*. Similarly, in the city of Samarkand, most *imom khatib* told me that *mahalla* mullahs were under their direct authority and that they could dismiss them if they did not have adequate religious knowledge. The imam of a registered mosque in an Iranian district of the city was planning to conduct a systematic examination of all the mullahs and *bibikhalfa* (female religious practitioners) in the *mahalla* in the vicinity of his mosque and was seeking an order from the provincial office of the Muslim Board to carry this out. Again, mullahs and the chairmen of *mahalla* committees did not share this view of their relationship. They considered themselves independent of the Muslim Board and the registered mosques and did not recognise the authority of the imams to appoint or dismiss them. At the same time, they generally obeyed directives from the *imom khatib* and the Muslim Board.

This ambiguity results from the tension between the formalised hierarchical structure of the Muslim Board and the accepted practice among local Muslims that any individual with adequate knowledge and appropriate personal character is qualified to cater to their ritual needs. Mullahs in the village of Pakhtabad defer to the *imom khatib* on religious matters, and he is respected by villagers for his religious learning. However, he has no exclusive claim to Islamic authority simply by virtue of his office. In addition to the *mahalla* mullahs, there are a number of other individuals in the village known for their Islamic learning. These include men known as *qori*, who have acquired the skill of chanting the Qur'an and are invited to perform on ritual occasions such as the *mavlud* (commemoration of the birth of the Prophet). If a household wishes to hold such an occasion on a grander-than-usual scale, they might invite well-known *qori* or renowned scholars from outside the village as well. The *imom khatib* is afforded respect and deference because of his character and religious learning on the same terms as these other individuals. However, official imams within the structure of the Muslim Board have the power of the state behind them. When they advise unofficial mullahs, they are also implicitly giving guidance on the government's own definition of acceptable Islamic practice.

An Imam's Dilemma

Central government seeks to use the establishment ulama of the Muslim Board as it uses the institution of the *mahalla* – as an extension of its executive rule. Official imams are expected to promote what the government considers legitimate expressions of Islam and to monitor the population for signs of 'extremism'. Yet the construction of Islam within state discourse, as subordinated within a locally authentic cultural and spiritual heritage, contradicts in fundamental ways the official imams' own conceptions of Islam. Through a study of the sacred texts, albeit within madrasas controlled by the quasi-state Muslim Board, they view Islam as a universal Truth that transcends geographical and cultural borders, even if allowances are made for local traditions. Much of what state discourse extols as an authentic Central Asian spiritual heritage is considered by madrasa-trained imams as the product of fallible human tradition (*urf-odat*) – survivals of pre-Islamic ritual. However, in an environment where the government does not tolerate anything it considers contrary to its version of acceptable Islamic practice and expects the official functionaries of the Muslim Board actively to support and enforce this view, imams and others who share their scripturally based understanding of Islam are forced to walk a fine line. Their freedom to condemn what they consider to be un-Islamic innovation is constrained.

This conflict is nowhere more apparent than in the practice of *ziyorat*, the visiting of the tombs of Muslim saints (*avliyo*) to seek their intercession in worldly affairs. Chapter 3 describes how the government celebrates the practice of *ziyorat* as an expression of a culturally authentic Islam that privileges its unique, Central Asian character. It has elevated historical figures in Central Asian Sufism as contributing to Uzbekistan's distinct national heritage. The government has monumentalised the tombs of these figures, and state officials have publicly engaged in *ziyorat*, turning the practice into a symbol of Uzbek nationhood (Louw 2007). It has sanctioned the publication of hagiographies of the lives of *avliyo* and the miraculous events and deeds associated with them (Schubel 1999). For *imom khatib*, however, the local practice of *ziyorat* comes dangerously close to polytheism. There are a large number of saintly shrines in and around Samarkand, and the head *imom khatib* for the city complained that visitors were praying directly to the *avliyo*, not to God. He did not consider visiting the tombs as in itself contrary to the *sharīʿa*. It is, he said, perfectly acceptable for Muslims to visit cemeteries to remind themselves of their final end, to address prayers to God and recite the Qur'an at the graves of *avliyo*, and even to dedicate these prayers in the name of the *avliyo* as a person who had been particularly close to God. He drew the line at the common practice of touching the physical structure of the tombs or taking water from the springs that are frequently in the vicinity of the tombs (this water is believed to have healing properties), as this smacks of idolatry.

Another imam in Samarkand held a similar view. He is a fairly young man and a native of Samarkand who graduated from the madrasa in

Andijan in the mid-1990s. He claimed to be a *sayid* (descendent of the Prophet) and also a descendent of the prominent Naqshbandi shaykh Makhdum-i Azam (d. 1542), whose tomb and mosque complex is located in the town of Dahbed near Samarkand. After graduating from the madrasa, he taught Arabic from 1997 to 2000 in a secondary school. When Arabic was banned as a school subject after the bombings in Tashkent in 1999, he became an *imom khatib* and was posted to his present mosque in 2001, initially as an assistant. Like all *imom khatib*, he is critical of practices he considers contrary to the *sharīʿa*, including the veneration of shrines and women's propitiatory rituals, such the *bibiseshanba*, which he attributes to ignorance of the true essence of Islam. At the same time, he expressed the view that seeking the intercession of *avliyo* could be effective, as these individuals are particularly close to God. They possess *karomat* (spiritual power), and requests from them were more likely to be granted. God would forgive the sins of others because of respect for such *avliyo*. He expressed the Sufi idea that certain individuals, by virtue of their perfection of character, are able to receive knowledge directly from God, knowledge that is distinct from that acquired through a formal study.

The position of these imams is, of course, complicated by the prominence the Karimov government gives to the shrines of certain prominent *avliyo* within its discourses. Many of the most prominent shrines in the city are under the administration not of the Muslim Board but of a state-founded organisation called Oltin Meros (Golden Heritage). This organisation asked the chief *imom khatib* of Samarkand to provide imams to recite the Qur'an for visitors at its holy sites. The *imom khatib* was put in a quandary, because he did not want to encourage practice he sees as outside the *sharīʿa*. At the same time, he was unhappy that those who recite the Qur'an at these sites were ignorant of true Islam. In sending the imams, he hoped that they would be able to discourage the bad practice of pilgrims. Krisztina Kehl-Bodrogi (2006) has provided a revealing account of the dilemmas faced by the official imams appointed by the

FIGURE 10. A *bibiseshanba* held to give thanks for a husband's return from successful employment in South Korea

Muslim Board to oversee a tomb and mosque complex in Khorezm, where the desire of successive imams to stamp out what they see as illegitimate forms of pilgrimage conflicts with implicit government support for this practice.[9]

The ambiguity of the language of tradition helps imams to negotiate this minefield. During Friday sermons, official imams call on Muslims to be united in following the Hanafi teachings, which they describe as having been handed down by the great scholars of the past, many of whom are celebrated by the government as contributors to the national Golden Heritage. They support the government line in condemning Wahhabis and the Islamic group Hizb ut-Tahrir, branded by the government as a terrorist organisation, as contrary to true Islam. In the spring of 2004, there was a series of shootings and suicide bombings around the country that targeted state law enforcement personnel. These were blamed on extremist Islamic groups by the government, and in the weeks following these incidents, sermons predictably focused on condemning these actions. Suicide bombers, the imams declared, were not martyrs but would be punished by God for all eternity. The sermons characterised Islam as a religion of peace and emphasised that true Muslims do not harm others in word or deed, nor do they involve themselves in politics. The current material difficulties that many in the country were facing were a test from God, and Muslims had to be patient and not engage in violent actions. Just as the government has told citizens to be on the lookout for deviant behaviour in their neighbours, imams, in their sermons, have exhorted parents to correct the attitudes of their children and neighbours to monitor each other's activities. The head imam of the province of Samarkand declared in a sermon I attended that every family is a madrasa, echoing the government's pronouncements that liken the *mahalla* to a 'school for democracy', instilling traditional Uzbek spiritual values (MIG, 67).

Imams promote the Hanafi tradition of Islam as locally authentic and in line with state discourse on cultural authenticity. From a position within this frame, they also condemn un-Islamic behaviour, as they understand it. In some of the Friday sermons I attended where the imams appealed to Muslims to be united and to reject groups such as Hizb ut-Tahrir or Wahhabis who sowed conflict, they also warned against the false claims of Christian groups who were attracting converts with false promises and financial incentives. They warned Muslims against seeking out healers or soothsayers who dealt with spirits (*jin*) as contrary to the *sharīʿa*. These practices are characterised as mistaken tradition and un-Islamic innovation – an understanding of tradition that is very different from the government's secular construction. Fundamentally conflicting visions of truth and authenticity are overlooked behind public and vociferous support of the government.

The establishment ulama do not uncritically adopt the government's construction of a local Central Asian Islam. However, like their counterparts in the Soviet period, they present their interpretation of Islam as consistent with state ideology. They praise Uzbekistan's Islamic heritage, endorse the interpretations of the Qur'an by the great Islamic thinkers who historically have resided in the region, and condemn the violent actions of religiously based opposition groups as misguided and un-Islamic. They characterise many of the practices adopted by local Muslims as *bid'at* (illegitimate innovation) – customs they claim have crept into local practice because of the enforced ignorance of the Soviet period – yet their freedom to condemn them is limited by the state discursive construction of cultural authenticity.

I'm Not a Wahhabi!

The late perestroika era and the initial years of independence was the period of greatest freedom and dynamism in Uzbekistan in relation to Islam. Mosque attendance increased dramatically, and people openly organised the ritual gatherings they had held more discreetly in earlier years. A lecturer at Samarkand State University recalled that students had asked for and received a prayer room in the university building and even remembered hearing the call to prayer over the intercom system in some government departments. In 1996, a group of lecturers at another higher educational institute in the city, along with their friends and relatives, financed the building of a mosque and helped with construction work. A vice-rector who had made the hajj pilgrimage to Mecca contributed the bulk of the money for this project. They registered it as a Friday mosque with the Muslim Board, and it was attended mainly by staff and students of that institute.

However, as government policies towards Islam became more repressive, this trend reversed. The prayer room in the university was withdrawn, and by the time I embarked on my first period of field research in Uzbekistan in September 1998, broadcasting the call to prayer by loudspeaker had been banned.[10] After the Tashkent bombings in early 1999, the vice-rector who had donated money to the building of the mosque was demoted to ordinary lecturer. The rector told him that the money should have been spent on improving the facilities at the institute rather than on a mosque.[11] The present imam at that mosque told me that in 1996 it had been full of teachers and students but that this changed after 1999:

> Then the state imposed restrictions on religion. The teachers were afraid to come, and they told the students not to come either. They told them that if they went they couldn't study at the institute. They were afraid that one of them might become a Wahhabi. But we don't teach anything bad in the mosque. The state monitors us. There's nothing happening here which shouldn't happen. After that fewer people came to the mosque. People who had strong faith remained, the rest with weak faith left. Again they started doing the things they did in the age of ignorance (*johil davr*), drinking vodka, taking bribes. . . . But when you die you will be asked if you prayed, if you knew God, if you fasted. The world of material concerns (*mol dunyo*) will pass. It is temporary.

On the occasions when I attended prayers at this particular mosque in 2004, there were usually about forty people of varying ages at the Friday noon prayers and only a handful of older men at noon prayers on other days.

During the spring of 2004, there were further bombings and attacks, mainly targeted at the police, which the government attributed to Islamic extremists. Shortly after the first incident, agents from security services visited the mosque in the *mahalla* where I was living in the old city of Samarkand, at the time of the evening prayers, and noted down the names and addresses of all those present.[12] One of my friends at that time was a devout Muslim, a young man who prayed at that mosque daily and was learning Arabic from the imam. He told me that he was avoiding the mosques and the main streets for a while because of the heavy police presence. He habitually wore a black felt cap, a style often favoured by devout Muslims, instead of the Uzbek-style *do'ppi* (a black cap embroidered with white thread) and felt that he would be a target for their attention. Indeed, a few days later when I was walking with him in a neighbouring *mahalla*, we were stopped by the *oqsoqol* (chairman of the *mahalla* committee), who advised him not to wear his cap because people would think he was a Wahhabi. He continued to wear it, however.

An atmosphere of apprehension surrounds everything associated with Islam. At the same time, a great many people continue to engage actively in Islam, praying regularly at mosques, holding funeral ceremonies and *mavlud* gatherings in honour of the Prophet, and visiting shrines of Muslim saints. I came across a number of young men like my friend in the previous paragraph who were studying Islam from *mahalla* mullahs or imams or from the numerous freely available government approved publications and recordings of sermons. Particularly in the village of Pakhtabad, many young men were becoming *qori* (reciters of the Qur'an) and were much in demand at religious gatherings. State measures to control Muslim expression have not so much reduced religious practice in a crude way but rather altered the manner in which practice is expressed. In the current atmosphere of fear and vulnerability, the label 'Wahhabi' has come to represent any religious expression of which people are unsure – any expression that does not fit into the category of established 'tradition', the clearly acceptable, the harmless – and consequently may make those associated with it a target for the state security services.

Fear of being labelled as Wahhabi affects the way people choose to express themselves as Muslim, but it can also be instrumentalised within personal rivalries. An account of the building of another mosque is illustrative. This took place in the village of Pakhtabad and was located next to the existing Friday mosque but was planned on a grander scale. It remained unfinished and unused, however, and people sometimes referred to it as the 'Wahhabi' mosque. Building work started in 1992 with money that apparently came from Saudi Arabia or Kuwait (although people I asked were not sure). It was organised by a group of villagers who might be described as reformists. Most of this group of seven people were well educated. The chief organiser of the mosque project was an engineer, and another prominent member was a Russian language teacher known for his fluency in a number of languages, including Arabic, as well as for being very knowledgeable about Islam. They believed that people should study Islam directly from the Qur'an and hadith and were critical of many village practices. For example, they argued that the series of ceremonies that occur on the Thursdays after a person dies, and on the twentieth and fortieth days, were un-Islamic, and that there should be only one short funeral ceremony. They argued about this with other villagers, including the imam of the Friday mosque who was the leader of the 'traditionalist' camp. The building of the new mosque seems to have brought these rivalries to a head.

In 1995, this group was denounced as Wahhabi, and building on the new mosque came to a halt. The catalyst for this was the government closure of a mosque in Andijan that members of this group attended. It had been identified by government authorities as controlled by Islamic extremists. The traditionalist camp in the village used this as an opportunity to isolate the reformists. The Russian teacher, fearing arrest, fled to Russia. Although the others remained in the village and were left alone by the state authorities, the imam and his group organised a social boycott that lasted until a year or so before my second period of field research began in 2004. They were not invited to village events such as marriage and circumcision feasts, and people were encouraged to avoid any events they held.

A factor that might have contributed to the identification of this group as Wahhabi is that approximately when building work started on the new mosque, a meeting was held at the Friday mosque adjacent to it. The aim of the meeting was to organise the village into a new form of governing structure they called an *amirlik* (emirate). Each *mahalla* in the village was to have a *yassaul* (judge), with a *yassaul boshi* (head judge) for the whole village. These *yassaul* were to ensure moral behaviour and maintain order in their areas and were to be integrated in a hierarchical structure to the ruler. This plan came to nothing, however, as the police arrived the next day and, in cooperation with the imam of the Friday mosque, prevented it from going any further.

Unfortunately, I was only able to obtain knowledge of this conflict at second hand, even though many people involved are still in the village, including the imam I had met on a number of occasions. This is still a highly sensitive topic, and I was unwilling to attract the attention of the security services to myself or to those with whom I was associated by openly investigating the incident. The circumspection I was forced to observe no doubt affected my research. On the other hand, it would have been impossible to conduct research on the sensitive topic of Islam without it.

Villagers with whom I did manage to talk about the mosque meeting claimed that it had been organised by people from outside the village. It occurred near the time of the events associated with the political group Adolat in the city of Namangan referred to earlier in this chapter, and the subsequent government clampdown on that group, and it is possible that it was organised by Adolat or a similar organisation. However, most of the reformist group within the village are unlikely to have been suspected by the law enforcement agencies of having anything to do with this movement or with Islamic political movements in general, because they were never arrested. The imam and the other traditionalists were able to use the prevailing atmosphere fostered by central government of vigilance against the threat of Islamic extremism to discredit and isolate them.

The government's discourses on good and bad Islam, its appeals made through the media and the official religious structures to maintain constant vigilance against alien forms of Islam and extremism, and the repressive use of state coercion have created a sense of existential vulnerability surrounding religious practice. This is exacerbated by the ambiguity in the law about what is permissible and what is not. The law permits individual and communal practice of religion in the home, but any such practice might be interpreted as the gathering of an unregistered religious group. It is up to local authorities to decide what is and is not permissible, and in so doing, they are guided by the government's opposition between culturally authentic practice and dangerous, foreign extremism.

The label of Wahhabism extends beyond the clearly Islamic. It is sometimes even applied to the activities of Christian groups, especially if they include members with a Muslim family background. An Uzbek student in Samarkand who was attending a Protestant Christian group told me that his father was worried that the Bible he brought home to his village might be Wahhabi literature. Even though the Bible is not banned or considered extremist literature by the government, I was aware of a case in the city of Samarkand in which a member of the Baptist church had been arrested for possessing the Bible at home. The pastor of his church announced this during a Sunday service, saying that the arrest was illegal and that when the case came to trial, the man would be freed. I was aware of a number of other Christians from Muslim family backgrounds who had been accused of being Wahhabi by neighbours in their *mahalla*, including members of the group the Uzbek student attended. This student showed the Bible to an *eshon* (a person who claims descent from the Prophet or prominent figures in Islamic history) who recognised it as a Bible and reassured the student's father that it was from God and that there was no harm in reading it. However, after the bombings and attacks on police in the spring of 2004, his father forbade the student from visiting the group.

The conflict between different interpretations of Islam in Pakhtabad illustrates how individuals can use the ambiguity and insecurity created by the state discursive construction of cultural authenticity to characterise opponents as Wahhabi and thus draw the attention of the law enforcement bodies upon them. In Samarkand, I came across a group led by a charismatic healer to whom I will refer as 'the Teacher'. He called his group a 'school of life' and seemed to draw on elements of Islam, Christianity, and Buddhism in his philosophy for attaining spiritual enlightenment (I will return to this group in Chapter 5). A large part of his practical message involved healing physical and psychological pain and suffering and opening up the way to success in life. The Teacher described how, in 2001, he had given courses on his philosophy in the Centre for Spirituality and Enlightenment (*ma'naviyat va ma'rifat*), a nationwide network of centres to promote the government's ideas about national spiritual development. Students had paid the equivalent of about U.S.$20, although the Teacher claimed that the director of the centre had pocketed all of this and he had received nothing. The head imam for the province of Samarkand objected to his teaching and informed the authorities in Tashkent that he was teaching Wahhabism. This imam must have known that the courses were not concerned with politicised Islam, much less Wahhabism, but he used the accusation to launch the investigation. The teacher told the investigators that he didn't speak Arabic and didn't even perform the *namoz* (Muslim prayers), and the Wahhabism charge was dropped. However, he was charged with teaching without a licence and fined the equivalent of approximately U.S.$300. The courses were stopped. At the time I met him, he was still not officially registered as a religious organisation, although he continues to operate from his home.

In another case, a village outreach worker for a local NGO in Samarkand offering help to the victims of domestic violence described how she initially encountered hostility from the district government officials and *mahalla* leaderships who accused her organisation of creating Wahhabis. This charge was levelled because they offered seminars to women informing them of their rights under the law and raising awareness of the issue of domestic violence. She and her organisation were only accepted after they demonstrated that they were able to offer concrete benefits to the community and forward the interests of local government officials. They offered medical and psychological help to victims, but the decisive factor was that they were able to mobilise aid from a foreign organisation to build a school in cooperation with the local *mahalla* committees and the district government. This allowed these officials to claim credit for fulfilling directives from central government to provide schools in their area.

Jan Gross, writing about the Soviet occupation of Poland during the Second World War, has described the privatisation of the state and the public domain under totalitarianism. Through the mechanism of denunciation, individual citizens were able to employ the coercive capacities of the state to settle personal disputes with neighbours (Gross 1982). The practical hegemony of state discourse forces, and also enables, citizens to conduct local disputes in terms of good and bad Islam. These are flexible frames that are given substance within actual social relations. The labels 'Wahhabi' or 'extremist' are invoked in local disputes over Muslim practice to position opponents in relation to the critical notion of cultural authenticity.

Aside from actually engaging in politically oriented religious activity, there are no fixed markers that would identify a person as being a Wahhabi. Human Rights Watch has reported that young men with beards are treated as suspicious by law enforcement organs (Human Rights Watch 2004), but a number of young men in Pakhtabad had long 'Islamic-style' beards and were in fact devout Muslims, something of which everyone was aware. They were not arrested or harassed by the police. Rather, what is Wahhabi is contextually determined. Bearded young men in the village of Pakhtabad who were established *qori* (reciters of the Qur'an) are safe from the Wahhabi label because they participate in a conventional and clearly nonpolitical mode of Muslim expression rooted in village practice. The same is true of officially appointed imams. When conducting my research, I found that officially appointed imams were among the most open and easily approachable.

An official imam in Samarkand told me that when he graduated from the madrasa, he had not wanted to work as an imam because he felt he would be more effective in spreading Islam as a teacher of Arabic:

When I finished, I didn't want to work in religion at first. This was because I thought that if I was a teacher of Arabic language in a *maktab* or a *litsei* (forms of secondary school), then during the classes I could bring the boys to Islam. If you sit in a mosque and do *ma'ruza* (sermon), few young people come, only two or three. I wanted to teach young people the way, to teach them the difference between *halol* and *harom* (Islamically permissible and forbidden) because the youth are our future. So I worked in an academic *litsei* for three years, from 1997 to 2000. I taught Arabic language and also added the hadith and the *odob akhloq* (morality) of our religion in the course of the lessons. Then in 1999 there were explosions in Tashkent. After that, the government stopped all Arabic lessons in *maktab* and *litsei*. . . . They said it was extremist Islamic groups. Our government didn't want people going over to extremist groups through the language. Some of the Arabic teachers were from that branch (*oqim*). Because of them, they closed us all down. But these extremist groups, these attacks are not Islamic. People don't have the right to do them. There's a hadith, the prophet was asked who was a Muslim. He replied a Muslim is he who in his speech and actions does not cause harm (*ozor*). But how many people were killed in the bombings? This is forbidden in Islam. So I was made unemployed. I had two specialisations in my diploma, Arabic teacher and *imom khatib*. I had to change over to my second profession.

Qori and officially appointed imams are able to express themselves as Muslim in ways that in other institutional and social contexts would render them vulnerable to being labelled as Wahhabi. However, because of the ambiguity about what constitutes extremist Islam and the arbitrary manner in which law enforcement agencies target individuals as extremist, people can never be sure that they might not be rendered vulnerable to the charge if they step outside the boundaries of what is clearly traditional religious practice.

This is not to say that people are merely passive victims. The cases I have presented show that many young men continue actively to engage with scripturalist Islam and find relatively safe positions from which to express their religiosity and promote their own interpretations of Islam. The 'Teacher', the founder of the new movement of spiritual enlightenment I mentioned earlier in this section, continues to operate from his home and counters potential opposition from neighbours in his *mahalla* partly by taking a full part in community life and contributing to *mahalla* projects. During the *navro'z* (New Year) celebrations, he prepared large quantities of the traditional dish of *halisa* (a paste made from boiled meat and wheat) and distributed it to residents. The women's NGO worker managed to overcome the initial opposition of local government and *mahalla* officials by supporting their agendas.

The government's discourse on Islam does not simply shape the religious subjectivities of citizens so that they adopt uncritically its construction of Islam as part of a national spiritual heritage. As subsequent chapters will make clear, Muslims in Uzbekistan contest interpretations of correct practice and come to their own understandings of Islam. The government's discourse is hegemonic in the sense that it shapes the terms in which citizens must present themselves as Muslims in relation to the state. The opposition between good and bad Islam has made tradition and cultural authenticity key frames within which religious practice must be located to avoid the attention of the coercive apparatuses of the state. Anything that does not clearly fit into this category is open to the charge of religious extremism and Wahhabism. This has been tragically demonstrated in the arrest and conviction of the group of businessmen in Andijan city accused of belonging to the 'extremist' Islamist group Akromiya and the subsequent massacre of hundreds of demonstrators by government forces. The significance of this incident is that the state authorities used the charge of religious extremism as the pretext for prosecuting them and justified their subsequent actions against the demonstrators in similar terms.

In neighbouring Kyrgyzstan, Muslims are openly exploring different discourses and interpretations of Islam. Julie McBrien has described how life-cycle celebrations such as weddings have become contexts in which Kyrgyz Muslims experiment with different ideas about what it means to be a Muslim. They explore alternative understandings of Islam through adopting particular forms of dress, and travelling preachers (*davatchi*) and study groups have become widespread (McBrien 2006a, 2006b). Although McBrien notes that debates about the nature of Islam are often framed in terms of extremism and tradition, as they are in Uzbekistan, individuals are much freer to explore openly alternative interpretations. In Uzbekistan, however, just as during the decades of Soviet rule, the open and free circulation of many of the ideas and theological trends that are debated wherever there are Muslims continues to be severely restricted.

tandir, the mud-brick ovens found in every house compound in the village. The bread for an occasion on this scale may also have been ordered from one of the specialist bakeries. We were served with the customary green tea; *lag'mon*, a noodle soup with meat; and *osh*, a rice pilau dish made with carrots, mutton, and cottonseed oil. These dishes were prepared in enormous cauldrons (*qozon*), which each *mahalla* collectively owns.

At one end of the courtyard, eight men were seated at a low table set on a raised seating platform (*so'ri*). There were six *qori* (Qur'an reciters) and two imams, one of whom was the *imom khatib* of Pakhtabad's registered Friday mosque. The second imam was from outside the village. A former *imom khatib* of a mosque in a nearby town who was locally known as a preacher, he had been specially invited to lead the event. After the meal, he delivered a sermon that located the *aqiqa to'y* within the *sharīʿa*, the Qur'an, and Sunna of the Prophet as it is interpreted within the Hanafi school. He explained that children were a blessing from God, not a purely human creation and that sheep were slaughtered to give thanks and to accrue religious merit (*savob*) through feeding others 'in the way of God' (*ilohning yolida*). Only one sheep was slaughtered for a girl and two for a boy, not because girls are less valued in Islam, but because the parents of a girl should also slaughter a sheep at her *nikoh* (wedding), so one should be saved for this event. He told the guests that the Prophet called girls a joy, even more so than boys.

The preacher then went on to remind the guests that this was one of the *mavlud* months, a time to remember and contemplate the birth and life of the Prophet. Every prayer said for the sake of the Prophet would count as ten normal prayers, he stated. The preacher recounted an event in the Prophet's life when he was invited to perform the *janoza*, the funeral prayers, for a recently deceased person. The Prophet asked if the dead man had any debts that had not been repaid and whether there were any descendents who could pay them off. The angel Gabriel appeared and asked the Prophet to continue with the *janoza*, saying that he would pay

FIGURE 11. Baking bread in a *tandir*

the debt. The Prophet, surprised, asked why this man was so honoured, and Gabriel replied that he was the man who had most proclaimed the greatness of the Prophet in the entire world. Gabriel then took the Prophet aside and they conversed. The angel told him that there were seven levels of hell, each with its own name and reserved for a particular type of person. The seventh and worst was reserved for people from the Prophet's *ummat*, the community of Muslims who commit sins. The Prophet was brokenhearted, and they both began to weep. After Gabriel departed, the Prophet closed the doors to his house and would not see anyone. He wept for three days without eating or drinking. News of this spread, and his closest followers came to him, including Abu Bakr (who became the first Caliph, leader of the Muslim community after the Prophet's death) and Ali (the son-in-law of the Prophet and the fourth Caliph). The Prophet refused to see them, and they began to weep as well. The carpet on which he sat had turned to mud with his tears. Finally, his daughter Fatima persuaded him to confide in her, and then she too wept. When the others asked her why the Prophet was weeping, she said it was because of his love of the *ummat*. Gabriel appeared and told them that because the Prophet was weeping, all of the angels were weeping, too.

While the preacher was recounting this event in the life of the Prophet, I noticed that two of the younger men at a nearby table were weeping in response to what they were hearing. Looking around, I saw that they were not alone – that here and there, other guests were weeping, including one or two of the *qori*, the Qur'an reciters, on the raised platform at the end of the courtyard. This was an expression of public piety that I had not previously seen in Uzbekistan, and I was somewhat taken aback. I had become accustomed to the reserve people usually adopt in their public expression as Muslims, not least because of the oppressive environment associated with anything that might be interpreted as 'foreign' or 'extremist', which I have described in previous chapters. An event like this, however, is a relatively safe location for pious expressions of this sort. It is firmly located within the category of Central Asian tradition, and the presence of the two *imom khatib* lent the event a certain degree of state authorisation, as these were representatives of the quasi-state structures charged with the definition and regulation of legitimate practice.

FIGURE 12. The *aqiqa to'y*, with the *qori* seated in an alcove at the centre back of the picture

After the sermon, the invited *qori* took turns chanting in Arabic verses from the Qur'an as part of the *mavlud*. The men's part of the event drew to a close after this, and members of the host household distributed squares of cloth to the guests to wrap up rounds of *non* bread, sweets, nuts, and other food that was left on the table to take home to share with those of their households who had not attended. The men then filed out; cars were ordered for the two imams, the most honoured guests; and the hosts bade farewell to their guests at the gate. As the men were leaving, the women started to arrive. They celebrated the event separately, occupying three or four interior rooms. They sat along the walls on the floor on flat, narrow, cotton-filled mattresses (*ty'shak*) around a large tablecloth (*dasturkhon*) laden with food. The women's part of the event differed in other ways as well. They were not present for the sermon or the Arabic recitation of the Qur'an. Women hold their own *mavlud*, which are presided over by women ritual specialists known as *otincha*. As a rule, women's *mavlud* in Pakhtabad do not involve the Arabic recitation of the Qur'an, but the *otincha* might recite poetry in what some of them called 'Turki', Uzbek language written in the Arabic script.

Household life-cycle rituals and celebrations have become a site where scripturally founded conceptions of Islam and what it means to be a Muslim are entering into the consciousness of people in Pakhtabad. Julie McBrien has described how some Muslims in a small town in Southern Kyrgyzstan are purposefully rejecting local ways of organising wedding celebrations and adopting a model they consider to be based on the guidance of the *sharīʿa*, excluding alcohol and music, segregating men from women, and inviting Muslim preachers (McBrien 2006b). She describes how they provide attendees with an opportunity to experiment with alternative ways of being Muslim and to engage the preachers in question-and-answer sessions. Weddings have become a site for public debate about the nature of Islam and Kyrgyz culture and of appropriate ways of being Muslim; some opponents of the new weddings characterise them as extremist and Wahhabi. In Pakhtabad, although a similar dynamic seems to be at work, public debate is muted. To label an individual or a practice extremist in Uzbekistan involves much higher stakes than in neighbouring Kyrgyzstan. In this situation, experience itself is a privileged site for moral reasoning.

To recognise that Muslim selves are developed within experience is nothing new. Muslims everywhere are confronted with multiple discourses on the nature of authentic Islam. Cognitive deliberation plays a prominent part in the judgements Muslims make between the range of objectified values and established interpretation, but values and discourses are apprehended in the light of individual life circumstances – through dreams, possession by spirits, and in the course of day-to-day interaction, as a number of anthropologists have made clear. Katherine Ewing has described how Muslims in Pakistan are confronted with multiple ideological and theological formations, including scientific secularism, modernist developmentalism, various trends of Islamic reformist thought, and the practice of Sufism and ideas of sorcery attack. She argues that individuals do not adopt fixed and coherent identities with reference to one or another ideology. Lived selves are always in motion, constituted within a dynamic narrative grounded in an individual's life experience and in relation to multiple Others (Ewing 1997).

I want to develop further the idea that understandings about Islam and Muslim selfhood are grounded in experience by examining the moral nature of experience. How is experiential reasoning morally persuasive? Following Charles Taylor, I have taken the moral to be defined by transcendence, the judgements an individual makes with reference to standards that exist independent of or above the contingencies of a life. The quality of transcendence may be provided by the values and schemes presented in different discursive constructions of Islam. It is also provided in experience itself, in the transcendent locations in reference to which experience is apprehended. In Uzbekistan, the relative absence of public debate has directed me to look more closely at this experiential aspect of moral reasoning.

Sociality as a Moral Source

In Chapter 1, I argued that individuals come to an understanding of what it means to be a Muslim partly through the sociality of interaction with others. A person is a Muslim by organising the marriages and settlement of children, holding life-cycle rituals with the involvement of kin and neighbours, and contributing to communal projects such as renovating a school or building a road or mosque in the *mahalla* – in short, by participating fully and appropriately in day-to-day interaction in the community. The *aqiqa to'y* described in the beginning of the chapter is an expression of sociality. It is one instance of the ongoing participation by the hosting household within the sociality of kin, neighbours, and friends in Pakhtabad along with wedding or circumcision feasts, *mavlud* commemorations, or *hashar*, the contribution of labour to joint projects. Households as a whole are represented in the event through their senior members, and others are included through the distribution of the food parcels guests take away with them.

Tohirjon once commented to me if a researcher only observed the everyday meals people consumed in their own homes, he would probably conclude that villagers in Pakhtabad must be seriously undernourished. He had been helping me carry out a survey of consumption, income, and expenditure of households in his *mahalla*, and this no doubt prompted him to reflect from my own location as an outsider and researcher. Breakfast in his household consists of little more than bread and tea. At lunch and dinner, the staple again is often bread and a thin potato soup with a very small amount of meat. A household of average wealth may have *osh* two or three times a week, but very little meat is eaten. This everyday *osh* is much less rich than the festive version served at the *aqiqa to'y*. He pointed out, however, that during the spring and summer, he attended some sort of *to'y* or other communal feast, where the food was of a much higher nutritional standard, at least once a week. *To'y* are occasions for communal consumption but also for shared expenditure. Households often contribute one or two kilograms of meat, or more frequently the equivalent in cash, to their neighbours' *to'y*, or they pool this money to buy a carpet or some other household object. The extent of this mutual contribution to each other's *to'y* varies and is not only confined to neighbourhoods. Sometimes groups of school or university classmates form a circle and contribute a certain amount, usually the cash equivalent of a fixed amount of meat, to the *to'y* of each member. Events like the *aqiqa to'y* take place within a mesh of mutual obligation and reciprocity wherein economic, affective, and kinship ties, the social and the sacred, cannot be untangled.

The idea that ritual practice reflects or enacts what might be called a moral community is well established in the social sciences. In Durkheim's thinking, the moral is more or less equated with the social. Altruism – whatever raises the individual above egoistic concerns and sensory appetites – is the basis of society, and religion is for Durkheim an objectification of society's collective ideals (Durkheim 1964, 1973, 2001). Roy Rappaport has argued that ritual is the fundamental social act. The performance of what he calls liturgical ritual establishes a public order, conventional rules and norms, and the obligation of those who perform the ritual to conform to them (Rappaport 1999, 107–38).

Among anthropologists of Muslim societies, Robert Launay argues that ritual practice expresses the existence and nature of moral communities. This might be the universal, impersonal, and egalitarian *umma* (Ar.), the community of Muslims equal before God, which transcends political, geographical, and cultural boundaries. Rituals that express this universal moral community are those recognised by all Muslims as required by the *sharīʿa*, such as prayer and fasting.[1] Alternatively, the moral community expressed in ritual might be local and particularistic, with ritual practice delineating boundaries and expressing differentiation in social identities and qualities of the person (Launay 1992). Within the competing discourses on Islam in any locality, rituals of this latter type are likely to be condemned by scriptural 'purists' as un-Islamic innovation and merely local tradition. Nevertheless, for those who take part, they are often important performances of Muslim selfhood.

In the context of Central Asia, Islam has sometimes been described as a collective identity rather than an individual 'faith'. Sergei Abashin (1997) has argued that individuals identify themselves as Muslim through membership of the community as a whole. A person is Muslim by birth rather than by belief, and the practice of Islam is a collective enterprise. Although the young, as a rule, do not pray or participate in ritual, it is for the older members of the household to do this on their behalf, just as in Pakhtabad, only the senior members of a household will attend an event like the *aqiqa to'y*. A common pattern for men is to start observing ritual prescriptions more regularly after they reach the age of about forty. Abashin has argued that this situation has been changing since the end of Soviet rule. With the spread of scripturally founded knowledge, ideas of individual responsibility and 'correct' textually legitimated practice are becoming more evident.

The link I am making between sociality and the development of Muslim selfhood is rather different. The above analyses take ritual or religious practice to be an enactment of a social system that exists independent of the individual. The link is between two separate objects, Islam and the object of society or moral community. Daily life and local forms of social interaction are invested with significance and morality by being placed within an Islamic frame (Lambek 1990, 23). I suggest an alternative understanding – that sociality itself is a moral source. I am exploring the creativity of moral reasoning that takes place through ongoing experience, and the transcendent nature of experience that gives it a moral quality. As an analytical concept, sociality differs from society in that it is immanent in the person and his or her intersubjective engagement in the social and material world. A Durkheimian understanding would locate transcendence in the superorganic nature of society as an object above and beyond the individual. I seek to explore the transcendent quality of experience itself, in the immersion within a sociality that exists within and between persons, that is at the same time apprehended as extending beyond the contingency of any individual life. By participating appropriately in a household or wider community, which can extend to include the state (Rasanayagam 2002b, 2003), individuals are immersed in a web of relations and obligations that locate them outside their own lives, a location that enables moral reasoning. Moral selves are not just reflections or enactments of a preexisting social order but are creative and continuously developing understandings that emerge from experience.

Direct Experience of the Divine

Sociality is not the only transcendent location that gives experience a moral quality. Another is the direct experience of the Divine. In Uzbekistan, this is not limited to the extraordinary – confined to the mystical experience of particularly enlightened scholars or to specialised ritual practices such as the Sufi *zikr*. Direct experience of the Divine can be a part of everyday living, dreams, experience of illness, or awareness of the body. At the same time, experience is not purely interior, a quality of the individual mind separate from social existence, but is mediated, even constituted, through interaction with others. Katherine Ewing has pointed out that that the phenomenology of dreaming is shaped by cultural codes or templates that are broken apart and recombined in dreams as individuals develop self-representations (Ewing 1990). In Uzbekistan, dreaming and visions are apprehended within a model for experience that allows them to be understood as direct contact with the Divine or spirit entities. As mentioned in the Introduction, this is likely to relate to the long history of Sufism in the region, as well as with reference to dreams and visions within the Qur'an and the tradition of the Prophet. In recent years, charismatic Protestantism has also begun to influence how converts understand immediate bodily experience as a reflection of their personal relationship with God.

There are a number of ways in which individuals encounter the Divine directly, some of which are spontaneous, such as dreams, and others that are cultivated through intentional processes. One of the latter, which seems clearly derived from Sufi ideas, is the practice of undergoing a *chilla*,[2] a period of fasting and isolation during which an individual seeks knowledge or healing directly from divine sources, often mediated through spirit agents. It can be undertaken by anyone, and many who do so claim to have been visited during the *chilla* by the spirits of prominent Muslim saints or deceased ancestors who gave them Islamic knowledge or physical objects, such as a Qur'an or prayer beads. A common claim is to have miraculously learnt how to read the Qur'an in the Arabic script as a result of undergoing a *chilla*. It is also a stage in the process during which a person identified as having spirit helpers gains knowledge and control over them in order to work as a healer or to foretell the future.[3]

A common context in which individuals encounter the Divine is during *ziyorat*, visiting the tombs of 'saints' (*avliyo*), a practice with a long history in Central Asia (Abashin 2001; Kehl-Bodrogi 2008; Louw 2007; Poliakov 1992; Privratsky 2001; Snezarev 2003). *Avliyo* are typically prominent historical figures, well-known Sufi masters or religious scholars, but in the case of tombs of only local significance, the precise identity of the *avliyo* may not be known. People in Uzbekistan visit the shrines of *avliyo* to obtain their intercession in overcoming some sort of problem, perhaps an illness or difficulty in conceiving a child, to ensure the success of a business venture, or to pass exams. Visitors sometimes sacrifice a sheep or a chicken at the tomb, or they may promise to hold a special feast if their wishes are granted. Maria Louw has described how sacred spaces can be sites where individuals directly encounter signs of the Divine. By sacred space, she means not only the tombs of *avliyo*, but also dream encounters with saints and ritual space created by propitiatory ceremonies such as the *bibiseshanba*. Louw argues that they provide focal points for creative reflection on the moral shortcomings of contemporary society. She uses the term 'Muslimness' to refer to the everyday practice of Islam and to the way Islam is understood and practiced within everyday lifeworlds as opposed to the textually defined Islam of the ulama. Muslimness, she argues, is a morality in the making. By reflecting upon saintly hagiographies, individuals reevaluate their own lives and the contemporary society from which they have become alienated. They reorient themselves in moral space and develop alternative narratives within which they feel integrated and valued (Louw 2007).

A moral source, as I am developing the concept, is not in itself 'Islamic'; it is a transcendent location that confers a moral quality to experience. Direct encounters with the Divine are apprehended by many in Uzbekistan within a moral narrative that develops a Muslim self, but the inherent creativity of experience opens up the possibility for alternative narrative frames. During my research in the city of Samarkand, I met an individual to whom I refer as 'the Teacher', introduced in Chapter 4. This man was in his mid-fifties when I met him. He was born in a village near Samarkand, studied construction at institutes in Dushanbe in Tajikistan and in Samarkand, and had worked in construction as a painter and brigadier (work group leader) for fifteen years. He described how, in 1991, he was visited by a number of spirit beings, including angels and Jesus, who took him up to the highest levels of heaven, where he encountered God. He described this process as a rebirth, an opening of his consciousness that enabled him to perceive the knowledge that comes from the stars and planets. The influence of Sufi philosophy is clear in this account and in his ideas that God is pure energy present in each person, and that knowledge of the Divine is not open to rational thought but must be felt through interior awareness. He also incorporates ideas from a number of other philosophical traditions. He used the Sanskrit term 'chakra' to refer to levels of consciousness, and he sees himself as a second Jesus who needs to gather twelve disciples around himself. These are to be women, because Jesus, with his twelve male disciples, had saved only men.

It would be easy to view this individual as a faintly ridiculous figure and dismiss him as an eccentric case, irrelevant to a discussion of the spiritual life of the majority of the population. However, to do so is to privilege our own conceptions of what counts as 'real' spirituality or religion. From the late Soviet period onward, and particularly after the dissolution of the Soviet Union, a great diversity of religious philosophies became available to Central Asians. These include not only a range of ideas within the tradition of Islam, but also a number of Protestant churches, the Krishna movement, and the Baha'i. Novel groups that incorporate elements of Islam, local practices such as the veneration of ancestors, and

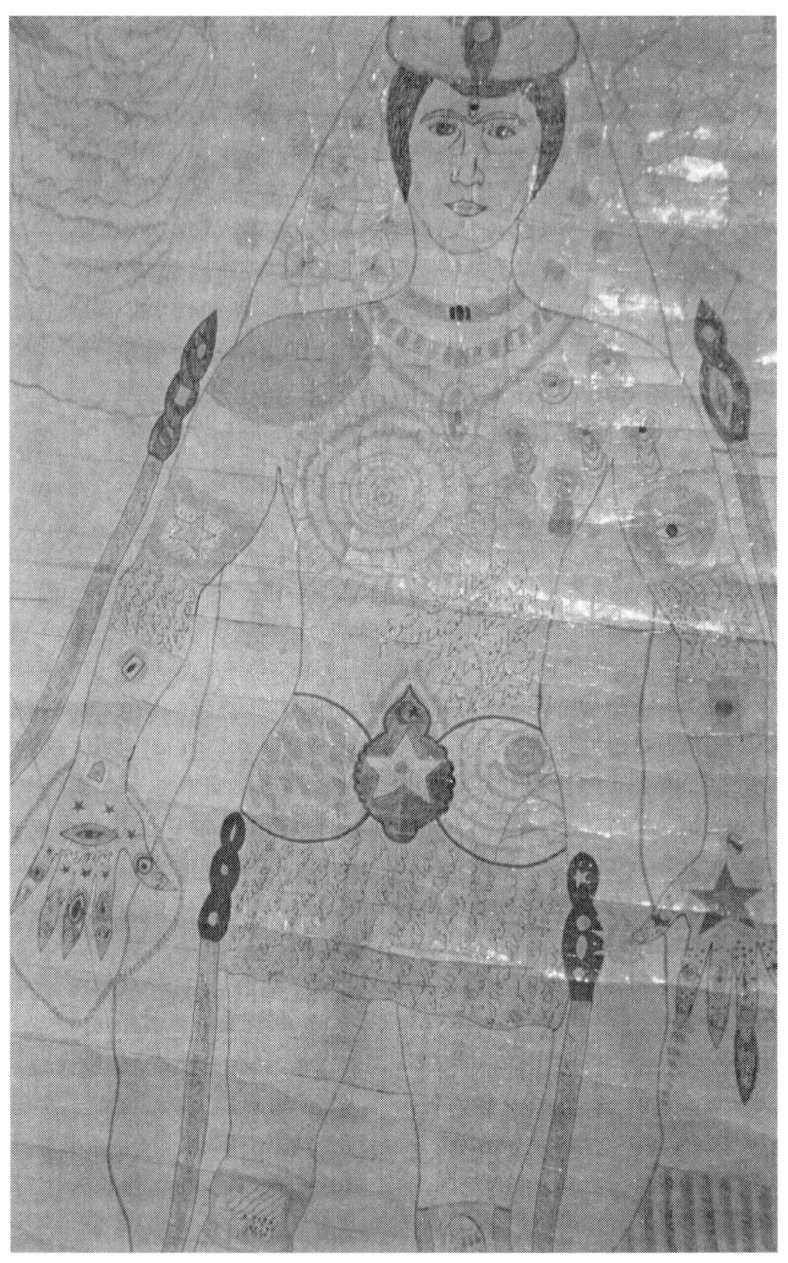

FIGURE 13. The Teacher's drawing of his vision of God during one of his spiritual journeys

ideas from other philosophies have developed, recruiting members from both the indigenous and Russian-speaking populations (Jessa 2006). The Teacher is part of this larger exploration of spirituality and moral selfhood. He has attracted a small circle of dedicated followers for whom he provides a coherent vision that places their physical and psychological condition within a transcendent moral frame. A central element in his teaching is the idea of healing. Physiological and mental suffering, tension in interpersonal relations, and failure in life in general are caused by the negative energy resulting from both personal dissatisfaction and wrongdoing. Individuals need to change their attitudes, express love towards those around them, and ask forgiveness for their own sins and those of their ancestors. This improves not only their own condition but also heals those around them. The Teacher denies that his movement is a religion. Religion, he claims, teaches fear of God, whereas he teaches people to love God. He describes his group as a 'school of life'.[4] In the past, he taught courses on his ideas in the municipal centre for 'Spirituality and Enlightenment' (*ma'naviyat va ma'rifat*), a nationwide network of centres established to promote the government's ideas on national spiritual development. He awarded diplomas after a six-month course of study and claims to have taught approximately 2,000 people in his classes before he was closed down by the state authorities when he was accused of spreading Wahhabi ideas.

The experience of bodily, social, and psychological disorder is an important medium through which individuals encounter the Divine. Whereas the Teacher claims to have ascended to a higher level of consciousness that allows him direct access to God, for his core followers, healing is the primary means through which the Divine becomes apparent to them. Most people who encounter the Teacher limit their involvement to seeking healing and do not become committed followers. His followers learn to apprehend disorder in their lives as directly resulting from their own behaviour, and bodily sensations are ascribed meaning. Each sign of the zodiac is associated with a particular part of the body so that, for example, people born under the sign of Virgo feel pain in their bowels when they are discontented or angry, whereas for those born under Aquarius, the legs are significant.

Two of his followers are illustrative. They are both *bibikhalfa* (female Muslim religious specialists) from Samarkand who officiate at women's ritual occasions. Fatmakhon is now retired. She was born in Samarkand and studied journalism at a higher educational institution in Dushanbe in the late 1960s. After graduation, she returned to Samarkand, married and had children, and worked as a journalist and schoolteacher. She described how she had suffered continually from a young age from a condition she described as her heart being squeezed (Rus. [*u*] *menya serdtse szhimalos'*). Doctors were unable to help her. When she was approximately seventeen years old, she had a dream in which she was presented with the Qur'an, indicating that she should study it and become a *bibikhalfa*, but she initially was embarrassed about doing this because she thought that it was something only uneducated women did in order to make a little money. At the same time, her family members were active Muslims, and she had performed the *namoz* (Muslim prayers) regularly from the age of seven. Four years previous to our meeting, she had been put into a three-day *chilla* to cure her condition, during which she miraculously became able to recite the Qur'an in Arabic, although she did not understand its meaning. After this, she became a *bibikhalfa*, reciting the Qur'an at women's ritual occasions, and she also began to heal people through the Qur'an. She described her healing abilities as a gift from God that she did not understand, but she was unable to heal her own condition. A year after becoming a *bibikhalfa*, she attended the Teacher's classes, and he put her into another *chilla* in order to ask forgiveness for her sins, which cured her affliction. Since then, she has stopped performing the *namoz* and instead performs a ritual developed by the Teacher intended to invoke forgiveness of sins. This mimics some of the movements of the *namoz*, such as bending down to touch the head on the ground and chanting 'There is no God but God' in Arabic (*lā ilāha illā allāh*).

The second woman had a similar history. She also comes from a religiously active family of mullahs and *bibikhalfa* and had been ill for a number of years with kidney problems, for which she had undergone operations in Tashkent and Moscow. She was registered as disabled, and she claimed that in 1985, doctors told her that she did not have long to live. She had undergone a *chilla* eleven years before our meeting, in which she was given a book of Qur'anic verses in a dream and learnt them by heart. However, her illness was not cured. During one of her visits as a *bibikhalfa*, a women told her about the Teacher's courses, and she attended them. The Teacher put her, too, into a *chilla*, after which her kidneys stopped bothering her. Both women describe their previous hostile relations with their husbands and mothers-in-law and their resentment about the domination they had experienced by the men in their lives, either husbands or brothers. Their hatred of men, they claimed, had caused them to be ill, but they recovered after they asked forgiveness for their past attitudes. Interestingly, both women continue to work as *bibikhalfa*, attending ritual occasions such as the *bibiseshanba* among women who view the ritual as a Muslim one and the *bibikhalfa* as fellow Muslims. They claimed that the women welcomed the advice they gave during these occasions and that they had passed on the Teacher's ideas about the causes of suffering and the need to seek forgiveness, although they said that they avoided ideas the women would find too outlandish.

In a study of the phenomenology of healing among charismatic Catholics in the United States, Thomas Csordas has described what he terms 'embodied self processes' through which individuals construct themselves as devout Catholics in relation to a divine Other. Sufferers develop a 'somatic mode of attention', a cultivated awareness and anticipation of physical symptoms and an active response to them. Experience of suffering and its alleviation is interpreted as experience of the sacred (Csordas 1994). Csordas argues that disorder and its alleviation can be a medium through which the Divine is encountered in daily existence and the ongoing flow of social interaction. Moreover, awareness is shaped within a 'habitus' developed through membership of a group. The two *bibikhalfa* from the 'school of life' have learnt to attend to bodily, psychological, and social disorders as resulting from their own negative attitudes and those of their ancestors. They have learnt to apprehend experience in a particular way and to link this experience to their own motivations and actions within the moral frame the Teacher has developed. Similarly, individuals, often from Muslim families, who have joined Protestant Christian churches frequently give accounts of long quests for relief from illness. A reason many converts give for initially joining a particular church was that they found healing in that group after visits to doctors, trips to the shrines of Muslim saints, and the efforts of mullahs proved unsuccessful. Through membership of a church such as the Pentecostal, which lays great emphasis on the link between bodily healing, faith in Jesus Christ, and proper conduct, converts learn to reinterpret past illness and suffering as evidence of a previous sinful life and to understand their deliverance from this as resulting from their turning towards God and renouncing sinful ways.

Divine Truth Materialised and Entextualised

For Muslims in Uzbekistan who develop their understanding of Islam through a study of scriptural sources, a large part of what I have described in the previous section is heterodox, non-Islamic tradition that has crept into the local practice of Islam over the centuries. In previous chapters, I describe how imams and others who follow a scriptural interpretation criticise elements of local practices, such as the veneration of saints or the extended feasting and commemorations connected with life-cycle events. Madrasa-trained imams characterise what they see as non-Islamic practice as deriving from the pre-Islamic tradition of Central Asia and blame the ignorance of Central Asian Muslims in large part on the suppression

FIGURE 14. A self-professed *bakhshi* in Samarkand using fire and candles in a healing ritual

of Islam during Soviet rule. For example, the common practice of lighting candles on Thursday evenings, or its modern equivalent of switching on electric lights, to welcome the spirits of deceased relatives; the custom of the bride and groom of circling a fire during a wedding; or the use of fire in healing rituals are attributed by some imams to the influence of Zoroastrianism, which existed in the region prior to Islam. This echoes the classification by Soviet ethnographers of many local ritual practices as pre-Islamic survivals. The grounding for this criticism is God's revelation transmitted through the Prophet and expressed in the Qur'an and Sunna. I want to extend our understanding of this as a moral source to the material world as Divine creation, entextualised in the Qur'an.

The natural world is invoked as evidence of the Truth of Islam not only by madrasa-educated imams but also by ordinary Muslims. A number of people in Samarkand referred to a discovery they attributed to the oceanographer and filmmaker Jacque Cousteau that salt and fresh water can remain separate when they come into contact. This, they said, was already referred to in the Qur'an, evidence that it encompassed all scientific knowledge. An imam from a village near Pakhtabad, when explaining his reasons for deciding to study at the madrasa in Andijan, stated:

If you look at history, you have al-Bukhoriy, al-Khorazmiy, al-Beruniy, al-Termiziy, these were perfect (*mukammal*) people from the point of view of both worldly and religious knowledge. Why? Because first they learnt religious knowledge well. Everything is in the Qur'an . . . engineering science comes from the Qur'an, the knowledge of geographers and geologists, medical knowledge, everything is in the Qur'an. So anyone who knows the Qur'an well will embody all this knowledge. Because Muslims don't understand Islam well enough, they have to go abroad, to America, England or elsewhere to study. I have heard that the books of al-Beruniy and al-Khorazmiy were taken from Asia and are kept in a library in England. These people were very spiritually developed. Through knowledge of the Qur'an they embodied all sorts of knowledge. The Qur'an is a wonderful thing. If we read and study the Qur'an well, we Muslims will not need anything else. For example, the car factories, or the reason planes fly, or trains, all this is in the Qur'an.

As noted in the Introduction, the idea that all scientific knowledge is encompassed within the Qur'an is not unique to Uzbekistan. In a similar vein, Qur'anic injunctions, such as the need to perform the ritual ablutions before prayer and to pray five times a day, are considered by many Muslims I met in Uzbekistan to be not only the will of God but also conducive to good health and hygiene. The same is true for practices attributed to the Sunna of the Prophet – for example, the directions for how to drink tea involve pronouncing *bismi llāhi l-raḥmāni l-raḥīm* (Ar. in the name of God the Merciful and Compassionate) before, *al-ḥamdu lillāh* (Ar. thanks be to God) after taking a sip, and doing this three times.

A *qori* (Qur'an reciter) in Pakhtabad explained that this practice was good for the health because it prevented people from drinking tea too quickly, which he believed could damage the liver.

In criticising the extended series of funeral commemorations, the imam of a Friday mosque in a village near Pakhtabad understood the injunctions of the *sharīʿa* to be inherently rational. He pointed out that the companions of the Prophet held only one event three days after his death. He not only criticised the extended commemorations on the grounds that that they are non-Qur'anic innovations, but also pointed out that they are clearly irrational because they can impose a financially ruinous burden on poor families. There is nothing in Islam, he stated, that could cause hardship to believers. He similarly criticises what he considers to be excessive spending on wedding celebrations and the associated dowries and gifts, when both bride and groom are given a large amount of clothes and household goods. The imam claimed that this could rise to U.S.$5,000, which leads to economic ruin and prevents families from improving their material condition. This, he claimed, was a result of people's ignorance of the true essence of Islam.

In making a distinction between genuine and mistaken belief and practice, imams in Uzbekistan construct an opposition between the Truth of the *sharīʿa*, or the pathway of a good life as revealed in Qur'anic revelation and the practice of the Prophet, and contingent human tradition (*urf-odat*). This is clearly in conflict with state discourses that subordinate Islam to a humanly created Central Asian tradition. The fine line imams are forced to walk in staying true to their understanding while also supporting state discourses is discussed in Chapter 4. Divine Truth is opposed to human ignorance and error. The universe is a creation of God, and the Qur'an is the entextualisation of that creation. Truth is present in both the material world and the sacred texts, and a person needs only to achieve a correct understanding of the nature of the world and the meaning of the texts. Failure to observe the proper precepts of the *sharīʿa* therefore is due to ignorance or weakness. Correct practice and personal conduct is framed not so much in terms of belief for these Muslims as in terms of proper knowledge.

As with other moral sources, the material world need not always be understood in Islamic terms. Entextualised within the Qur'an and Sunna, the material world is objectified as a primary reference for Islamic reasoning. However, as a transcendent location for experience, the material world is open to diverse understandings.

The Moral Quality of Experience

The *aqiqa to'y* described in the beginning of this chapter was not only an expression of an ongoing sociality but also was an enactment of a more actively self-conscious commitment to a textually informed interpretation of Islam. However, as is evident in the account I have given, women and men participated in the *aqiqa to'y* differently. The textually founded Islamic elements of the event were confined to the men's participation. The recordings of sermons, the live sermon, and the Arabic recitation of the Qur'an were not part of the women's celebration. This reflects what might be seen as a gender distinction in the practice of Islam, with men given more ready access to scriptural interpretation. Women do not as a rule attend the mosque, except at major festivals, so they do not hear the Friday sermons that are a major source of scriptural knowledge for ordinary Muslims. Although a number of madrasas have opened since independence, they cater almost exclusively to boys and men, and the Imom al-Bukhoriy Islamic Institute in Tashkent has only a limited number of places for women.[5]

Imams with whom I spoke sometimes commented on women's relative ignorance about genuine Islamic knowledge and criticised female ritual specialists as little more than charlatans, interested only in making money. Whereas the weeping of men during the *aqiqa to'y* was an expression of appropriate piety, the wailing of women during funerals, which was common in Samarkand, was criticised by some of the men at these

FIGURE 15. Women mourning at a fortieth-day funeral commemoration

events as an imitation of Shiʿi practice by women who were ignorant of correct Sunni Islam. An imam in Samarkand explained that the practice of wailing at a funeral is specifically banned within the *sharīʿa* and that *bibikhalfa* make women do this. It was a source of *fitna*, or disorder, which came from the ignorance (*ilmsizlik*) of women. Women had less knowledge, in his view, because of their weaker intellect (*aql*), compared to men, although he recognised that some women in Uzbekistan had gained genuine learning.

Regardless, it would be misleading to suggest that there are separate, gender-defined Islams in Uzbekistan. The criticism by imams of women's ritual practice is part of a more general attack on *bid'at* – illegitimate innovation in the local practice of Islam. In the context of household and local community, the ritual events that women hold are part of the same ongoing sociality in which men are immersed. They address the welfare of the household as a whole, not just the concerns of female members, and are financed from the same budget as men's rituals. Households operate on a common budget, and women would not be able to hold separate events without the active support of male members.

The *aqiqa to'y*, therefore, worked on a number of levels simultaneously. It was part of the meshwork of sociality in which distinctions between sacred and social, kinship ties and material exchange, and even a separation in the ritual practice of men and women are difficult to sustain. At the same time, it was located firmly within a textually founded interpretation of Islam, and the hosts had made a conscious effort to organise the event in this way. The event also had echoes of interaction with spirit or divine agency in the way that food on the table was wrapped up and taken away to be consumed by others who had not participated. At all the *mavlud* and other rituals I attended where the Qur'an was recited or a *zikr* chanted, items such as salt and water were placed on the centre of the tablecloth. These items, it is believed, would become infused with the blessings of the spoken words, although many who participate in these rituals would not agree with this understanding.

It is difficult to draw a clear distinction between a category of Muslims in Uzbekistan who have universalist, scripturally oriented understandings of Islam and others whose understanding of Islam is embedded in local cultural practices. Participants at ritual events like the *aqiqa to'y* may understand it in different ways, but this does not prevent the event from being an enactment of their belonging to a shared moral community. The *aqiqa to'y* remains a shared model for experience that allows for a productive and meaningful interaction among participants. Even if some Muslims have little direct knowledge of the sacred texts, they recognise the superior knowledge of madrasa-trained imams, and imams are included within the flows of sociality through their participation. Since independence, more and more villagers have been making the pilgrimage to Mecca, which takes them beyond local sociality and situates them within a global community of Muslims. Men who attend the main mosque for communal prayers on Fridays listen to a sermon by the madrasa-educated *imom khatib* on proper Muslim conduct. Through their mosque attendance, they participate in a community that defines itself as Muslim through communal prayer as prescribed within the *sharīʿa*, independent of local sociality. An increasing number of individuals in Pakhtabad, like the Hoji-bobo who hosted the *aqiqa to'y*, have gone further in striving to lead a Muslim life more self-consciously based on scriptural interpretation, but this does not separate them from their kin and neighbours who have not taken this step.

In this chapter, I have sought to examine the moral quality of experience. This is provided by moral sources that locate experience outside the contingencies of an individual life. They are produced within what might be called local cultural imaginaries, models for interaction, social institutions, cosmologies, and models for experience. They do not determine how experience is interpreted but offer possibilities for apprehending experience as transcendent and therefore a medium for moral reasoning. The narrative reasoning by which individuals develop moral selves out of the indeterminacy of experience is discussed in Chapter 6.

SIX

Moral Reasoning through the Experience of Illness

Chapter 5 discussed the moral quality of experience, and in this chapter I explore its creativity. Experiential reasoning is not only a self-conscious, cognitive activity of the mind but is inherent in life as it is lived. It takes place within embodied, intersubjective engagement in a social and material world. At the same time, experience is not 'neutral' or unmediated but is refracted through models for action, cosmologies, and local histories that make possible particular qualities of experience. It is creatively configured and made meaningful within a developing narrative frame.

I have chosen illness as a context for examining moral reasoning because it introduces an obvious break into the flow of experience. It presents a point of discontinuity, an interruption and challenge that demands attention (Good 1994; Mattingly 1998). Perhaps because of this, a significant body of literature has developed that seeks to explore personal illness as an experience through which sufferers and those around them construct meaning. Arthur Kleinman has distinguished between illness, disease, and sickness. The former is the subjective experience of suffering – how sufferers themselves perceive affliction and how this is shaped through cultural orientations and within social networks. Disease is the objectification of the sufferer's complaint by expert practitioners through the lens of their particular form of practice, whether they are doctors trained within a Western biomedical tradition or the healers described in Chapter 7 who work with the aid of spirits.

Sickness is the political economic understanding of disorder, the correlation between particular diseases and socioeconomically defined population groups. It encompasses issues such as oppression and economic deprivation (Kleinman 1988). For Kleinman, illness is not simply disease located in the physical body or a psychological disorder of the mind. It is implicated in social and cultural worlds, in relations of power, and in moral evaluations.

Culture and Experience

The term 'culture-bound syndrome' has been used to convey the idea that conceptions of disorder and strategies for treatment are produced within specific cosmologies, ideas about the nature of the person and interaction with human and nonhuman agents in the environment. These influence how immediate perception is recognised as being a particular type of encounter, emotion, or state, and how it demands attention. For example, an experience in one cultural context of an encounter with spirit beings in a dream or waking vision – an interaction with agents external to the person that produces 'real' physical effects – may, in another cultural context, be the product of an internal psychology or even a psychological disorder.

In Uzbekistan, a condition referred to as a 'fallen heart' (*yurak tushgan*) might be an example of such a 'syndrome'. Symptoms are typically lack of energy, strength, and motivation, a pervasive tiredness during which the sufferer wants only to remain lying down at home. It can lead to more serious illness and hospitalisation. This recalls a family of conditions often described as 'soul loss' in a number of societies around the world, commonly associated with sudden shock or fright in which part of a person's vital essence is believed to have left the body (Desjarlais 1992; Greenway 1998; Wikan 1989a). A fallen heart cannot be treated with biomedical intervention, and after it is diagnosed, often after hospital treatment has proven ineffective, the sufferer needs to seek the aid of healers who work with the help of spirits or someone able to recite verses from the Qur'an. They might visit the tomb of a saint to recite the Qur'an there and wash themselves in water from an associated sacred spring. In addition, as in a number of Muslim societies, contact with *jin* is, for many people, a cause of disorder. In the Qur'an, *jin* are described as one of the three types of intelligent beings created by God, the other two being humans and angels. Although the Qur'an refers to both Muslim and unbelieving *jin*,[1] just as there are Muslim and non-Muslim human beings, in the context of illness, *jin* are generally considered malevolent and are associated with dirt and pollution, dwelling in toilets or in washing areas, and feeding from polluting substances such as sexual fluids, blood, and saliva. Certain conditions are associated with them, including madness and paralysis of facial muscles, and illness caused by *jin* is not treatable by biomedicine. This category of illness and its treatment, which falls outside the sphere of biomedical intervention, is collectively referred to as *eskicha* (the old ways) or *musulmonchilik* (Muslimness or Muslim ways).

However, I am not interested in identifying locally specific syndromes or disorders with coherent etiologies and treatments. The perspective of the experiencing self reveals how cultural models do not act as scripts that individuals merely follow, treading well-worn paths of illness and treatment. That is perhaps what Kleinman refers to as disease – the objectification by expert practitioners of the sufferer's experience of disorder in accordance with a particular system of knowledge (although we see in Chapter 7 that expert practitioners also draw creatively from multiple cosmologies). Rather, I want to explore how local cosmologies and cultural models for illness afford possibilities for particular qualities of experience. They provide ready-to-hand objectifications of immediate perception, such as bodily pain, and contribute to what Robert Desjarlais has called 'aesthetic sensibilities'. Desjarlais describes these as the 'tacit cultural forms, values, and sensibilities – local ways of being and doing – that lend specific styles, configurations, and felt qualities to local experiences' (Desjarlais 1992, 65). Aesthetic sensibilities pattern how people make sense of their lived world, their bodies, and their social environment and shape the way people experience and express suffering so that there are embodied ways of being ill and healthy. I am not suggesting that sufferers are determined by their sensibilities so that they act without conscious volition in standard ways. Instead, I want to foreground the creativity of experience that enables moral reasoning. Cultural models, cosmologies, and sensibilities provide a repertoire of human and nonhuman characters and modes of experience that are creatively refashioned within an individual's narrative construction of his or her life and self. I discuss this further through the illness experiences of Ilkhom-aka, a sixty-year-old retired knife maker in the village of Pakhtabad.

Moral Reasoning through Experience

Ilkhom-aka became a blacksmith in the collective farm at the age of sixteen, and after military service he worked as a knife maker in a nearby town, producing for private sale in the bazaar. At the age of forty he began performing the five daily prayers and now regularly attends the Friday mosque in the village for the midday prayers. He says that he was a Muslim before, although he had not observed religious obligations, such as abstaining from alcohol or pork, and had only prayed at major festivals. He blames his former lack of religious observance on work commitments and the antireligious atmosphere during the Soviet period. It is a fairly common pattern in the village for men to start observing religious prescriptions more actively at approximately age forty when they begin to take part in ritual events within the community more actively as representatives of their households.

While discussing his views on *bakhshi*, healers who invoke the help of spirits, he recounted his own experiences of illness. His daughter had suffered from epilepsy beginning at the age of twelve and died in 1991. He recounted his search for treatment during a period of ten years before her death, during which he had taken her to medical doctors as well as to a number of different healers in the Fergana Valley. He also had been ill during this time, suffering from a fallen heart, and whilst in hospital he had a dream in which he saw the house of a *bakhshi* of whom he had no previous knowledge. He sought it out for his daughter and slaughtered a sheep there (many healers mark sufferers with the blood of chickens or sheep as part of the healing process). He was put into a fifteen-day period of fasting and isolation (*chilla*) for his condition. One night during the *chilla*, he had a dream in which he vomited bile (*safro*) from his stomach, and in the morning he felt much better. He continues to visit this *bakhshi* periodically for healing. He recounted an occasion when he accompanied his elder brother's daughter to another healer who also works with *jin* to address her difficulty in conceiving a baby. This healer, to whom he referred as a *tabib*, did not use blood or the practice of *chilla*, but instead employed passports as a medium for divining the causes of disorder. During this visit, Ilkhom-aka's stomach hurt, and he interpreted this as indicating that the *jin* called down by the healer conflicted with those of the *bakhshi* who initially had cured his illness. After his daughter died, he once more became ill, with a pain in his side, and visited his regular *bakhshi*, who put him into a *chilla* for three days. On the evening after completing it, he performed the ritual ablutions (*tahorat*) and the evening prayers at home and then lay down to sleep. He described how a black man and woman appeared while he was still awake, read the Qur'an over him, and then left. They were followed by a man dressed as a doctor in a white coat and a woman dressed as a nurse who came in a white cloud. They performed an operation on his side, and in the morning he felt fine. These were the spirits sent by the *bakhshi*.

Ilkhom-aka's experience of illness and healing encompasses multiple 'streams of knowledge' (Barth 1993). He resorts to all the traditions of healing available to him, including the state health care system and the varied types of healing associated with the sphere of *eskicha*. Even the

FIGURE 16. A diviner who works with spirits helping a client with family problems in a village near Pakhtabad

experience of being healed by spirits incorporates imagery from the biomedical system, as spirits take the form of medical doctors and nurses and perform operations, imitating the practice of hospital treatment. His experience of distress and healing is shaped within a world in which spirits are present in the environment and interact with humans. However, this cannot be understood just as an instance of 'culture-in-the-making' in the way Barth has suggested.[2] Barth describes this as a pragmatic process whereby individuals interpret actions and events with reference to a stock of knowledge, drawing on varied traditions of knowledge to find practical solutions to practical problems. Interpretations are collectively arrived at and introduce incremental innovation into the stock of shared knowledge, but this analysis omits the moral dimension. Experience is apprehended within a moral narrative.

Ilkhom-aka's encounters with spirits take form within his ideas about a good life that emerge through his interactions in his immediate community and his engagement with wider discourses. An important aspect of his moral self is a self-representation as a good Muslim, regularly performing the five daily prayers and attending communal prayers at the mosque. A large part of what might be called his circle of significant others is made up of other religiously observant men with whom he comes into contact at the mosque or at the ritual events in which he represents his household. Imams during Friday sermons regularly condemn the activities of *bakhshi* and those who consort with *jin* and exhort people not to turn to them for healing or prophesy. Although the existence of *jin* is not questioned, this mosque-based 'orthodox' view emphasises that healing comes from God directly and not through the intervention of intermediaries and that a person's fate is only for God to know. Ilkhom-aka's attitude to his healing experience is ambivalent. The visions he has experienced in dreams and his encounters with spirits have persuaded him of the reality of *jin* and the efficacy of treatment by those who control them (*jinkash*), but he also maintains a certain moral distance. He initially displayed embarrassment about admitting to visiting the *bakhshi* and talked about how she 'binds *jin* and harmful things' (*jinlar baylaydi . . . zararli narsalar baylar ekan*), displaying an awareness that the activities of the *bakhshi* were illegitimate. However, he stressed that it all depended on a person's purpose or aim (*maqsad*). He emphasised that he had refused to become a healer himself and only undertook the *chilla* for healing and not to gain access to, and control over, the *jin*. This is a line he has drawn himself that allows him to take advantage of his healing treatments while continuing to locate himself within a moral narrative in which being a good Muslim, as understood in his mosque circle, is an important part.

Ilkhom-aka's experience is similar to that of Rifat-aka, a former teacher of about the same age. Rifat-aka worked in retail in a nearby town until he came to teach in one of the schools in the village in 1980. His father had died in 1985, when he was forty, after which he started to perform the daily prayers (*namoz*), just as Ilkhom-aka had. He stated that every Muslim house needed someone who read the *namoz*, and he had learnt about Islam by attending communal ritual events and from talking to men with Islamic learning (*domla*) at these occasions, and from books. Like Ilkhom-aka, his encounters with spirits have convinced him of their reality. Rifat-aka recounted an occasion in 1994 when he had been praying in the mosque and an elderly man with a full beard wearing a turban came and stood in front of him without speaking and then disappeared. That evening at home he recited the Ya-Sin sura from the Qur'an, one that is associated with healing, something he does every day to maintain good health. On this occasion, the elderly man appeared again. When he asked a *domla* about this later, he was told that every letter in the Ya-Sin has a guardian (he used the Arabic term *muwakkil*) and that the purity of these beings is transferred, bringing healing and aid. In line with the mosque-based interpretation of Islam and correct Muslim practice, Rifat-aka condemns those who work with *jin*, claiming that they are only interested in making money. At the same time, his own experience has convinced him of the reality of spirits. He asserts that everyone has their own angels (*farishta*), some of whom are good and some bad. Normally we do not see our spirits, but some, such as healers, have learnt to control them. Spirits tell those who control them what they have heard in the world above, and this is how diviners obtain knowledge. As a good Muslim, however, he avoids healers who work with *jin* and relies only on the Qur'an for healing.

The experience of these two men is constituted within local cosmologies and models for illness that afford possibilities for particular qualities of experience. These include the biomedical state health care system and the variety of discourses within Islam. They live in a world in which spirit beings are real and surround humans in the everyday environment. This is not only validated within the practice of healers who invoke the aid of spirits, but also by the teachings of mosque-based Islam. Disorders caused by *jin* are untreatable by biomedical intervention and can only be cured by recourse to those who control *jin* or through the healing powers of God channelled through the Qur'an. Dreaming is open to being apprehended as a direct encounter with the Divine or spirit beings.

Local models, cosmologies, and sensibilities provide a repertoire of human and nonhuman characters and models of experience, but Ilkhom-aka and Rifat-aka have developed their own individual understandings of the nature of the spirits they have encountered. They locate them within a developing narrative of their life and self. This is more than a retrospective, cognitive interpretation of past events. The spirits that Ilkhom-aka and Rifat-aka encounter are immediately apprehended as *jin* or angels within their continuingly developing moral narrative frames.

The Narrative Understanding of Self

The perspective of embodiment directs our attention to the way Ilkhom-aka experiences his social and material world through his body and extends reasoning beyond self-conscious reflection. It suspends the conceptual separation between mind and body, the physical and the intangible, rational thought and emotion. These dualities, Scheper-Hughes and Lock have argued, are historically developed constructions and are not 'natural' categories. Their notion of the 'mindful body' (Scheper-Hughes and Lock 1987) is intended to help us understand how global processes, such as relations of power, or a society's ideas about personhood and other conceptual categories, are inscribed upon the body (Scheper-Hughes 1992; Wikan 1989a, 1989b). An embodiment perspective reveals that 'thinking' is not solely an activity of the self-conscious mind, but that emotion and experience too are modes of reasoning. They have been described as 'embodied thought' – thought or knowledge felt within the body (Rosaldo 1984). Moral reasoning is integral to experience, and it is misguided to locate it only in cognitive reflection, opposed to an unreflective engagement within the flow of life.

However, the perspective of embodiment does not capture fully the moral dimension of experience, how experience is objectified as having particular moral significance. To explore the relation between experience and meaning, I follow a number of anthropological studies of illness that make use of the concept of narrative. Narrative theory builds upon an opposition between an idea that events occur in mere succession with no inherent meaning or direction, and the creative synthesis of events, as well as the characters involved in them, into a meaningful plot leading to a particular conclusion. Paul Ricoeur has referred to this as 'drawing a configuration out of a succession' (Ricoeur 1991, 22). This opposition derives from a distinction made by Aristotle between history and poetry. The former is a representation of the sequential succession of actions as they occur and thus is concerned with the particular. Poetry, by contrast, is structured as a plot and presents a coherent whole, with a beginning, middle, and end. It addresses the universal and has a pedagogic purpose. It represents what could happen or what *ought* to happen rather than merely recounting what *is* (Aristotle 1987). Therefore, there is a contrast between life lived historically as a sequence of events and the narrative construction of *a* life leading to a particular, morally evaluated end.[3]

Narrative theory concerns the fashioning of meaning from indeterminate experience that is potentially open to any number of interpretations, and the context of illness lends itself to an understanding of this process as intimately involved within the body. Sufferers and those around them invoke locally meaningful models and categories to make sense of illness, to locate themselves and others within an ordered, moral world where responsibility can be assigned and action can be judged as virtuous or culpable (Good 1994; Hunt 1998; Kleinman 1988). The intimate connection between meaning and embodied experience as evidenced in the context of personal illness leads to the question of the self. Narrative theory points to how illness propels sufferers to reflect upon their personal biographies, to place themselves within a plot leading to a morally evaluated outcome.

The plot, the moral story in which the self is located, is not stable but subject to continuous reinterpretation in response to ongoing experience and through interaction with others who are also immersed in plots, with their own motives and desires. Experience is indeterminate, potentially open to objectification in multiple ways, and memory of past experience is reassessed in the light of an ongoing present (Good 1994, 135–65; Lambek 1993, 383–92). Cheryl Mattingly has described this as the moral uncertainty of operating from multiple points of view. The relation between experience and meaning is not provided by narrative coherence, she argues, but by narrative drama, where individuals are confronted with unexpected events and developments that overturn their previous narrative structures (Mattingly 1998). The self is thus in a constant process of development, oriented within multiple moral frames that are continually in a state of becoming.

An embodiment perspective reframes the problem of the relation between the universal and the particular. It collapses Aristotle's separation of history and poetry by suggesting that moral reasoning with reference to the universal occurs within embodied, ongoing experience of life as it is lived. Carrithers and Mattingly have argued separately that immediate understanding and action are themselves narratively structured, so that life as lived is never a mere succession of events that requires a separate narrative construction to transform it into a life lived within a moral story; moral evaluation and reflection are inherent to experience. Carrithers locates this quality in the evolved nature of humans as social beings. What he terms 'sociality' is manifested in an innate propensity for humans to engage with and respond to each other. Others are apprehended not just in the context of immediate interaction, but within an 'unfolding story' in which they are constructed as characters motivated by particular moods and intentions and immersed in plots (Carrithers 1992). Mattingly develops a similar analysis. She rejects the idea that there is such a thing as 'raw' experience, a prelinguistic or prenarrated sequence of events, that is made meaningful through a secondary narrative interpretation. Action itself has a narrative structure. Actors operate within their own motives and plots, seeking desirable outcomes and endings and reading the actions of others as also immersed in plots of their own (Mattingly 1998).

An Islamic Revival Narrative

The entire self is involved within moral reasoning and reflection, and it is not helpful to treat (abstract) thought, action, emotion, and bodily sensation as distinct conceptual spheres. Memories of past experience are constantly reevaluated in the context of the present. Personal accounts about 'rediscovering' Islam are particularly illustrative, and I return to the experience of Abdumajid-aka, introduced in Chapter 3, a lecturer in mathematics at Samarkand State University and director of a secondary school, who was in his late fifties at the time of my field research. His account is representative of many Muslims in Uzbekistan yet at the same time illustrates how the creativity of experiential reasoning produces a highly personal moral narrative, so that he has come to his own unique understanding of Islam.

Abdumajid-aka was born in Samarkand, the seventh of eight surviving children. His father was a builder and carpenter, and Abdumajid-aka described him as semiliterate (Rus. *polugramotnyi*) because he only read the Latin script.[4] Abdumajid-aka's father did not perform the five daily prayers (*namoz*), praying only occasionally, and neither of his parents instructed him in religious observance or even discussed Islam with him. Abdumajid-aka said that they were afraid that his school or other state authorities might have found out about it because it was forbidden by law to encourage children to observe religious practice. He recalled how, when he was ten or eleven years old, he and his schoolmates had been forced by their teachers to eat sweets during Ramadan so that anyone who had been keeping the fast would be forced to break it. Abdumajid-aka attributes his knowledge of Islam as a child, such as it was, to his mother, who performed the *namoz* regularly at home and often read the Qur'an. She had not attended state schooling, but as a child she had taken part for a number of years in a class for girls given by a *bibikhalfa*, a female religious practitioner who officiates at women's rituals. There she had learnt how to recite the Qur'an and had memorised a large part of it and also learnt the appropriate recitations for ritual events such as funerals, weddings, and women's propitiatory ceremonies, such as the *bibiseshanba*. She had never practiced as a *bibikhalfa* outside her own household, however, as her husband had not allowed it.

Abdumajid-aka described the awareness of Islam that he gained through childhood as something that he gradually became steeped in (Rus. *propityvalis*'). He knew there was a God because his of mother's regular prayer and from daily ritual actions such as pronouncing *bismi llāhi l-raḥmāni l-raḥīm* (Ar. In the name of God the Merciful and Compassionate) before every meal and *omin* at the end. However, he said that he understood this in terms of 'tradition' rather than a conscious religious commitment, just as he wished his Russian neighbours *Khristos voskres* (Rus. Christ has risen) at Easter time. His parents had arranged for him to be circumcised when he was six years old, which was almost universal among the indigenous population in Soviet Central Asia, even for Communist Party officials. However, he recalls that the ritual and accompanying celebration (*sunnat to'y*) was more what he considered a traditional than a religious event, something done to fulfil societal expectations. He recalled a schoolmate with a Russian mother and a Tajik father who had not been circumcised because his mother had not allowed it. When his father started to arrange a marriage for him, it was remembered that they had never organised a circumcision celebration, so the young man was not considered a Muslim and had to find a Russian wife. Abdumajid-aka stated that what was considered significant was that he had not undertaken a *sunnat to'y*, making him an unsuitable marriage partner, rather than that he did not observe the tenets of Islam, indicating to him that the *sunnat to'y* for most people at the time was a cultural marker and not an enactment of religious commitment.

Abdumajid-aka described how this unreflective stance changed during his time at university in Samarkand in the late 1960s, where he attended the inevitable courses on philosophy, political economy, and atheism. He described this as a period when he started to develop his intellectual thinking, and he frequently makes reference to his analytical, rational approach to reasoning. He found the Marxist materialism he encountered in his courses convincing and went through a period when he no longer believed in the existence of God. However, he described how, over time, this changed and how, paradoxically, the more he studied philosophy, the more he pondered the nature of God. He has eventually arrived at his particular understanding of the Divine, which he emphasises results from his independent conclusions from books he has read, his experience, and critical reasoning. He sees God as a universal or absolute consciousness (Rus. *mirovoi razum*). He believes that all living things occupy a graduated scale of consciousness. Humans have a greater potential for developing this consciousness than animals, and between humans and God, the absolute consciousness, are beings such as the angels. His conception of the Divine is not bounded within Islam, however, but encompasses all religious systems:

> I image God as . . . complete understanding that has to bring order into our disorder. This may be by the help of different religions, maybe through Islam, Orthodox Christianity, Judaism, or Baha'ism. I liked their constitution. I think that in the future religion will develop in such a way it will develop general social principles for conduct in society. Religion first develops for a certain group of people, and then gradually becomes a kind of constitution for all humanity, which people accept in their spirits. It won't be important to pray in a mosque or a church. The principles of behaviour will be important. Religion was a carrier of ideology and in the future this will be the case as well. This ideology will direct people, a general ideology, not like the state ideology which changes. Religion lasts longer than government ideology.

> The conflicts between Arabs and Jews, and in Northern Ireland has to find a solution, because the time is ripe. Each era has its own religion. The principle of tolerance is in every religion.

At the same time, Abdumajid-aka places himself firmly within an Islamic frame and recounted the process through which he came to develop an active commitment to Islam. He blames the breakdown of his first marriage in 1986 on the director of a state enterprise and Communist Party member who made him critical of the hypocrisy of professed communists who said one thing and did another. He contrasted this with the support he received at the time from his sisters, who are active Muslims. By the early 1990s, he began, in his words, to 'find his place in life'. He became director of a secondary school, remarried, and established a second family. He became well known and respected in Samarkand and was elected chairman of his *mahalla* committee in 2003. As *mahalla* chairman, he plays a leading role in organising and managing ritual events in his neighbourhood, such as funerals and weddings. He attributes his present well-established position in part to his belief in God. The early 1990s in Uzbekistan was a period of a general awakening of interest in Islam, with an unprecedented availability of Islamic literature, and he recalls obtaining books in 1996 on the ritual prescriptions of Islam and on how to perform the daily prayers. During the month of Ramadan that year, he had a dream in which he was attending an *iftor*, the breaking of the daytime fast, in a relative's home. His nephew, the imam at a prominent mosque in Samarkand, was present in the dream, as was an old man with a white beard and turban who invited the guests to pray after the meal, saying that those who had not performed the ritual ablutions (*tahorat*) should in any case join in, but should remember to come prepared in the future. Some time later he mentioned this dream to one of his sisters, a *bibikhalfa*, who told him that the dream was significant and advised him that if he found himself in a similar situation in the future, he should perform the prayers. The next year the situation did in fact occur during an *iftor* gathering, and Abdumajid-aka has performed the daily prayers ever since.

In common with Ilkhom-aka and Rifat-aka in the village of Pakhtabad, Abdumajid-aka developed a more active engagement with Islam as he began to occupy a more prominent and senior position within local society. It is common for men to start representing their households at ritual events within their neighbourhoods and to take the lead in pronouncing blessings and prayers at communal meals and other similar gatherings as they reach a certain age. At minimum, this means adopting the modes of deportment expected at these occasions and learning appropriate formulas to recite, although, of course, this does not mean that every individual adopts an active commitment to Islam as he grows older.

Abdumajid-aka's experience of bodily disorder and healing has informed his development of a moral self, and his past experience of illness is reassessed within his present understanding. He recalled how, in the late 1960s, when he was a university student, his brother was afflicted by what he referred to as 'inflammation of the trigeminal nerve' (Rus. *vospalenie troinichnogo nerva*) around his eye that caused half of his face to be paralysed. His brother was a senior university lecturer at the time and was able to access good doctors through his network of contacts. However, despite attempting a number of biomedical treatments, the problem was not solved. Eventually, one of his relatives suggested that they go to a healer called Qori Najmi. This healer recited verses from the Qur'an over Abdumajid-aka's brother, hit him with his prayer beads to expel the evil spirits, and blew upon him (an action referred to as *suf suf*). He told them to come again early the next morning, because his first breath of the morning was the strongest. After four of these treatments, the facial paralysis disappeared. Abdumajid-aka visited this healer on a number of occasions in the following years, including in 1974, when his baby daughter was suffering from sores on her scalp and fainting fits that were not responding to hospital treatment. They were cured after a number of sessions with Qori Najmi. During my field research I came across a number of similar accounts of partial facial paralysis that were not responsive to medical treatment but were cured by recourse to healers who recited verses of the Qur'an over sufferers or by healers who worked with spirits.[5]

These experiences of illness, healing, and dream encounters are similar to those of Ilkhom-aka and Rifat-aka, but Abdumajid-aka understands them in very different terms. He occupies a location outside the encounters from which he can objectively reflect upon the motives and subjective perception of the actors involved and determine what is actually taking place.

Qori Najmi has Islamic learning, but he's educated not in the madrasa, but in a *qorikhona*, where they learn to read texts out loud. He only has a surface knowledge of Islam, not as deep as he would have received from a madrasa education. He has no medical qualifications, so he does not know how his healing works. He thinks that when he reads a prayer, God allows him to heal people. However, in actual fact, in my own opinion he has a very strong biopole which is able to influence the biopole of other people. Because he continually prays, he fills himself with energy. There is energy which is in the universe, which he uses. When he performs the prayers early in the morning, he receives this energy and then gives it out, so the first person gets more of this energy than the later ones. He notices this but explains it as his first breath being stronger. The person sitting before him only thinks of getting better, and is completely subordinate to the healer. They are attuned to each other, and then Qori Najmi stimulates the internal potential energy which exists in every living thing. This is written into the genes. There is a blueprint for how the organs of the body should work.

Abdumajid-aka claims that he no longer takes medicines when he feels ill, but instead relies on prayer. In a state of prayer, he believes, a person directs himself entirely towards God, asking for healing of a particular part of their body and this awakens the internal reserves for self-renewal and healing that are present in all organisms. Thus, people who pray regularly are healthier, and he feels much healthier himself, no longer suffering from chronic liver and stomach problems as in the past. In addition, he asserts that undertaking the ritual ablutions (*tahorat*) five times a day before prayer imposes a regime of hygiene and cleanliness that helps to maintain good health. This 'scientific' or 'modernist' understanding of the beneficial effects of the *tahorat* contrasts with a view held by many others that the state of ritual purity it provides acts as a protection against the malign influence of *jin*. Moreover, his assertion that healing comes from a person's internal reserves, and that a focus on God in prayer stimulates this human potential, would not sit comfortably with the view of many Muslims that healing comes directly from God.

Abdumajid-aka has developed his particular conception of the Divine through his own bodily experience of disorder and healing, the instances of healing he has witnessed in the course of his life, through memories of childhood and the religious practice of his family members, through his present social position, and through his own studies. His educational and professional background have developed in him a self-reflectively analytical stance. At the same time, Abdumajid-aka lives in the same world as the two men from the village of Pakhtabad. All three feel themselves to be good Muslims who pray regularly and observe the tenets of Islam to the best of their ability. They have reached a stage in life when they occupy a more prominent position in their social circles as representatives of their households, and Abdumajid-aka is also the director of a secondary school and chairman of his *mahalla* committee. They all recognise and experience dreams and waking visions as real encounters with divine agency and acknowledge the healing power of the Qur'an through those who are able to read it. Abdumajid-aka's self-representation as a committed Muslim and community leader would be understood and accepted by the two men from Pakhtabad, and his successful recourse to the healer Qori Najmi would be intelligible to them. At the same time, all three men have highly individual understandings of what is going on in these encounters and have developed individually particular Muslim selves. Many of Abdumajid-aka's views on the nature of the Divine would at best be confusing for the other men. Remaining within a common frame of Islam, and with reference to the same models of illness and disorder, each has located himself within a particularised moral narrative.

Personal Fortune and Divine Judgement

Moral reasoning occurs though all experience, not only illness. Any encounter or occurrence is apprehended within a moral narrative, including climatic phenomena such as a highly unusual and intense hailstorm that occurred in June 2004 while I was conducting field research in the village of Pakhtabad. The storm lasted for about ten minutes, during which hail the size of ping-pong balls bombarded the village, destroying crops and punching holes in some corrugated iron roofs. A few days later, a forty-four-year-old *qori* (Qur'an reciter), whom I call simply Qori-aka, attributed the storm to the villagers' ignorance and neglect of Islamic obligations, specifically the obligation to give *ushr*, which he explained as the duty to distribute one-tenth of agricultural production to neighbours or the poor.

> Most people now don't know about *ushr*, because we have gone far from the Prophet. We've forgotten lots, and gone far from Islam. Now people are gradually starting to explain these things, but what the Prophet has told us has already happened. The hail was God's power. God has said that he has placed a responsibility on the rich to give to the poor. He will ask us on the day of judgement whether we have given the poor their due. Because people haven't given *ushr*, there are misfortunes. This is laid out in a hadith.

Qori-aka is from a family recognised in the village for their knowledge of Islam. His great-grandfather had studied at a madrasa in Bukhara before the Soviet period, had been the imam in the Friday mosque in the village, and had taught a number of people from within the village and outside, including the present imam. Qori-aka himself has never formally studied Islam at a madrasa. This would have been very difficult during the Soviet period. Instead, he has studied the Qur'an from his family, from others with religious knowledge (*domla*) in his neighbourhood, and from books printed before the Soviet period. He had begun performing the five daily prayers from the age of twenty, and was one of the few young men who did so during the Soviet period. He recalled only one or two others who prayed regularly in the factory where he had worked.

Just as he attributes the hailstorm to divine agency, Qori-aka believes that illness is sent by God as punishment for a person's wrongdoing. This is not necessarily a bad thing, in his view, as every human being will inevitably do wrong at one stage or another, and suffering in this world expunges a person's sin. 'The illness takes a person's strength, his colour. Then God gradually gives back the strength and the colour and the sins are forgiven.' In these instances, Qori-aka develops his understanding of Islam through the experience of natural phenomena. The material world, as God's creation, is the transcendent source that constitutes his understanding as moral.

Tohirjon, my host in Pakhtabad, like Qori-aka, apprehended misfortune or success in terms of personal moral conduct. My position in the village was largely mediated through him, and I became integrated within his own household and social network. He facilitated much of my research by introducing me to his neighbours and acquaintances and arranging for me to teach in his school, where I was able to expand my social contacts. He would invite people I wanted to meet to his home or accompany me to meet them elsewhere. He had been chosen for a place on a one-month training course in the United States for village teachers organised by an international NGO, and he attributed this to the fact that he had helped me in my own research. I was a Christian, so he had been sent to a Christian country.

Similarly, Tohirjon attributed the popularity and success of his private university entrance preparation classes, which even attract high-paying students from a nearby town, to the fact that he sometimes teaches children in the village for free who cannot afford to pay for the lessons.

He is proud of the fact that a relatively large proportion of his students have obtained *byudjetnyi* (Rus.), places at universities around the country. These are state-supported places exempt from tuition fees and with a modest subsistence grant that are awarded to those with the best test scores. A number of his students managed to obtain fee-paying places as well. He contrasted his success with an exam preparation centre in a nearby town, where the number of successful students was only a few greater than his own despite operating on a much larger scale and charging higher fees. For Tohirjon, this success validated what he perceived as his more honest and conscientious approach to the courses. The large town teaching centre, he claimed, did not actually conduct any real teaching at all, but just acted as an intermediary between the students' families and the higher educational institutes, using the fees to pay bribes in order to obtain the question papers in advance or to secure places in other ways. This is a very uncertain venture, as more often than not, the question papers obtained in this way are not genuine. The papers are issued centrally from the capital, Tashkent, at the last minute to prevent this sort of corruption.

In fact, Tohirjon also engages in this practice. During the period of my field research, he charged U.S.$700 dollars for the course, which included U.S.$150 in actual fees and a U.S.$100 bonus if the student attained a state-sponsored place. The rest was used to obtain the tests in advance. However, he maintained his self-representation as an honest, dedicated teacher through the fact that he, unlike those in the larger town centre, actually put a lot of effort into teaching his students and produced real results, with some of his students entering university without the need for bribes. Moreover, he contributed to the collective good of his community by offering free courses to some of those in need.

While Tohirjon sees his good fortune as flowing from his positive participation with others in his community, he also believes the inverse to be true. In Chapter 1, I recount his view that the physiological disorders and other misfortunes of some of his neighbours are punishments from God for their past corrupt practices in the collective farm. After a conversation with a neighbour on this topic during which the neighbour denied that illness resulted from inappropriate moral conduct or from *jin*, but was the result of poor material conditions, poverty, and inadequate diet, Tohirjon declared that this neighbour did not fully participate in society. He did not have a job with any form of collective (Rus. *kollektiv*) and had no cooperative spirit that would induce him to think in more communal terms. Instead, he made a living by just keeping cows. This activity has become popular for those who can afford it. In a situation in which state salaries are very low, and practically nonexistent in the case of the collective farm, keeping cattle is a reliable form of investment and saving that, moreover, does not involve much cooperation or interaction within a larger community. Tohirjon himself fattens calves for sale as a strategy for accumulating enough capital to provide for the marriage of his four daughters.

Like the other individuals discussed in this chapter, Tohirjon lives in relation to multiple models for illness. He understands illness as divine judgement upon personal conduct, but he also accepts that affliction can be caused by inadvertently offending the *jin* that exist unseen all around us. He was careful to tell me not to spit in the washing area in his house, as this is where *jin* gather, and spitting would anger them. Before attending the *aqiqa to'y* in a neighbouring *mahalla* described in Chapter 5, he insisted that I perform the *tahorat*, the ritual ablutions. When I questioned the necessity of this, because I am not a Muslim, he stressed the importance of maintaining a ritually pure state as protection against *jin*. He recounted a story he hazily remembered about a Russian bulldozer operator who became paralysed after digging up a cemetery his Uzbek Muslim colleagues had refused to touch for fear of offending the spirits.[6] 'We always have to be careful of high powers (*yuqori kuchlar*), divine powers (*ilohi kuchlar*), or angels. They don't care if you are a Muslim or not a Muslim, a young person or an old one, a *qori*, a learned person. If you offend them, they will harm to you.' These orientations, however, do not prevent him from recognising the efficacy and causal logic of biomedical treatment. When members of his family become ill, he might consult a state-employed doctor who lives in the village and take them to a hospital if this is needed, visit a healer who works with spirits, or invite someone to recite the Qur'an over them. He often resorts to all of these options. His mother, who lives in his household, heals clients with the aid of spirits, and many of his neighbours come to him for the administration of injections that have been prescribed to them by doctors because he has acquired some skill at this.

Tohirjon is able to understand his own experience and that of others in different ways – as encounters with spirit agents, as governed by the natural laws of a material world, or in terms of participation within flows of sociality. Local cosmologies and models allow for particular qualities of experience. This is apprehended as meaningful within an individual's ongoing moral narrative and produces particular understandings of Islam and moral self. It is the creativity of experience that affords space for reasoning, and this is discussed further in Chapter 7.

SEVEN

Debating Islam through the Spirits

In this chapter,[1] the theme of illness is continued, but the perspective shifts from sufferers to the practice of healers who work with spirits. Within the cosmologies of healers, experiential reasoning is given objective form. The government's efforts to monitor and control religious expression have stifled public debate and the free circulation of interpretations independent of its own discourses, but Muslims in Uzbekistan are still able to develop their own understandings of Islam and contest the practice of others. We have seen that imams criticise much of the practice of Central Asian Muslims as un-Islamic innovation, but their criticism is muted by the government's celebration of an authentic Central Asian cultural and spiritual heritage. Those who do not speak from the security of the quasi-state regulatory structure that *imom khatib* enjoy are even more vulnerable to charges of extremism if they proselytise too vociferously.

In this environment, criticism of the practice of healing and prophesy with the help of spirits is 'safe'. The postindependence government has not incorporated these practices within its idea of cultural authenticity. Healing with spirits falls outside the categories of Islam, religion, culture, and politics produced in state discourse and therefore is less likely to attract the attention of state officials and organs. It has become a site where debates about what it means to be a Muslim can take place in relative freedom.

Healing with Spirits in Uzbekistan

The healers I encountered in Uzbekistan evoke spirits to diagnose and treat illness in others and for purposes of prophesy. Spirits do not take physical possession of the bodies of the healers, but healers remain autonomous and fully conscious. They might be described as inhabiting an expanded or altered consciousness that enables them to see and converse with spirits while displaying no change in outward demeanour (Stephen & Suryani 2000). At the same time, interaction with spirit beings is not confined to discrete occasions of healing or prophecy but is continuous within the lives of healers. Some claim that when they were children they were able to see strange beings invisible to others. They encounter and converse with spirits in dreams and waking visions, and many discovered the existence of their spirits through an illness experience. This illness was caused by the spirits and recurs if the person does not practice healing. In some cases, the spirits are fulfilling a greater mission through the healer, calling the people of Uzbekistan back to Islam after decades of Soviet-imposed atheism. Healers might be said to embody the spirits in the sense that through their relation with the spirits they establish and maintain an ongoing moral state (Lambek 1993, 316–20).

A brief account of healing with spirits during the Soviet period provides a historical context for current practice. Gleb Snezarev provides one of the most detailed descriptions. Basing his account on fieldwork he conducted in the 1950s, he describes what he calls remnants of shamanism and its demonology in Khorezm province in northeastern Uzbekistan (Snezarev 2003). He describes varieties of supernatural beings, including *jin* and *pari*, among others. *Jin*, in his account, are malevolent beings that cause harm to people who encounter them. They are found in such places as abandoned villages, houses, and mosques; in cemeteries; in the manure of horses and donkeys; and in ash. *Pari* both harm people and have a benevolent attitude; they are classified as Muslims and unbelievers. Men and women who were called by *pari* to serve as shamans were referred to as *parikhon* or *folbin* in Khorezm and as *bakhshi* among Kyrgyz and Kazaks. This call sometimes came in the form of a dream in which the chosen person was offered one of the objects used by shamans such as a tambourine or whip, and those who were called risked illness or madness if they refused. In addition, upon accepting the call, the shaman had to visit a saint's tomb to receive the saint's blessing – again, often through a dream. Snezarev provides a detailed account of the various healing rituals shamans used to expel the problem-causing *jin* with the aid of the *pari* spirit helpers, including the placing of chicken blood on various parts of the patient's body as food for the *pari*.

Like Snezarev, Vladimir Basilov draws a distinction between what he describes as shamanic practices and Islam in pre-Soviet and Soviet Central Asia. Shamans were healers who expelled illness-causing *jin* and divined the future with the aid of spirit helpers. He characterises the history of shamanism in Central Asia from the late nineteenth century onward as one in which it became Islamised. Shamanic cosmology was enriched by Islamic imagery, and shamans repositioned themselves within an Islamic frame. For example, they demanded that their clients carry out the same ritual ablutions before their healing ceremonies that they would before performing Muslim prayers; they used the Qur'an and Muslim prayer rugs in their divination and healing rituals; and they claimed that their healing spirits were prominent figures from Islamic history or cosmology, such as the angel Gabriel. Basilov also describes the hostile attitude of many Muslims towards shamans for contravening the doctrines of Islam and the opposition of some shamans to Islam. These shamans criticised the wearing of protective amulets that contained verses of the Qur'an written on pieces of paper, claimed that their spirits forbade them from becoming a mullah, or stated that they could not say the name of God when making offerings to the spirits. For the most part, however, Basilov describes a situation of peaceful coexistence and assimilation. Muslim figures such as mullahs adopted elements of the shamanic tradition and used spirit helpers. He describes Sufism, with its traditions of ecstatic trance states and its scorn for the normative strictures of ordinary Islamic practice, as particularly open to incorporating elements of shamanic practice. Sufi spiritual leaders, Basilov states, accepted shamans among their followers and allowed them to combine shamanic divination with Sufi practices such as the *zikr* (the chanted repetition of the name of God). Shamans, for their part, presented themselves as exemplary Muslims, and some considered it essential to obtain initiation from such Sufi masters (Basilov 1992).

Snezarev and Basilov attempt to differentiate between what they implicitly assume to be Islam proper and pre-Islamic shamanic practices that have been assimilated within it. There are two reasons why I do not agree with this approach. Firstly, this implies the objective existence of a 'pure' Islam, of which these practices do not form a part. This dismisses the subjective experience of the healers who construct themselves as Muslims precisely through their interaction with spirits. Moreover, to assert that certain practices are pre-Islamic survivals is to make a theological claim (Launay 1992, 5). Rather than focusing attention upon the process through which Muslims themselves construct moral selves and debate and negotiate the nature of Islam, the analyst implicitly prejudges local debates with his or her own notions about how the boundaries of Islam should be drawn. A more productive approach is to look at how individuals come to their own understandings. This means taking seriously the diverse perspectives of Muslims in their own terms.

Secondly, classifying the practice of healing as shamanism sets it apart as a field of knowledge and practice with its own specialist practitioners, separate from 'lay' experiences of spirit beings. However, everyday encounters with spirits in dreams or during visits to the tombs of saints draw on the same cosmologies and histories as those of specialist healers, and both are enactments of moral reasoning through which individuals develop an understanding of what it means to be a Muslim. What distinguishes specialist healers is their more explicit reflection on encounters with spirits. The cosmologies healers develop present in objective form and thus make more readily accessible to conscious reflection and manipulation, the processes of moral reasoning that are largely implicit within experience. Like practices anthropologists have described using the labels of witchcraft, sorcery, or spirit possession, healing practices are creative interventions within ongoing, immediate concerns through an appeal to power that transcends the present. An important characteristic of this 'magical' practice is its ambiguity. Healing with spirits, witchcraft, and sorcery can be morally evaluated in both negative and positive terms, often both at the same time. This renders them creative media for debating and contesting what is true Islam and who is a good Muslim.

If we want to explore the creative dynamic of healing practices, we need to take the subjective experience of these practices seriously in their own terms. As the healers locate themselves firmly within Islam, we need to be open to exploring how debates about what it means to be a good Muslim are carried on through interaction with spirits. Even from Basilov's own account, it is clear that identifying different types of shamanic or Muslim healing practices as distinct categories is problematic. In the present-day context, the labels used to describe healers and their spirits are not objective descriptors. They are morally loaded labels through which the practice of healing with spirits and the healers themselves are characterised as truly Muslim or excluded from genuine Islam. It is common for healers to be referred to by others using a term they personally disavow.

Taking Spirits Seriously

Much of the anthropological literature on spirit possession and sorcery has aimed to reveal the rational motivations underlying the seemingly exotic. There is a sometimes implicit, sometimes openly stated assumption that spirits and magic do not exist as empirical realities, so that the task of the social scientist is to uncover what is indeed real, namely, their observable social effects. Emphasis is placed upon the motivations and strategies of actors involved and the structural position of spirits and magic within a social system. This was most clearly evident in the British structural functionalist tradition of anthropology, in which witchcraft accusations were commonly interpreted as expressing the tensions generated by a society's social structure (Middleton 1963; Nadel 1952). Similarly instrumentalist assumptions underlie more recent analyses in which spirit possession is understood as a means for socially marginalised groups within society – often women – to exercise a degree of agency or to establish a social network that offers them the support, autonomy, and authority they lack in wider society (Doumato 2000; Lewis 1998). Alternatively, the practice of healers who work with spirits or magic has been analysed in terms of personal charisma and the strategies healers employ to convince clients of the efficacy of their treatments and in terms of their competition with other healers (Bellér-Hann 2001; Lindquist 2001a).

These analyses have provided important insights into the dynamics of healing and into the societies within which they are located. Healers as well as those who employ sorcery, or accuse others of doing so, are often motivated by such strategic and instrumental concerns. Moreover, in societies where women have limited autonomy outside the enclosed space of the home, networks formed through possession cults, groups formed for visiting shrines, or regular ritual gatherings women hold to invoke divine or spirit intercession can give those involved a means of expression they otherwise would not enjoy. However, by excluding the subjective reality of spirits and magic, creativity of moral reasoning is also excluded. It is true that a moral dimension is often part of instrumentalist or functionalist analyses. Lewis has made a distinction between central and peripheral possession cults, where the former represent and enforce the dominant morality and are the province of more powerful sections of society, whereas peripheral cults are amoral. Structural functionalist analysis typically makes a similar claim that witchcraft allegations act to enforce social norms. But morality here is seen as static rules and norms that leave little space for creativity and diversity.

The issue of morality takes centre stage in the more recent literature, which studies witchcraft and sorcery in relation to conditions of modernity. This literature suggests that far from being forms of primitive, premodern thinking that should be displaced by the advancement of scientific knowledge, sorcery and occult practices are in fact produced within the local experiences of global capitalism and the politics of the modern nation-state. In these terms, occult practices and spirit possession are understood as moral commentaries of the dispossessed within colonial and postcolonial societies, as resistance to their situation of inequality and exploitation (Comaroff & Comaroff 1999; Moore & Sanders 2001; Ong 1988; Taussig 1977), as well as a critique of the political power and corruption of politicians (Meyer 1998). Insightful though these analyses are, they, too, gloss over the possibility of the reality of magic. Occult practices and spirit possession are not studied on their own terms but are regarded as really being about something else. They are taken to be meta-narratives arising out of a more tangible (and more apparently rational) economic or political reality. Dynamism is located in changing political economies that are objectified and reflected upon within sorcery discourses.

In order to fully appreciate the creativity of magic and how this creativity enables processes of moral reasoning, we need to open ourselves to its reality for those involved (Boddy 1988; Kapferer 2003; Lambek 1988). This is the approach adopted by a number of recent studies of spirit possession and sorcery in Muslim societies. By taking spirit agents seriously, rather than attempting to 'decode' spirit possession as an allegory or reflection of processes external to it, Jennifer Nourse has been able to explore possession as an arena in which the Lauje in Indonesia come to differing understandings of what it means to be Muslim. Whereas reformist Muslims, mainly immigrants to the area but also some local Lauje, criticise belief in spirits as a pagan practice that denies the fundamental unity of God, Lauje who take part in possession rituals emphasise the collective nature of spirits as refractions of a single essence created by God, and therefore consistent with monotheistic Islam. An additional voice is that of elite Lauje followers of a Sufi tradition who establish their authority and identity as true Muslims through their mastery of knowledge of the spirits as separate, individual entities with their own natures and powers (Nourse 1996). It is only by accepting the subjective experience of all parties in their own terms, Nourse argues, that we can free analysis from the limiting perspective of individual strategies and competition over authority and power.

Nourse's ethnography touches on an important aspect of magic that creates particular space for creativity, namely its ambiguity. The spirits are located within the experience of the Lauje Sufi elite in a fundamentally different manner than the way in which they inhabit the mediums themselves. Although their utterances during possession rituals through the bodies of the mediums emphasise their collective nature, the Sufi elite take these occasions as opportunities for displaying and expanding their own esoteric knowledge by discerning genuine from fake spirits, reinterpreting their utterances for the audience, and attempting to discern and individuate the spirits' origins and identities. All participants are involved within the same possession episode, but experience is not uniform and they develop contrasting Muslim identities through their interaction with spirits.

This quality of ambiguity has been pointed out in accounts of sorcery and spirit possession in a wide range of ethnographic contexts. The power of sorcery is often viewed as amoral, so that it can be used both to inflict harm and protect. Healers and those who provide protection against sorcery attacks are frequently held in suspicion as being potential sorcerers themselves. This is true even when the power involved is attributed ultimately to God or is located within the text of the Qur'an (Barth 1993, 257–60; Bowen 1993b; Lambek 1993, 121–33). Similarly, possession complexes among previously non-Muslim groups incorporated within a Muslim dominated polity have been shown both to negotiate an accommodation with Islam and even reflect the hegemony of Islamic ideals, while at the same time being a forum for expressing resistance to Islam and to validate alternative non-Muslim identities and moralities (Masquelier 2001; McIntosh 2004).

The ambiguity of magic is the ambiguity inherent in the indeterminate nature of experience itself. Magic brings this into sharp relief. Bruce Kapferer makes the point that sorcery is located in the lived-in world. It does not present an abstract model through which contingent events can be understood, merely offering explanations for misfortune or expressing interpersonal conflict. Rather, sorcery brings to bear on crises and suffering in the lived-in world cosmologies that articulate the ontological state of humans in the world and the forces motivating individual action. It aims to effect material interventions in ongoing life-concerns (Kapferer 1997). Healing cosmologies and histories manifest the reasoning inherent in experience. Moreover, Kapferer argues that a person's subjective experience of sorcery arises from a consciousness grounded both in the body and the world. Consciousness is not only reflective thought, but arises from an embodied existence in a lifeworld as well as a person's relations and interaction with others, much of which is not explicitly reflected upon (Kapferer 1997, 222). For Kapferer, sorcery is a manifestation of consciousness. In Chapter 6 I argue that moral reasoning is innate to experience, whereby indeterminate, contingent experience is apprehended within an unfolding moral narrative. This takes on objective form in the cosmologies healers invoke. The dynamic process of moral reasoning is laid bare in the creative work of healers as they develop Muslim selves through their interaction with spirits.

Healing Cosmologies

As I show in Chapter 6, individuals draw on a variety of domains of knowledge in apprehending their experience of illness and encounters with spirits. Healers in Uzbekistan similarly invoke within their healing practice an eclectic mixture of Islamic cosmology and practice, Sufi ideas about chains of the transmission of knowledge, ideas from what might be termed 'New Age' healing such as bioenergy, as well as imagery from the biomedical tradition. This mixture of imagery and practice is not unique to healing in Uzbekistan but has been observed among healers in a variety of settings from Kazakhstan and Russia to Bali (Barth 1993; Bellér-Hann 2001; Lindquist 2001b). Kapferer has described sorcery practices as 'metacosmologies' in the sense that they break apart elements of different cosmological frames and recombine them in novel ways, so that they are major sites for invention (Kapferer 2003). The creative dynamic of healing with spirits offers a means for healers to construct themselves as Muslims in the face of critics who claim that they stand outside true Islam.

The ethnography on healing with spirits I present here was recorded in and around the village of Pakhtabad. Gulnorahon is a fifty-year-old woman who lives and works in a town in Andijan province located approximately ten miles from Pakhtabad. I have chosen to relate her story because it is particularly rich in creative imagery and includes features common to most of the healers I encountered, although imagery and practice vary from healer to healer. Gulnorahon described her ancestors on both her mother's and father's side as 'white bones', descendents of the Prophet or of Muslim saints, and recalled performing the morning *namoz* (Muslim prayers) with her grandmother in her childhood. She graduated from a higher educational institute and works as a schoolteacher. At the age of twenty-five, she became ill and had a series of heart attacks, which persisted for ten years and resulted in the partial paralysis of her face (a condition people often associate with the influence of *jin*). In 1989, when she was thirty-five, after recovering from a heart attack in a clinic in the city of Andijan, the doctor who treated her suggested that she turn to a 'spiritually pure person' who could cure her by reading the Qur'an over her and that she turn to 'our own *musulmonchilik*' (Muslimness).

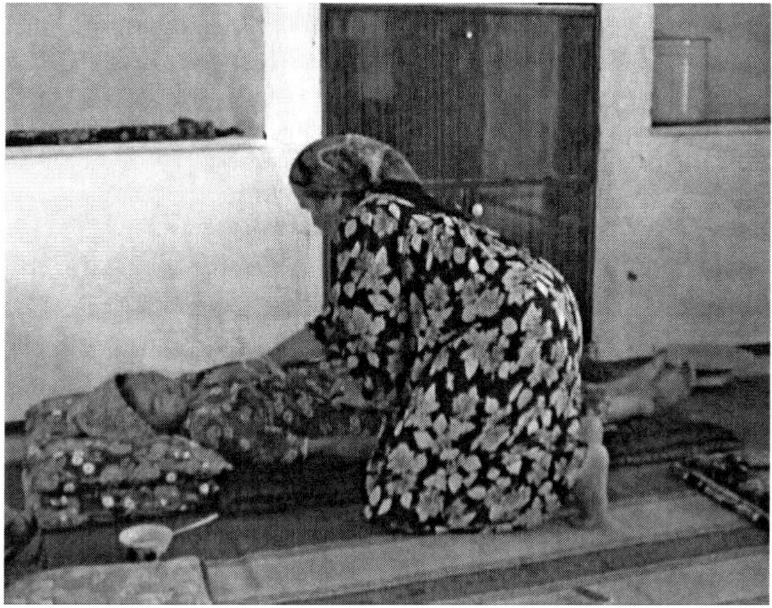

FIGURE 17. One of Gulnorahon's apprentices treating a fallen heart in Pakhtabad

Gulnorahon recovered after a healer in Kyrgyzstan cleansed her of the hostile spirits possessing her.

During the healing process, Gulnorahon had a dream in which a woman gave her seven objects connected with healing, including prayer beads (*tasbeh*) and a knife. When she subsequently related the dream, the healer summoned the spirit, asked her name, and identified her as Lojim Poshsha Hojaona, one of Gulnorahon's ancestors who had performed the hajj pilgrimage to Mecca seven times and become a healer (*tabib*) herself. The healer identified Gulnorahon as a healer and became her master (*ustoz*). Gulnorahon learnt healing practice with her and was also shown how to heal by an *oqsoqol* (old man) who appeared to her in dreams. In fact, Gulnorahon said that in her childhood, she had dreams where she saw spirit beings but she did not know what they were at the time. In 1990, her master gave her the *duo* (blessing and permission) to 'work in Islam, purity (*poklik*), to perform the prayers five times a day, to work in a *halol* (ritually pure) manner, not for monetary gain in this world but for God'. She gave her the prayer beads, knife, and other tools of healing, and also the spirit of her ancestor Lojim Poshsha Hojaona as a spirit helper.

In 1991, after working as a healer for a short period, Gulnorahon completed a three-month course at an 'extrasense' centre in Tashkent that her master from Kyrgyzstan had also attended. At the centre, she studied, as she put it, how to perform the Muslim prayers, religious knowledge (*ilm*) from a *domla* (person learned in Islam), anatomy and physiology from a doctor, and how to heal spiritually. She received a diploma. The centre was founded by a retired university professor who had been on the hajj and who had herself graduated from the parent centre in Moscow with which the Tashkent centre had been affiliated during the Soviet period. After independence, it was registered with the state authorities and in fact became a private firm belonging to the founder.[2] When I asked Gulnorahon why she felt the need to attend the course, she replied that she needed to obtain official documentation (*hujjat*): 'If you gather people they will ask you if you have any documents. I am a teacher as well, and because there are all sorts of worldviews, this diploma gives me lots of strength'. She added that her documents gave her the right to check up on people who practice her form of healing in Andijan. She claimed that there were a lot of charlatans pretending to heal people for money, whereas she had read the Qur'an and had a *duo* (blessing) from a master. In fact, Gulnorahon was the only healer I encountered who had attended any sort of institutionalised training or had paper qualifications. Most had obtained a *duo* from another healer or through a dream encounter with an ancestor, Muslim saint, or some other spirit being.

In the course of her healing, Gulnorahon relies on her spirit helpers, which she refers to as *azizlar* (saints) or *otakhonlar* (sing. *otakhon*: ancestor). The fact that she and other healers refer to their helping spirits in this way rather than as *pari* is significant, and I will return to this issue in the next section. She has a principal *otakhon* named Hurshid Mahsum who was also given to her (*qo'y bergan*) by her master in Kyrgyzstan. This *otakhon* has a 'deputy' named Karim Polonoglu Nusrotilloh Qori, and they call on other *azizlar* as necessary. Gulnorahon uses her *azizlar* to diagnose patients' illnesses and to inform her as to what healing actions she needs to perform, such as reading a specific passage from the Qur'an. 'I will read and they will stand behind me. Together we will heal, and . . . they will tell me how to massage, to give heat, to pass biopower.' With a Russian patient, Gulnorahon recounted how her principle *otakhon* called 'the head of the popes' from her (the Russian's) own nationality (*millat*). Her head spirit has told her that he has spirits from every national group.

Gulnorahon's healing contains a mixture of elements pertaining to Islam, knowledge of biomedicine and anatomy, and what might be called 'New Age' philosophy.

People get lots of illnesses from getting frights, stress. Blood doesn't circulate properly and a person can go mad, blood doesn't go to the brain. Hardened blood goes to the organs. Medicine can't detect this. We raise the heart with water and with hands (passing heat and bioenergy through the hands). Then we use lead (she drops a small amount of molten lead into a bowl of cold water and makes a diagnosis of the state of the patient's inner organs from the shape the lead takes), and after we've raised the heart two or three times the blood vessels will loosen, the circulation will improve.

In fact, Gulnorahon and the healers she trained were the only healers working with spirits I encountered who referred explicitly to 'bioenergy'. I surmise that this is because she and her master had attended the training institute in Tashkent, and Gulnorahon had incorporated this knowledge within her healing practice. In describing how she worked with her spirit helpers, she explained:

I'll do two *rakaat* of the *namoz* (cycles of prayer) to give them strength to do the job. For example, I'll place three *oqsoqol, otakhonlar* on the first person to come. If there's a problem with the internal organs, a doctor *otakhon* will come, give injections and heal. I'll ask them to give light from the third planet to the place which is cold. They will clean the client. This is not seen, you have to believe. I will cut the *jin* out with my knife and the black things will fall off the person. The *otakhonlar* will sweep them up, and a person from the second planet will come and take them away.

In addition to healing with spirit helpers, Gulnorahon prepares herbal medicines and also dips paper on which verses of the Qur'an are written in tea, which the patient drinks.

The cosmology and practice of most healers I observed share a set of central features, many of which are also described in the ethnographic accounts of healing in Uzbekistan during the Soviet period that I referred to earlier in this chapter. These include the initiatory illnesses by which the sufferer is identified as a healer, self-identification as coming from a line of healers so that healing is seen as a natural quality of the person transmitted by blood, obtaining the blessing and sometimes training from established healers, and often being visited in dreams by ancestors or Muslim saints who might also pass on certain objects used in healing, such as a Qur'an or prayer beads. Despite the wide variation in individual practice and cosmology, these shared features unite the diversity of individual practice into a tradition of healing shared by practitioners and clients. Tradition in this sense is not a bounded and fixed body of knowledge and practice, mechanically reproduced from generation to generation, perhaps incorporating elements from other such traditions and shedding some of its own with the passage of time. This sort of conception would encourage an 'archaeology' of healing, which attempts to identify a pure essence continuing through time and to identify which elements of contemporary practice are part of the core and which derive from other traditions. Healing cosmologies and practices clearly have histories, and tracing these can be a worthwhile endeavour. However, limiting analysis to tracing the genealogies of discrete cultural artefacts overlooks how healing practices arise from the concerns of the present and articulate moral reasoning in relation to it. Healing practices constitute a tradition in the sense that they are a model for experience and practice, similar to the models for illness discussed in Chapter 6. It is not a mechanically followed script, but it is re-created within experience and made meaningful within moral narratives. It renders the practice of healers mutually intelligible to other healers, their clients, and critics.

What was in fact most striking and consistent in the healing practice I observed is the insistence by healers that their spirits and healing power come from God. Gulnorahon stressed that she was working in the service of God (*ilohning yolida*). The blessing she received from her master was presented in these terms, exhorting her to work in a religiously pure manner and not for monetary gain. She presents herself as a devout Muslim, performing the prescribed five daily prayers and adding two extra prayer times as well. Her spirits, she declares, ask her to call those who come to her for healing to lead Muslim lives, to perform the prayers and the ritual ablutions so that they can live in a state of purity.

> My *azizlar* told me to put a prayer rug in front of them and I told them to go and pray after they were healed. In this way lots of people have returned to Islam. When they prayed, the illness went. This is a spiritual (*ruhiy*) thing. By reading (the Qur'an), purifying, the illness goes and people begin to perform the *namoz* (prayers). This is one way of entering Islam and strengthening it. I tell people to read the *namoz*, to learn *ilm* (religious knowledge), to walk with the *tahorat* (in a state of ritual purity), and to pray. This is a light to the people.

Gulnorahon is not only asserting that her practice is fully in conformity with Islam, but also that she is contributing to God's work by bringing people back to Islam. Through their relations with spirits, healers are addressing the question of what it means to be a Muslim, which became a vital concern for many Muslims with the end of Soviet rule. They are addressing critics who claim that their practice is un-Islamic and developing Muslim selfhood.

What's in a Name?

Since the end of the Soviet Union, the number of people in Pakhtabad who have obtained an education in the sacred texts of Islam has increased. They may have studied in one of the country's madrasas or taken lessons from those who have. Since independence, a number of books written by Islamic scholars have become available that provide information on the correct form of prayer and how to apply Islamic morality in the conduct of daily life, and cassette or compact disc recordings of the sermons of prominent preachers are readily available as well. The influence of this textually based interpretation of Islam has spread, as more people attend Friday prayers at the main mosque, and religiously educated preachers are invited to deliver sermons at household life-cycle celebrations. Prominent targets for criticism by these Muslims are healing or prophesy with the aid of spirits. The existence of *jin* and other spirit beings such as angels is not usually denied by these critics. Rather, they condemn the claim that healing can be obtained from a source other than God, as well as the attempt to discern a person's fate, which is for God alone to know.

The views of a young *imom khatib* in Pakhtabad village are indicative of the sort of criticism levelled against healers. This imam was in his early twenties at the time of my field research in 2004. He had recently graduated from the state-registered madrasa in the city of Andijan, where he had studied for four years after leaving school, and had been appointed to the officially registered Friday mosque in a neighbouring village by the provincial branch of the Muslim Board. The imam makes a distinction between a *bakhshi* or *folbin* and a *tabib*. The first two he condemns as *harom*, forbidden according to the guidance of the *sharīʿa* because they invoke the help of *jin* to heal, whereas healing only comes from God. A *tabib*, on the other hand, treats illness with plants. These are provided by God and act as an intermediary for divine healing, which makes their use permissible. The imam recognises the reality of *jin* as one of the three beings obliged to pray to God, the other two being humans and angels.

He also acknowledges the ability of *jin* to cause illness and attributes to them the condition of facial paralysis mentioned in Chapter 6. He stated that they are attracted to dirt, such as saliva and sexual fluids, but that people who maintained a religiously pure state and behaved in a correct manner had nothing to fear from them. To be cured of illness caused by *jin*, he stated, the sufferer needs to go to a religiously learned man (*domla*) who can recite verses from the Qur'an and knows the language of the *jin* so that he can tell them to leave the sufferer alone. The ambiguity of spirits is apparent here. On the one hand, the imam denies the claim that healing can come from any source except God, but on the other hand, he also acknowledges the power of *jin* to cause illness. He therefore condemns healers for working with *jin*, but at the same time, he recognises their effectiveness in relieving disorders caused by them. What seems to determine whether a practice is religiously permissible or not for the imam is whether the healer cooperates with the *jin* (which is inadmissible), orders them to depart by reciting verses from the Qur'an, or avoids them altogether by using plants.

However, as is evident from the account given above of Gulnorahon's healing practice, the distinction the imam makes between different healing practices is not so clear cut. Gulnorahon and other healers who work with spirits typically incorporate the recitation of Qur'anic verses as well as herbal remedies in their treatments. I came across only one individual in Pakhtabad who described himself as a *tabib* and was generally referred to as such by others in the village. He was an elderly man in his eighties. In his healing practice, he combines a number of the techniques that are clearly separated by the imam, and his case illustrates how porous boundaries are, making it problematic to talk about healing traditions as distinct and bounded. The *tabib* identified himself as descended from a long line of healers, some of who worked with spirits in God's way and others who treated sufferers using herbs (*giyoh*). He told me that healing was in his blood lineage (*zot*). He only uses medicines produced from herbs and animal products, although his grandfather had been helped by two spirits whom the *tabib* described as five-year-old boys. These spirits are connected with a mulberry tree in his garden, which he claimed is 150 years old. The *tabib* referred to his grandfather as a *qori*, a person who recited the Qur'an, but he also recollected how he employed 'black magic' (he used the Russian term *chernaya magiya*) to 'bind' people and cause affliction. He stated that the two child spirits who had helped his grandfather were still present in the mulberry tree and gave him knowledge. He cannot control them, however, because he has not undertaken the forty-day period of isolation and fasting (*chilla*), as his grandfather had done, although he was contemplating putting his own grandson through this so that he could take on the spirits and follow him in his healing practice. The *tabib* distinguished between different methods of knowledge (*ilm*), including technical knowledge used in the state hospitals, knowledge of plants and herbs, and Islamic knowledge his grandfather had used. He attends communal prayers and performs the early-morning and evening prayers daily, but, unlike Gulnorahon and many other healers I encountered, he claimed that his own healing had nothing to do with Islam.

For this elderly *tabib*, different types of knowledge (including the ability to read the Qur'an) could be used to heal, inflict suffering, or see into the future and are completely separate from his own practice as a devout Muslim. By contrast, the young imam newly graduated from the madrasa judges healing practices through the prism of what he considers to be genuine Islam, as, in fact, do Gulnorahon and many other healers, although the imam would condemn their practice as un-Islamic. This seems to be a generational difference. The *tabib* began his healing practice in the 1970s, when questions about the correct conduct for Muslims and the influence of textually based interpretations of Islam were not as prevalent as they have become since the end of Soviet rule. He does not construct himself as a good Muslim through his healing practice and his relation to spirits, as other healers do, and he sees them as distinct spheres. However, many in Pakhtabad, like the imam, interpret healing with spirits though the lens of what they perceive to be proper Islamic practice. They ignore the assertions of healers that their spirits are not *jin* but *azizlar* or *otakhonlar* sent from God.

Another person critical of healers who work with spirits is Qori-aka, the forty-four-year-old man mentioned in Chapter 6 who is from a family known in Pakhtabad for religious learning and whose great grandfather had been the imam in the Friday mosque in the village. Qori-aka believes that reading the Qur'an can bring healing to those who genuinely believe and follow its precepts, and he condemns those who work with *jin* as contrary to Islam. However, like the imam, his attitude to spirits is ambivalent. He stated that the *sharīʿa* cautions against attempts to subordinate *jin* and that healing could not be achieved in this way. At the same time, he acknowledges that in the past great men of religious learning had gained knowledge through spirits. Qori-aka was sceptical about the claims of healers that their spirits were *azizlar* or *otakhonlar* sent from God, because he did not believe that these healers had any real Islamic learning in contrast to the great figures of the past. He accused them of merely fooling people in order to make money, a charge commonly levelled against healers.

The young imam and Qori-aka are among those in Pakhtabad with the closest engagement with the sacred texts of Islam. If their attitudes to healing with spirits are ambiguous, those of other villagers are even more so. Some in the village recognise healers who work with *otakhonlar* as in conformity with Islam and condemn those who deal with *jin*, whereas others consider *otakhonlar* to be merely the spirits of the departed who have no power to intervene in the affairs of the living and accuse healers who invoke them of trying to fool people in order to make money. What remains consistent are the ideas that working with *jin* is not something a good Muslim should do and that those who work with *jin* are called *bakhshi* or *folbin*.

The ambiguity associated with the nature and power of spirits makes the identification of which spirits are illegitimate *jin* and which are *otakhonlar* sent from God, who is a *bakhshi* who works with *jin* and who is a *qori* who merely acts as a medium for channelling the power of God, far from straightforward. *Bakhshi*, *folbin*, *qori*, *jin*, or *otakhon* are therefore not categories of healer or spirit that can be applied in an objective manner with reference to the observable characteristics of a particular healing practice or the nature of a particular spirit. They are morally loaded labels that define the practice of a particular individual as legitimate or illegitimate, in conformity or in contravention of genuine Islam. In this respect, they work in a similar manner as the labels 'traditional Islam' and 'Wahhabism' that the government uses to characterise religious practice as good or bad.

The ambiguity of naming is particularly evident in the practice of healers themselves. The terms people generally used to refer to healers like Gulnorahon are *bakhshi* or *folbin*. However, healers themselves denied being *bakhshi*, stating that *bakhshi* and *folbin* worked with *jin*, 'bound' people, cast spells to block people's success, and worked for the sake of money. In contrast, most of the healers I encountered emphasised that they did not work with *jin*, which were evil, but with *otakhonlar* and *azizlar* sent from God. They stressed that they never demanded money from their clients, but accepted whatever it was in their hearts to offer. While they professed the purity of their own spirits and practice, they would often characterise other healers as morally suspect.

Moral Reasoning Objectified

Gulnorahon has developed an understanding of herself as a Muslim in large part through her encounter with spirits. Her understanding of healing cosmologies is not a static tradition she has simply inherited but is a creative production of experiential reasoning. Healing with spirits is a fruitful context for exploring the creativity in experience because it is objectified and made visible within the cosmologies invoked by healers.

The experience of Zuhrahon, a healer in Pakhtabad who worked with *otakhon*, is particularly revealing because her healing practice began in the late Soviet period and thus spans the period of changing attitudes to Islam in the village. Zuhrahon was forty-one years old at the time of my field research and was married to a teacher in one of the schools in the village. Her grandmother had also been a healer. She first became aware of her spirits at the age of six when she developed a problem with one of her eyes. After a course of unsuccessful treatment in a clinic in the city of Andijan, her parents took her to a woman she described as a *bakhshi* who informed her that the problem was caused by two spirits, one of her father who was still living at that time, and the other of his deceased younger brother. This meant, according to the *bakhshi*, that Zuhrahon would have the ability to heal with these spirits, and in fact her illness would recur if she did not practice as a healer. As she was still a young child, however, the *bakhshi* called on the spirits to leave her alone until she was older.

In adulthood, Zuhrahon suffered from a number of recurring illnesses. In 1983, after the birth of her first child, she lost sight in both her eyes, and again hospital treatment was ineffective. Her original healer had died, so Zuhrahon went to another *bakhshi* who lived near her parents' home. This *bakhshi* placed chicken blood on her and told her that if her problem was not a medical one but was from *eskicha* (the old ways), the blood would disappear and she would be healed. After this treatment worked, the *bakhshi* placed Zuhrahon into a *chilla*, a period of complete isolation for three days during which she read the Qur'an, and a further seven days during which she was able to move around the house but not venture outside. The *bakhshi* then gave her the *duo* (blessing and permission) to start working as a healer. However, Zuhrahon was still only twenty-one years old and had only one child, a relatively junior member of her husband's parents' household, and she felt uncomfortable practicing as a healer in front of her mother-in-law. She actually began healing after the death of her father in 1986. She again fell ill, but this time she was unable to walk. She was taken to a male healer in a neighbouring district whom she insisted was not a *bakhshi* but a religiously learned man (*domla*) who healed by reciting the Qur'an. This person wrote passages from the Qur'an onto paper and instructed her to dip these in water and drink the water for forty-one days. He also put her on a diet of bread, raisins, and nuts for forty days. He told Zuhrahon not to practice as a *bakhshi*, not to 'bind threads' (*ip baylama*), and not to do any other kind of 'bad work'. However, when her problem returned seven days after she ended her diet, he agreed that she could practice as a healer. He helped to open her up to her spirits by reading verses from the Qur'an. Although he offered to enable Zuhrahon herself to see her spirits, she was too frightened to go so far and is content only to hear and talk to them, although she knows that they are men with white beards who carry prayer beads (*tasbeh*), because she has seen them in dreams.

Despite placing herself firmly within an Islamic frame, Zuhrahon avoids the use of the Qur'an, and her experience of using it in the past has reinforced a belief that it is dangerous for her. She considers reciting the Qur'an a male activity and greatly respects the male reciters (*qori*) who can do so without fear. The only women who read the Qur'an, she claimed, are *poshshakhon*, or descendents of the Prophet. A number of *otincha* in Pakhtabad supported this gendered distinction and expressed the view that women were incapable of *qiroat*, the formal chanting recitation, but could only read the text with normal intonation. At women's religious gatherings, there is less recitation of the Qur'an in Arabic than at men's gatherings. Zuhrahon has been told by a *qori* that if she reads the Qur'an for healing, she will become insane. On one occasion, she was persuaded to recite Qur'anic verses in order to invoke good fortune for her brother-in-law. They had just been to the home of another healer who also works with spirits but whom Zuhrahon said both harmed and helped people. She said that this healer's spirits did not get along with her own (*to'g'ri kelmaydi*). When she read from the Qur'an later at home, she was able to see the spirits of this healer and became very frightened.

On consulting a prominent male healer in the village, she was advised not to recite in the future.

The development of Zuhrahon's understanding of Islam is discernable in her encounters with spirits and her healing practice. She was healed in childhood and identified as a healer by a *bakhshi* and obtained the permission and blessing to practice healing from another. At the same time, she has been told not to cast spells upon people in the way of a *bakhshi* by men she considers to be of greater spiritual strength and learning than herself and is aware of the negative association between the *bakhshi* and *jin*. Like the *tabib* described earlier in this section, Zuhrahon began her relationship with spirits and healing in the Soviet period before the textually based interpretations of Islam that condemn working with *jin* became so widespread in Pakhtabad. Her experience of receiving healing and permission to heal herself from a *bakhshi* leave her ambivalent about them, so that she acknowledges that they can do good as well as 'bind threads' to harm people. She insists that she is not herself a *bakhshi* but works with *otakhon* who are 'clean' (*pok*) and only do good works. By asserting that her own spirits do not get on with those of other healers she considers to engage in suspect practice, she is asserting her own religious purity and coming to terms with the warnings of the male healers she has encountered in the past, as well as the increasingly widespread knowledge that working with *jin* is incompatible with leading a good Muslim life. Her understanding of herself as a good Muslim is objectified in her encounters with the spirits of healers she considers suspect. She recalled an occasion when she had visited one such healer for treatment who had promised to send her people to heal Zuhrahon at home. When Zuhrahon went to sleep, she saw two well-dressed old men with white beards come into the room:

They were not my people, they had horns. They stood beside me and turned their *tasbeh* (prayer beads). The old man behind me touched me and I felt a strong electric current. I was scared. They gave me an injection. Then in the morning I had no pain. My brother went to the woman and asked what happened, and she said she had sent her people, but they had horns. They were probably *shaitonlar* (devils). I don't know if they were *devlar* (demons) or *jinlar*.... My people don't like her people. I don't know but they really cured me.

Although healers universally distance themselves from *jin*, they do not all claim that their own spirits are *otakhon*. Fatimahon, a sixty-three-year old healer in a village near Pakhtabad, described herself as both an *otincha* and a *parikhon* (a person who heals with the aid of spirits). She recounted being visited by the spirits of Imom Hassan and Imom Hussain, the grandsons of the Prophet Muhammad, after being chronically ill for eighteen years with an illness 'given by God'. These spirits presented her with a Qur'an and continued to visit her for twenty years, during which time they taught her to read the whole of it. As a result, she became an *otincha*, reciting the Qur'an at women's gatherings and giving Qur'an lessons to girls. At the age of fifty-seven she was struck down with another illness given by God, during which she was taken to the seventh level of heaven by angels and shown all the *aziz avliyolar* (saints). When Fatimahon related this to another *otincha*, she was told that she was to become a healer, and since then she has healed people with the aid of the two grandsons of the Prophet. Fatimahon, too, distanced herself from association with *bakhshi*, saying that they use the blood of sheep and chickens and that she and others like her only work with *ilm*, religious knowledge. She also belittled the *otakhon* of other healers, saying that they would disappear in time because they had no *ilm*:

Well, you have different *millat* (nationality), we have our Uzbek *millat*, and Tajiks have their *millat*, Russians are different. Our *azizlar* have different *millatlar* as well. Because I was given *ilm*, mine come from God. Ours won't disappear. They are the grandsons of the Prophet. Those of the *bakhshilar* and the *otakhonlar*, they are also God's creations, but they are temporary.... Those people they show on the TV, they may be around for 20 or

25 years and then they will disappear, they haven't got strength. The *domlalar* (religious teachers) are ours; their ones don't know the Qur'an, they don't have *ilm* like us.'

These three healers – Gulnorahon, Zuhrahon, and Fatimahon – all construct themselves as good Muslims whose healing power and knowledge come from God. They differentiate themselves from *bakhshi* and deny that their spirits are *jin*. However, each has come to a particular understanding of Islam and their own Muslim self through their engagement with spirits, and this is objectified in the cosmology and imagery they invoke. Gulnorahon has incorporated into her healing elements from 'New Age' philosophy and biomedicine that she learnt at the training institute in Tashkent and also invokes the authority of quasi-state officialdom in the form of her diploma from the institute of healing, which physically resembles those awarded by universities. She has received religious knowledge (*ilm*) both from her formal education and from the spirits themselves and sees herself as a missionary, calling people to return to the true path of Islam after the years of Soviet repression. She criticises other healers as charlatans, interested only in money and with no official training or knowledge, and even claims the right on the strength of her official documentation to inspect and regulate their practice just as a state functionary would. Zuhrahon has more modest aspirations, although she also distinguishes herself as religiously pure. She places herself on a lower level in a spiritual hierarchy, with men of religious learning and descendents of the Prophet at the top. Fatimahon bases her claims to pure Islam on a mastery of religious knowledge. In her case, this has come directly from the grandsons of the Prophet, and she belittles the *otakhon* of healers like Gulnorahon and Zuhrahon as lacking real knowledge. She views their spirits as newcomers with no real knowledge who, unlike her own spirits, will not stand the test of time.

All three healers, as well as critics of their practice, such as the young imam and Qori-aka, evoke common criteria for evaluation. They lay claim to a mastery of Islamic knowledge for themselves and accuse others of ignorance, having pecuniary motives, and acting outside the bounds of true Islam. Gulnorahon, Fatimahon, and many of the other healers I encountered are responding to the criticism of their practice by imams and others who adopt a scripturally based interpretation of Islam. Despite the exhortations of imams during Friday sermons that good Muslims should not resort to people who work with *jin*, these healers establish themselves as good Muslims by claiming that their spirits are not in fact *jin* but spirits sent by God and that their healing is founded on a mastery of *ilm*, Islamic knowledge. Gulnorahon also draws on the legitimating power of 'official' documentation with her diploma from an institution she regards as having been registered with the state authorities, mirroring the authority invested in imams of registered mosques as quasi-state appointees who are charged with monitoring religious activities in their areas. They criticise other healers in the same terms employed by these imams, accusing them of consorting with *jin*, acting outside the bounds of what is permissible in Islam, having no real religious knowledge, and being motivated by a desire for material gain.

The increasing influence of textually based interpretations of Islam in Pakhtabad since independence is being played out within healing cosmologies. The existence of *otakhon* spirits themselves is an indication of this. As Basilov's account of the pre-Soviet situation makes clear, healing with the aid of spirits historically has been attacked as un-Islamic. With the growing influence of textually based interpretations of Islam in recent years, people have become more conscious that working or negotiating with *jin* is considered contrary to proper Islam. That almost all the healers I encountered in Pakhtabad stressed that their spirits, as *azizlar* and *otakhon*, were not the *jin* of *bakhshi*, is an expression of their own and their clients' changing ideas of Muslim selfhood. That this is a fairly recent development is supported by the claims of both healers and others in Pakhtabad and the surrounding area that *otakhon* only appeared in the last ten years or so. Even their critics use the novelty of *otakhon* as a pretext for attacking healers, mocking them as a new way to try to make money. As I noted above, ethnographers in the Soviet period wrote of spirit beings called *pari* who could be both harmful and benevolent to humans, whereas *otakhon* are unambiguously benevolent and sent by God. In fact, the phenomenon is so new that most of the healers who worked with *otakhon* do not have a specific name for themselves as healing practitioners.

Some of the healers working with *otakhon* linked their recent arrival with the revival of Islam in Uzbekistan. Gulnorahon stated that in the Soviet period, there were *bakhshi* and *qori* who read the Koran, but she had not heard of people working with *otakhon*. Her assertion that they were sent to strengthen Islam after the decades of Soviet repression was echoed by another healer in Pakhtabad who worked with *otakhon* and who was also an *otincha*.

As the day of judgement draws near, lots of people will become ill from the effects of bad *jin*. I was told this by a *parikhon*. That time has come now. People who say they cure with the power of God, with *azizlar*, will give healing. Why do I say this? In the past, lots of people used to die, now they don't, only a few in the past 10 or 15 years. This is because in the past people used to defecate or urinate in the fields. This is not allowed in Islam. And in the past they did this and there was lots of illness. All the fruit and vegetables were affected. Now because Islam is strong, and faith is strong, it's helping. . . . *otakhonlar* are increasing and healing people.

Individual healers, their clients, and critics all have individual understandings of Islam and the nature of spirits. This diversity is produced within the creativity of experiential reasoning, but the experience of different actors remains mutually intelligible. I turn to the topic of intelligibility in the next and final chapter.

EIGHT

Experience, Intelligibility, and Tradition

In my research on Islam in Uzbekistan, I have been impressed by a striking contrast. A subdued, even fearful atmosphere surrounds religious practice. The postindependence government has sought to closely regulate religious expression. It has attempted to subordinate Islam within its construction of a Central Asian national and spiritual tradition, the Golden Heritage at the heart of its ideology of National Independence. Interpretations of Islam not endorsed by the government are outlawed as extremist. I have described the atmosphere of existential vulnerability this has generated, wherein the label 'Wahhabi' has come to represent anything not deemed culturally authentic and which might attract the attention of the state security services.

There is, at the same time, a riot of exploration with regards to Islam and also expressed in the variety of Christian and other groups that emerged after independence and are attracting adherents. Muslims in Uzbekistan are creatively developing understandings of moral selfhood and of moral community resulting in a great diversity in interpretations of Islam and what it means to be a Muslim. In addition, registered and unregistered Protestant Christian groups are active and are attracting members from the indigenous, Muslim population, particularly in urban centres such as Samarkand. Groups like the Krishna or Baha'i have become established, and new spiritual movements outside these more formally institutionalised religions are emerging.

Anthropologists working in Muslim societies have frequently dealt with diversity in interpretation and practice through a discussion of the debates and struggles about definitions of 'correct' Islam. Some have given accounts of competing modes of knowledge and authority, often involving the spread of reformist movements and ideas in opposition to locally rooted systems of knowledge and its transmission (Bowen 1993a; Gardner 1999; Horvatich 1994; Lambek 1990). A recent productive move has been to develop the theme of piety, both as personal endeavour and public performance. These studies explore how individual Muslims cultivate appropriate dispositions and moral or pious selves through self-reflexive practices and disciplines that also are publicly enacted (Deeb 2006; Hirschkind 2006; Mahmood 2005). Magnus Marsden challenges the idea that Muslims occupy clear and distinctive positions, whether theologically informed or embedded in 'everyday' cultural practice. He describes processes of moral evaluation and reflection that involve the emotions as well as the intellect, and that complicate simple dichotomies between 'scriptural' and 'everyday' ways of being Muslim (Marsden 2005).

What is distinctive about processes of moral reasoning in Uzbekistan, however, is the absence of public and open debate. Because of the government's suspicion of religious expression outside the parameters of what it has constructed as culturally authentic tradition, public processes of reasoning are restricted and public acts of piety of the sort described in other Muslim societies risk attracting the unwelcome attentions of the state security apparatuses. The lack of open debate has directed me to look to experience itself as a site for moral reasoning. I have described the creativity of experiential reasoning – how diverse understandings of Muslim selfhood arise from the particularity of located experience. At the same time, disparate understandings remain *intelligible*. By directing attention to intelligibility, I am not concerned with defining Islam as an analytical object capable of encompassing diverse local practices. To the extent that Islam is objectified, this takes place within the narrative development of an individual moral self. Rather, I want to explore how Muslims with sometimes radically different understandings of Islam and what it means to be a Muslim can nevertheless recognise themselves and others as belonging to a common community of Muslims. Attention to the intelligibility of experience also extends the discussion beyond specifically Muslim self-understandings to process of conversion to Christian and other groups, as well as to the practical operation of state discourses.

The Intelligibility of Experience

In Chapter 6, I gave an account of Abdumajid-aka, the mathematics lecturer and *mahalla* committee chairman in Samarkand. He has come to his own, very particular conception of God. His understanding incorporates ideas that resonate with Sufi thinking in that he sees God as an absolute consciousness, a perfect instance of a more imperfect consciousness present within all living beings. He sees Islam as but one path to enlightenment that can also be attained through other religions and philosophies, such as Christianity or the Baha'i faith. He nevertheless locates himself firmly as a Muslim, a self-representation that is accepted by others. He prays regularly at a major mosque in the city near his home and is on good terms with the chief imam of Samarkand city, who is a member of his *mahalla* committee. As chairman, he plays an active and leading role in many of the Muslim ritual events in his *mahalla* and attends those in neighbouring *mahalla*.

The diversity of the understandings of Muslim selfhood that healers develop through their relationship with spirits is objectified in their spirit cosmologies. These cosmologies are sites where competing ideas about what it means to be a Muslim are debated. Healers almost invariably claim to be working in God's path, declaring their own spirits to be *otakhon* sent from God, whereas those of others may be *jin* or devils. Despite varying interpretations, the practice of healing through contact with divine agency, mediated by spirits or the Qur'an, is a form of experience intelligible to healers and their clients. In Chapter 6, I described how Ilkhom-aka and Rifat-aka in Pakhtabad developed their own differing understandings of Muslim selfhood through their encounters with spirits and experiences of illness. Both also regularly attend Friday prayers at the main mosque in the village and represent their households at communal ritual occasions. Although Ilkhom-aka has recourse to healing from those who work with spirits, which the imam of his mosque condemns as prohibited by the *sharīʿa*, this does not prevent him from being an active member of the community of men who regularly attend Friday prayers. This is fairly typical of Muslims in the village of Pakhtabad. Imams and others with scriptural knowledge of Islam routinely play a prominent role at ritual gatherings alongside others who understand these rituals in ways the imams would condemn as contrary to true Islam.

Multiplicity of intention and interpretation has been commented upon by a number of anthropologists working in Muslim societies, particularly in the context of ritual. Bowen has argued that an ambiguity of exegesis, an 'economy of professed ignorance' (Bowen 1993a, 318), allows Muslims with diverse and conflicting understandings of Islam to participate as co-members of a community. In the Gayo Muslim society he studied in Indonesia, he describes how less controversial rituals, such as daily prayer, take place in public space, while more contested rituals, such as those concerned with establishing communication and relations of transaction with spirits of the deceased, are pushed into discrete, private space where the ulama can pretend that they do not exist. Participants at a ritual event can have differing intentions and understandings of what is taking place. The host of a ritual feast may see it as part of a transactional relationship with ancestral and other spirits and privately dedicate it as such, perhaps placing ritual foods on the graves of ancestors, whereas 'modernist' ulama who recite verses from the Qur'an at the event can ignore this aspect and see the event purely in terms of offering prayers to God (Bowen 1993a, 229–50; Bowen 1997).

Andrew Beatty has described the multivocality of the *slametan*, a ritual meal held by Muslims also in Indonesia. Rather than the absence of stated intention observed by Bowen, in this ritual, the intent of the host is publicly stated at the beginning of the meal in response to which participants respond with a collective *Amin*, asserting harmony and social unity. The symbolism of this occasion, which is conveyed both in the opening address and in the composition of the foods served, is interpreted in diverse ways by those present. Pious Muslims interpret the symbolism in terms of scriptural Islam, whereas mystics read into the symbolism a deeper message that the human body and self is a microcosm of the universe and source of knowledge. A common ritual language accommodates a diversity of interpretation (Beatty 1996).

The productive ambiguity, the absence of explicit exegesis, and the multivocality of symbols that Bowen and Beatty have described no doubt enable Muslims in Uzbekistan with diverse, indeed individually particular, understandings of Islam to participate jointly in ritual occasions. Disputes about theological interpretation and correct ritual conduct do, of course, take place, as I have described in previous chapters. Individuals arrive at their own understandings of Islam but are aware of the debates taking place around them about what constitutes 'true' Islam and that their own views are not completely shared by others. The concept of the intelligibility of experience allows us to understand this in more positive terms than is suggested by an intentional ignorance and passive tolerance of difference. Intelligibility enables productive and creative interaction without insisting on a common interpretation and also extends beyond a specifically Muslim frame.

Beyond a Muslim Understanding

In Chapter 5, I described the charismatic healer and founder of a spiritual movement to whom I referred as the Teacher. His dreams and visions of angels, spirits, and figures in Islamic history (including, in his case, Jesus) are shaped within models for experience that are shared by others such as Ilkhom-aka and Abdumajid-aka. Whereas these latter two have apprehended their experience within a moral narrative of Muslim selfhood, the Teacher has developed an alternative narrative and has founded his own spiritual movement, which he thinks of as transcending religion. Many of his followers, such as the two *bibikhalfa* also described in Chapter 5, have joined his circle through their own experience of illness. Their illness and healing emerges from models for experience including interaction with spirits, undergoing the *chilla*, and becoming healers themselves, upon which others such as Ilkhom-aka also draw. Although the two *bibikhalfa* have developed moral selves that are not altogether Muslim, this does not prevent them from taking prominent roles within rituals other participants perceive as being Muslim. The shared model for illness and healing renders experience and practice mutually intelligible, even if it is apprehended within individually particular moral narratives.

A number of recent converts to Protestant Christian groups recounted similar dream or illness experiences, where they eventually found healing through membership in a Christian church. In Samarkand, I attended the meetings of a small, unregistered group of evangelical Protestant Christians. The group was founded in 2001, describes itself simply as Protestant of no specific denomination, and is made up of members from a variety of national groups including Koreans, Uzbeks, and Tajiks.[1] Because it is not registered with the state authorities, it is vulnerable to the intervention of law enforcement bodies. When I first attended the worship and bible study meetings of the group, they were held regularly in a private house. However, after the series of bombings and shootings targeting the security forces in Spring 2004, which the government blamed on Islamic extremism, and the subsequent crackdown on the activities of unregistered religious groups, attendance greatly declined and the venue began to shift from place to place, moving to other private homes and on some occasions to an unoccupied, partly constructed office building. The main pastor is Russian and preaches in Russian, but his words were translated into Tajik and Uzbek by established members of the group.

The account of a dream within the conversion narrative of an Uzbek member of the group is reminiscent of the dream in Abdumajid-aka's own narrative of return to Islam described in Chapter 6. For this young man, the dream encounter with Jesus was a pivotal moment. He described how, at the age of thirteen, he had become interested in Islam. He began to perform the daily prayers (*namoz*) regularly, visited imams to ask about Islam, and started learning Arabic. He planned to go on the hajj pilgrimage to Mecca and encouraged his immediate family to adopt Islamic practices, his mother to start wearing the *hijob* (Muslim head covering) and his father to perform the *namoz*. However, when he was sixteen years old, his aunt, who had become a Christian, took him to her church and gave him a booklet about Christianity, in which he read that the only path to heaven was through Jesus. He described what he called a 'war in his heart', and one night, before going to sleep, he prayed to God to give him guidance. That night, he had a dream in which he was with Jesus, who was dressed in white, with a crowd of people gathered around. In his dream, the young man was telling the people that this was Jesus and asking why they did not believe. It was as a result of this dream, he claimed, that he decided to become a Christian.

Ahmadjon is another member of this group. He is of Arab nationality[2] and became a Christian three years before the period of my research. As an Arab, he described how he had considered himself a 'real' (Rus. *konkretniy*) Muslim because he had the blood of the Prophet in his veins. He characterised his past life as a sinful one of heavy drinking and fighting. The turning point came when his mother became ill, which he now describes as a 'moral illness' (Rus. *moral'no bolela*) brought on by the sinful behaviour of her sons. Ahmadjon recounted the family's search for treatment. His father, a senior police officer, had used his contacts to take her to a doctor in the capital, Tashkent, who told them that his mother would either die within months or be paralysed. Seeking a cure, they asked mullahs to pray over her, visited the shrines of *avliyo*, and resorted to healers who worked with spirits, none of which had any effect. Finally they attended a Christian prayer group, and after this his mother recovered.

The model for illness and its treatment is one shared with Ilkhom-aka and other Muslims, and in Ahmadjon's case it facilitated a conversion to Protestant Christianity, but membership and regular attendance in the group has transformed Ahmadjon's conception of moral personhood to one that is not shared by Muslims I met in Uzbekistan. He has come to privilege an interior stance of intentional belief that is materialised in his outward behaviour and successful social interactions. The authenticity of belief is contrasted with an outward, unreflexive conformity to custom, and he characterises most Muslims in Uzbekistan, including converts themselves before they became 'believers', as 'cultural' Muslims with no real knowledge of the sacred texts and without a genuine spiritual commitment to Islam who routinely transgress the prescriptions of the *sharīʿa* and who take part in ritual practice simply because this is what is expected of them as a member of their family and local community.

Ahmadjon himself was inspired to continue attending the meetings of the Protestant group by hearing about the life of Jesus. He described the dilemma he felt at being from a Muslim national group yet believing in Jesus Christ, and how it would be impossible to continue living in the Arabkhona *mahalla*, where the residents are predominantly of Arab nationality. Neighbours in his *mahalla* accused him of betraying his religion and even of becoming a Wahhabi. He described how he fell out with many of his relatives and neighbours and was not invited to their ritual events and household celebrations. His response to this criticism was that he could not have sold his religion; because he had not had any belief in the first place, he could not sell what he did not have. In response to the claim that as an Arab or a Tajik a person can only be a Muslim, he replies that there is no nationality before God. He declares that although

Tajiks or Arabs might claim to be Muslims and see circumcision as proof, this is a lie, as most do not pray or fulfil the requirements of Islam.

He sees himself as having undergone a personal transformation since becoming a believer in Jesus Christ. He now no longer leads a sinful life and his mother is no longer ill. His entire extended household of sixteen members, including his brothers and their wives, have all become believers in Jesus, and relations within the household have improved. In fact, he claimed that much of the initial opposition of the *mahalla* has ameliorated, as his relatives and neighbours see how his behaviour has changed for the better. He claimed that he is once more invited to attend ritual occasions such as weddings and funerals. Initially he had thought about avoiding such events, particularly if there was alcoholic drink served. He felt that there was no room for what he called custom in his life, only for God and Jesus, but he has decided to attend these events so as not to cause offence. He claims that there are now hundreds of Christian converts in the Arabkhona *mahalla*.

In fact, the rosy picture of acceptance Ahmadjon painted during our initial conversations was qualified in the course of my regular attendance at the meetings of this group. Two weeks after my first visit, I attended a morning prayer meeting at Ahmadjon's home in Arabkhona. Most of his extended family was present except for his father, who was at the funeral of a neighbour. I was later told that at this funeral, Ahmadjon's relatives had tried to shame his father for allowing his family to convert to Christianity, saying that he could not control them and accusing him of betraying his religion. A local mullah had threatened to report him to the internal security services so that he would be arrested for encouraging people to convert. Proselytising is illegal in Uzbekistan, although the constitution guarantees freedom of religious belief. Other Arabkhona residents in this Christian group recounted how their neighbours had accused them of being Wahhabis. They described how they had been visited by the security services, who warned them against holding religious gatherings in private homes, and how the security services had visited a school in the *mahalla* and taken the names of all the children who had converted to Christianity. All religious groups have to be registered, but what is an unregistered, and therefore illegal, group and what is a legitimate gathering of neighbours and relatives for a ritual event in a private home is ambiguous. In effect, the law enforcement bodies use the government's category of authentic national heritage to make these judgements, but do so in a highly arbitrary way. The construction of tradition as national heritage, in the form of the label 'Wahhabi', can become a tool in local disputes to characterise parties as inauthentic or alien and therefore suspect.

Many of the themes of Ahmadjon's conversion narrative are echoed in others. Recent Christian believers commonly describe themselves as having considered themselves Muslims in the past, perhaps praying occasionally and attending the Mosque at the major feast days, but having no real belief. The ritual performance of most Muslims is dismissed as mere tradition, as these people also drink alcohol, eat pork, and fail to perform the five daily prayers. The Qur'an is described as confusing, difficult to understand, and containing many contradictions, whereas the Bible offers a clearer and more direct channel to God. Some echo the discourse of imams in asserting that many of the local practices of Muslims are not Islamic at all but are vestiges of pre-Islamic traditions, human creations rather than divine Truth, and they attribute the laxity of Muslims in Uzbekistan in part to the enforced atheism of the Soviet Union. Many are happy to take part in the ritual events held by their Muslim relatives and neighbours, even adopting the appropriate dress such as the *khalat* or *chopon* (a long robe worn over other clothes) that is customary at a Muslim funeral, because these customs have no meaning but are only of human, social significance. Many, like Ahmadjon, described past lives characterised by immorality, illness, and social failure, which transformed after they accepted Jesus into their lives and developed a committed belief.

The conversion narratives of Ahmadjon and other members of Protestant Christian groups construct a Christian believer wherein belief is an interior state, a personal and direct relation to God, in opposition to culture as an outward show or appearance. On one level, this is similar to the stance of the imams I describe in Chapter 4, in that tradition is constructed as a human product in opposition to God's Truth. However, imams characterise local Muslims who contravene the *sharīʿa* as ignorant, but Muslims all the same. The notion of interior belief (*e'tiqod*) is important, but all Muslims I encountered who referred to this considered it something unknowable to others, a matter between a Muslim and God. Debates about authentic Islam were framed in terms of correct knowledge, meaning that Muslims who contravened the *sharīʿa* needed to be educated. By contrast, Christian conversion narratives deny that most Muslims are in fact 'real' Muslims at all. The emphasis is upon sincere interior belief, which is embodied in an individual's physical health and morally upright behaviour, and evidenced externally in positive social relations and perhaps material success.

Ahmadjon's experience of illness and healing is made possible through shared models for experience. It is thereby intelligible to others, including those who place themselves within a narrative of Muslim selfhood, although Ahmadjon has developed a distinctively Christian narrative, and his sustained participation in a Protestant group has developed understandings of personhood and belief that differ from those of many Muslims I encountered. The intelligibility of experience is something that can be consciously manipulated to bridge the gap between Christian and Muslim frames, as shown in the following account of an Adventist pastor in Samarkand.

The pastor is of Iranian nationality, has graduated from an Adventist seminary in Russia, and was recognised as a pastor just as I first began to attend his church. He considers himself to be a 'Muslim Adventist', a Muslim who believes in Jesus, and develops this understanding through a critical study of the Qur'an and the Bible, through embodied practice in accordance with the prescriptions of both, and through a concept of tradition as a human creation separate from God and belief. He told me of his conversations with Muslims and imams in which he demonstrated to them that he habitually fulfils all of the requirements of Islam except the hajj pilgrimage, including praying, giving alms, not eating pork, not drinking or smoking, and not chasing after women. He would discuss with them how Jesus is recognised as more than an ordinary prophet in the Qur'an, in which he is referred to as the Word of God or the Messiah. Any Muslim, he declares, who seriously studies the Qur'an can become open to receiving Jesus into his heart, and he has argued with imams that being a follower of Jesus is fully Qur'anic. Problems only arise, in his view, from 'tradition', from people who consider themselves Muslim but who are not genuinely so because they have no real knowledge of the Qur'an and do not live in accordance to its prescriptions.

He also considers himself to be Muslim because he grew up as a Muslim and from childhood was socialised within Muslim celebrations and rituals. He is planning to circumcise his sons and hold the customary feast for relatives and neighbours, although without the alcohol and other traditions, which he argues, do not come from the Qur'an but are human inventions. He views this as an opportunity to show that he and his sons are Muslim – that they have not changed either their religion or nationality, but are just Muslims who believe in Jesus. He makes his own distinctions between tradition and belief and between being Muslim and following Jesus. Referring to the origins of the word 'Islam', he points out that a Muslim is a person who 'submits', giving his heart to God, as he has done. Using the imagery of modern technology, he once told me that his life was recorded on his hard disk. His hard disk was Muslim and couldn't be cleared, but his central processor belonged to Jesus.

The Idea of a Tradition

Talal Asad's paper 'The idea of an anthropology of Islam' was an important contribution to the development of the subfield of the anthropology of Islam. Asad suggested that Islam, as an object of study, should be approached as a 'discursive tradition that connects variously with the formation of moral selves, the manipulation of populations . . . , and the production of appropriate knowledges' (Asad 1986, 7). For Asad, a tradition consists of discourses.

> These discourses relate conceptually to *a past* (when the practice was instituted, and from which the knowledge of its point and proper performance has been transmitted) and *a future* (how the point of that practice can best be secured in the short or long term, or why it should be modified or abandoned), through *a present* (how it is linked to other practices, institutions, and social conditions). (Asad 1986, 14)

Rather than taking the category of Islam, or indeed religion in general, as a given, Asad argues that we need to understand it as an historically rooted discursive construction that is produced within relations of power (Asad 1993). Asad sees Islam as a discursive tradition seeking to define correct practice and interpretation, wherein 'orthodoxy' is not merely a body of opinion about the correct interpretation of texts but is a relationship of power. 'Wherever Muslims have the power to regulate, uphold, require, or adjust *correct* practices, and to condemn, exclude, undermine, or replace *incorrect* ones, there is the domain of orthodoxy' (Asad 1986, 15).

Discourse is a useful perspective for examining the efforts of the government in Uzbekistan to define and regulate 'legitimate' religious practice. But where the scope for public debate and expression is limited and where experience itself becomes a privileged site for moral reasoning, a discourse approach has limited purchase. I have suggested that the intelligibility of experience provides possibilities for meaningful and productive interaction and communication among individuals with diverse understandings of moral selfhood. However, Islam cannot be constructed as the object of study from an experience perspective, and I do not intend to do so. Not only would it be difficult to place the diverse understandings of Muslim selfhood I have been describing within a single frame of histories, texts, and practices that would have universal resonance for Muslims, but the intelligibility of experience also extends beyond specifically Muslim self-understandings.

I return to the idea of a tradition to develop further the concept of intelligibility. Asad has attributed his use of tradition to the philosopher Alasdair MacIntyre. In *After Virtue*, MacIntyre addresses the problem of the incommensurability of rival moral positions in modern Western society (MacIntyre 2007). He argues that the premises on which rival standpoints are founded are different, so that there can be no common evaluative framework within which rational agreement can be achieved between differing standpoints. In the absence of rational criteria, an individual's choice of a moral position is personal and emotive. What is important for our purposes is the concept of a tradition in MacIntyre's work, key to which is the idea of intelligibility. An individual life is intelligible to subjects and others within a coherent narrative that begins at birth and ends at (or continues beyond) death. In turn, the behaviour and intentions of individuals are intelligible only within what MacIntyre calls a 'setting', historically situated institutions, practices, and social milieu. Carrithers develops a similar idea when he describes sociality as the innate propensity of human beings to interpret the speech and actions of others as 'unfolding stories', in terms of what the subject imagines to be the plans and intentions of others immersed within their own plots (Carrithers 1992, 55–91). Plots, and therefore actions and intentions, can only be mutually intelligible when they are located within shared, institutions, histories, and practices, and they must share conceptions of possible futures and ends. As MacIntyre states, an individual's story is embedded in the historically developing story of the communities from which the individual derives his or her identity.

God for his or her actions and cannot make up for the sins of others. The same is true for other models for experience, such as obtaining healing through the recitation of the Qur'an. This might be subjectively understood as imploring God to grant healing, as calling upon the aid of the angels that stand behind each letter in the Qur'an, or, as Abdumajid-aka believes, as activating the inner energies that all living beings possess. Individuals hold diverse understandings of their experiences within their own moral narratives, which produce different understandings of moral selfhood. At the same time, the practice of different individuals remains mutually intelligible, arising as it does from a shared setting.

MacIntyre and Asad see a tradition as the limit of intelligibility. Meaningful dialogue and argument are possible within a tradition but difficult or impossible across traditions because different traditions are founded on different premises and evaluative frames. For Asad, Islam is itself such a tradition, but I have argued that in Uzbekistan, where experience is the privileged site for moral reasoning, intelligibility extends beyond specifically Muslim understandings. The setting in which individuals are immersed includes models for experience, histories, social institutions, the sociality of participation within a household and community, arranging for the marriage and settlement of children, and contributing to communal goals. The setting provides possibilities for experience that is apprehended creatively within diverse narratives of moral selfhood. These may be Muslim but do not have to be, and at the level of experience they remain mutually intelligible.

The Intelligibility of State Discourse

Finally, I would like to return to state discourse and how it might be rethought with the idea of intelligibility. At the centre of this discourse is the Idea of National Independence, an attempt to naturalise the independent state and the rule of the Karimov government though an ideal of cultural authenticity. The nation is presented as returning to a golden, spiritual heritage that embodies the natural character, values, and worldview of the Central Asian population, suppressed during the years of Soviet rule. The culturally authentic Central Asian family and community are invoked as a model for the state, and the often-quoted slogan 'from a strong state to a strong society' expresses the claim that a strong executive presidency is necessary to protect democratic ideals and individual freedoms.

Frequent reference is made in the speeches of the president to self-stereotypes that attribute such qualities as hospitality and industry to Uzbeks. For example, the multiethnic makeup of the population and the presence of ethnically and religiously defined minority groups is addressed through appeal to the Uzbek quality of hospitality, wherein the tradition of welcoming strangers will guarantee freedom and equality for all:

> Law and economics provide equal opportunities for all, while humanness, kindness, charity and mutual tolerance, respect and compassion are peculiar to Uzbeks – 'Uzbekness' known to everyone throughout centuries forms the atmosphere of benevolence and confidence. (Karimov 1995, 132)

Religious tolerance will be safeguarded by the inherently 'secular' nature of Central Asian Islam.

Economic and foreign policy are portrayed as being an inescapable fact of nature. Uzbekistan's climate, it is argued, predisposes the country for the production of cotton and also necessitates the need for a centrally administered irrigation system to make the land productive. Its geographical position at the crossroads of Eurasia and the historical legacy of the Great Silk Road dictate paths of foreign policy and trade networks (Karimov 1993, 17–38). Control of the republic from Moscow during the Soviet period is blamed for causing underdevelopment and dependency through ignoring these specific local circumstances. In contrast, the 'free market' towards which the reform process is ostensibly oriented functions according to natural laws, but a 'civilised' market is in tune with a nation's spiritual values and entails a large measure of central government control to protect vulnerable members of society.[3] Uzbekistan is following its own unique path and cannot copy the example of other nations.

I have argued that state discourses are hegemonic not because they succeed in shaping the subjectivities of citizens but insofar as they determine how individuals must present themselves in situations where the coercive apparatuses of the state can be invoked, and to the extent to which this influences how they are able to come to their own understandings of moral self and community. The concept of cultural authenticity is an effective tool of governance. In relation to religious practice, it is expressed in the opposition between Central Asian 'tradition' and Wahhabism, an alien religious extremism. The criterion of cultural authenticity facilitates the monitoring and control of the population. It is used by officials within the structure of executive government and the coercive apparatuses of the state to make judgements on the legitimacy of an individual's conduct, and can be invoked within local disputes.

State discourses draw upon symbols, institutions, and models for experiences that are shared by citizens and attempt to fix how they are interpreted. Individuals in Uzbekistan are nevertheless creatively reworking these within their own narrative understandings. Rather than seeing this in terms of an opposition between a top-down view of the state with a 'grassroots' view from the local level, Michael Herzfeld prefers to examine state ideologies and rhetorics of everyday life as a shared 'cultural engagement'. This tends to be concealed when the analysis is in oppositional terms of 'elites' and 'ordinary people' (Herzfeld 1997). He uses the term 'cultural intimacy' to describe those aspects of cultural identity, for example, British muddling through, or Greek mercantile craftiness, which provide insiders with assurance of common sociality. Governments might try to co-opt this symbolism as a means of legitimation or to command loyalty among citizens, who for their part utilise and recast these idioms in pursuit of their own goals, which are often at odds with state authority. It is because these concepts originate at the local level that they are of use to state authorities, but they are open to alternative interpretations by local actors as well.

A site for this tension in Uzbekistan is the practice of *ziyorat*, visiting the shrines of Muslim saints. Louw (2007) has described how the government has adopted key historical figures and their shrines within its nation-building narrative. These national forefathers are portrayed in state discourse as embodying an idealised and historically specific local 'Muslimness', which is presented as distinct from the alien ideologies of both Soviet communism and political Islamism. By publicly and conspicuously visiting the shines of the most important of these figures during national celebrations of their lives, senior government officials have adopted the local model for *ziyorat* as a performance of state building and demonstration of loyalty to the government. Louw shows how shrines are also creatively reworked within individual lives in ways that can contest official narratives. She argues that shrines and the historical lives of their occupants are focal points for reflection where individuals who find themselves materially and socially marginalised are able to establish an alternative moral sphere of existence within which they feel valued.

The government has similarly attempted to instrumentalise the institution of the *mahalla*, but this has not prevented Abdumajid-aka from developing a vision of the *mahalla* as a model for a moral community and an indigenous basis for democratic governance. His view of the *mahalla* and his role as committee chairman have put him in conflict with some local government officials in the city of Samarkand, who see the *mahalla* as an extension of their administrative control over the population. Abdumajid-aka's vision is also different from that of many members of the association of *mahalla* leaders, which he founded. Many of its members do not share his ideal of local democratic governance, but map the pattern of hierarchical executive government at the state level onto the *mahalla*, characterising themselves as little *hokim* (executive governors) whose job it is to maintain moral order and protect the interests of residents against outside forces. Despite these radically different visions and the occasional conflicts that arise, Abdumajid-aka does not see himself in opposition to the state but in cooperation with it in promoting the best interests of all citizens. All these individuals are able to interact and cooperate while retaining distinct understandings of this institution because their understandings are mutually intelligible within the context of a local setting, in MacIntyre's sense, in which the *mahalla* is a model for practice and community interaction.

The intelligibility produced within a shared setting goes beyond a bare and instrumental manipulation of cultural references and symbols. It makes possible meaningful and productive engagement, even among individuals who hold diverging motivations and understandings. It enables individuals like Abdumajid-aka to pursue their own ideals even in an overbearing and repressive political environment and allows others, less positively, to recruit the coercive apparatuses of the state on their side in local disputes. It allows imams to maintain their own understanding of Islam whilst also supporting government policies. The 'legitimacy' of government discourse need not be seen in terms of 'belief', of domination and resistance, or of acceptance and dissimulation. State discourses seek to fix the interpretation of Islam and local institutions such as the *mahalla* in particular ways, but citizens see the pronouncements of the Karimov government for what they are, self-serving attempts to legitimate authoritarian rule. They creatively develop their own understanding through experience. Nevertheless, government discourses engage in a meaningful dialogue with citizens. They are located within their everyday lifeworlds, in the sociality of household and community, in practices of shrine visitation and direct interaction with spirit agents and the Divine, and they speak to the experience through which individuals in Uzbekistan develop moral selves. State discourses are not necessarily 'believed' but they are understood.

Notes

Introduction

1 See, for example, the reports by the International Crisis Group (2005) and Human Rights Watch (2005).

2 These protests were reported by, among others, the BBC. See 'Uzbekistan's most orderly protest', BBC News 12 May 2005, http://news.bbc.co.uk/go/pr/fr/-/1/hi/world/asia-pacific/4540041.stm.

3 I base my analysis on a Russian translation of the text posted on the Web site of 'Tsentrasiya', http://www.centrasia.ru/newsA.php4?st=1093410660.

4 See, for example, Human Rights Watch (2004).

5 See, for example, Bauman (1993, 4–6). Also see Williams's hypothetical 'hyper-traditional' society, which is 'maximally homogenous and minimally given to general reflection' (Williams 1985, 142).

6 For a good account of the development of Islamic legal, see Wael Hallaq's *The Origins and Evolution of Islamic Law* (2005).

7 The philosopher Ṣadr al-Din al-Shīrāzī (d. 1640) identified five levels of humanity in relation to consciousness of the reality of Being. The most enlightened are those who have negated their own being to become open to the Truth. They are followed by philosophers who perceive God through rational thought. Third are people of faith, who are followed by those who merely follow the authority of others. The fifth and lowest level is occupied by those who rely on the physical forms and senses (Rizvi 2005, 233–4). For an example of an ethnography of a contemporary Sufi movement, see Werbner (2003).

8 Pakhtabad is one of three villages that make up the territory of a *qishloq fuqaroning yig'ini* (Village Citizen's Committee), known in Russian as *selsovet*, with a total population of about 23,000.

One: Islam and Sociality in Pakhtabad and Samarkand

1 For a discussion of the concepts of society and sociality, see Ingold et al. (1996).
2 See Ilkhamov (1998, 2000) for an account of agricultural reform. See also Trevisani (2007a, 2007b).
3 These are fruits and vegetables grown outside the cotton production plan, which therefore afforded greater opportunities for unofficial profits.
4 See also Kandiyoti (1999) for an account of patterns of household composition in Uzbekistan.
5 Networks of exchange extend to the collective farm so that people are able to gain access to land and other resources through their diffuse relations with brigadiers and others who control allocation (Rasanayagam 2003).
6 See Kandiyoti (1998) and Koroteyeva and Makarova (1998b) for more on women's *gap*.
7 The Uzbek names for these months are *rabiulavval*, *rabiussoni*, *jumodilavval*, and *jumodissoni*.
8 Lobacheva translates this into Russian as *obshina*.
9 Fathi has described the role of female religious authorities in Central Asia, to whom she refers as *otine* or *otunca* (Fathi 1997). See also Kandiyoti and Azimova (2004). According to my own observations, these female religious practitioners were known as *otincha* in Andijan and the village of Pakhtabad and *bibikhalfa* in Samarkand.
10 See also Basilov (1996).
11 For accounts of the government's policy on the *mahalla* since independence, see Kamp (2004), Noori (2006), and Sievers (2002).
12 The Soviet ethnographer Lobacheva notes that one of the terms used for similar social residential institutions in Khorezm was *matchitkum* or *matchitkaum* (Lobacheva 1989, 43). See also Geiss (2001).
13 The sudden interest on the part of the provincial government to restore supplies was likely tied to the spate of shootings and bombings targeting law enforcement officers a few months earlier in spring 2004, as a means of alleviating popular resentment against the government.
14 *Islom odobi va akhloqi* (Tashkent: Movarounnahr, 2001).
15 *Musulmon ayolning o'z eri oldidagi vazifalari.*
16 *Muslim Board of Uzbekistan* (Tashkent: Movarounnahr, 2001).

Two: The New Soviet (Central Asian) Person and the Colonisation of Consciousness

1 In the late Tsarist period, the region known as Turkestan, which was ruled directly by Russia, covered much of present-day Turkmenistan, Uzbekistan, Kazakhstan,

and Kyrgyzstan. The emirates of Bukhara and Khiva were much reduced in size and remained autonomous protectorates surrounded by Russian Turkestan. It was not until 1924 that the borders of the Central Asian republics were drawn in more or less their present form.

2 Class enemies included former landlords, wealthy peasants (Rus. *kulak*), former industrialists, officers in the Tsarist armed forces, and police, as well as religious functionaries.

3 See Ssorin-Chaikov (2003, 172f.) for an account of this policy among indigenous populations of Siberia.

4 *Eshon* are those who claim descent from the Prophet Muhammad or prominent figures in Islamic history and were attributed the power to channel blessing from their illustrious ancestors.

5 Stephen and Ethel Dunn have suggested a 'two-story' model of culture in Central Asia, whereby different values and systems of relations obtained in the public sphere, dominated by a discourse of socialist modernity, while the private, intimate sphere of the family retained a more 'traditional', prerevolutionary worldview (Dunn & Dunn 1967). Lubin (1981) adopts a similar analysis in relation to gender relations in Soviet Central Asia.

6 According to Ro'i, between 1945 and 1970, only eighty-five students graduated from the Mir-i Arab Madrasa, although many attended but dropped out. In the late 1970s, there were only thirty or so places at the Imom al-Bukhoriy Institute in Tashkent (Ro'i 2000, 601–04).

7 In the Soviet Union, an *oblast* was a provincial subdivision of a republic, and a *raion* was a district subdivision of an *oblast*. These were Russian terms. Since independence, they have been renamed using the Uzbek terms *viloyat* and *tuman*, respectively.

8 The *selsovet* was the lowest level of the Soviet government administrative structure, responsible to the *raion* level.

9 For similar accounts, see Privratsky (2001, 83–4), Poliakov (1992, 58), and Abashin (1997, 456).

10 In Pakhtabad, people refer to these female descendents of the Prophet as *poshsha* or *sayid*.

11 When I asked this man why people did not go to the *pir* directly, he replied: 'The *hokim* (governor) has his own deputies, and the *pir* has as well and takes things through them. It's difficult to get a *duo* (blessing) from a *pir*. They only give it to people they like'. His grandmother first caught the *pir's* attention when she was serving guests at a ceremony that the *pir* attended.

12 Babadjanov has given an account of Mahammadjan Hindustani, who established an informal school for the study of Islam in the Khruschev era (Babadjanov &

Kamilov 2001). Stéphane Dudoignon, Habiba Fathi, and Svetlana Peshkova have described the teaching activities of *otincha* (Dudoignon 2004; Fathi 1997; Peshkova 2006).

Three: Good and Bad Islam after the Soviet Union

1 See, for example, the publications of Islam Karimov (1995, 1997). See also the pamphlet outlining the Karimov government's new ideology to replace Marxist Leninism: *Milliy istiqlol g'oyasi* (Idea of National Independence).

2 In Turkey, the *mahalle* is a residential quarter in a town or and village that also constitutes a social unit in certain respects. The equivalent in Uzbekistan is the *mahalla*.

3 For accounts of the Egyptian case, see Gaffney (1991) and Starrett (1998).

4 Aihwa Ong has described how the government in Malaysia constructs a locally authentic Islam in this way (Ong 1999).

5 The booklet titled 'The Idea of National Independence' (*Milliy istiqlol g'oyasi: asosiy tushuncha va tamoyillar*) describes the national 'Golden Heritage' in these terms and portrays alien forms of Islam as a threat to religious and interethnic harmony.

6 For an account of similar processes in contemporary Russia, see Sokolovski (2005).

7 See Megoran (2002, 2005).

8 The Uzbek word *avliyo* is sometimes translated as 'saint' and refers to exemplary Muslim figures such as Baha al-Din Naqshband, who are considered by many local Muslims to have been particularly close to God and thus to have the ability to transfer *baraka*, divine grace, to living supplicants. It is derived from the plural of the Arabic word *walīy*, meaning 'friend', 'benefactor', or 'protector'. The Uzbek plural form is frequently added, making it *avliyolar*.

9 *Milliy istiqlol g'oyasi: asosiy tushuncha va tamoyillar* (Tashkent: Uzbekiston, 2001).

10 See also March (2003).

11 'Our nation is possessor of such traditional levers of stability of the society as family and mahalla (neighbourhood) – the basic support of our mentality. Family and mahalla enable the people to deal efficiently with numerous problems of the current transition period and preserve the continuity of the good old and pragmatic present' (Karimov 1995, 127).

12 The term *hokim* refers to the governors of provinces as well as the heads of city and district administrations.

13 Speech of President Karimov titled 'Will and Faith: A Test of our Faith' (reproduced in Karomatov et al. 2001, 169–82). See also Human Rights Watch (2004).

14 Personal communication from a *mahalla* committee chairman.

15 This is, in fact, a version of an existing scheme proposed by central government that has proven unattractive to most *mahalla* committees, because to participate, they would have been forced to take on responsibility for the considerable debt burdens of the past.

Four: The Practical Hegemony of State Discourse

1 See also Fathi (2006), Kandiyoti and Azimova (2004), and Peshkova (2006).
2 See also Khan (2003).
3 Malashenko estimates that 3,000 mosques were built or restored in Uzbekistan during the perestroika period, up to January 1992 (Malashenko 1994a, 111).
4 During my second period of field research from 2003 to 2004, I learnt that one of the students I had taught at the Foreign Languages Institute in Andijan five years earlier had been imprisoned for eleven years for involvement in religious extremist groups. However, his classmates insisted that he was merely a devout Muslim with no political involvement.
5 For an account of this group, see Khalid (2007, 156–60) and Naumkin (2005).
6 The Soviet Spiritual Directorate was initially renamed the Muslim Board of Mawarannahr in 1992 and became Muslim Board of Uzbekistan in 1996.
7 Resolution of the Cabinet of Ministers on the Rules for State Registration of Religious Organisation in the Republic of Uzbekistan of 20 June 1998 (No. 263).
8 The tasks of the Department for Fatwas is laid out in a booklet titled 'The Muslim Board of Uzbekistan' (Tashkent: Movarounnahr, 2001). I also discussed the sermons with a number of *imom khatib*.
9 See also Hilgers (2006, 87–92).
10 This ban was imposed in early 1998 following the incidents to which I referred earlier in the chapter in which several policemen were killed in the city of Namangan.
11 I was told this by a lecturer at that institute.
12 By visiting at the evening prayers, they ensured that they would encounter only the most devout members of the congregation.

Five: The Moral Sources of Experience

1 See also Henkel (2005).
2 The word *chilla* derives from the Tajik word *chil*, meaning forty.
3 See Kehl Bodrogi (2008) for an account of healing with spirits in Khorezm, Uzbekistan.

4 This emphasis on the movement being a school rather than a religion recalls the recollection of a Sri Chinmoi centre for spiritual education by a novice follower of Sufism in Samarkand. This was established in the city during the perestroika years. It was part of a worldwide network of such centres that were founded by the Indian mystic and philosopher Sri Chinmoi, himself a follower of the teachings of the Sri Aurobindo. It is possible that the Teacher was influenced by the ideas of meditation and self-revelation preached at this centre.

5 On a visit to this institute in February 2004, I was told that the institute had 20 girls and 120 boys.

Six: Moral Reasoning through the Experience of Illness

1 See, for example, verse 72.

2 He adopts the phrase from Obeyesekere (1981).

3 Mattingly provides an excellent discussion of Aristotle's distinction between history and poetry within a general discussion of narrative theory (Mattingly 1998, 28–30).

4 In the early years of the Soviet Union, the Bolshevik leadership introduced the Latin script for many Turkic languages, while Stalin imposed the Cyrillic script as universal in the late 1930s. For an account of Soviet language policy in Central Asia, see Kreindler (1995).

5 These descriptions recall a condition known as Bell's palsy, which often clears up by itself after some time without biomedical treatment.

6 Maria Louw has also reported coming across a version of this story in the city of Bukhara during her research between 1998 and 2000 (Louw 2007, 100).

Seven: Debating Islam through the Spirits

1 This chapter is a revised version of an article first published in the *Journal of the Royal Anthropological Institute* (Rasanayagam 2006a).

2 Galina Lindquist has described such institutes and healers who use bioenergy in Russia (Lindquist 2001b), and Bellér-Hann describes similar institutions in Kazakhstan that issued state-authorised certificates to healers (Bellér-Hann 2001).

Eight: Experience, Intelligibility, and Tradition

1 In Uzbekistan, following Soviet practice, an individual is a'citizen' (*fuqaro*) of the state of Uzbekistan, as well as having a 'nationality' (*millat*), an ethnonational designation. Thus, Uzbekistani citizens can be Uzbek, Tajik, Russian, Koran, etc.

2 'Arab' is a specific national designation in Uzbekistan, but these 'Arabs' claim to have migrated to Central Asia centuries ago, they do not speak Arabic, and their first language is Tajik.

3 'The social market economy corresponds to high ideals of oriental Islamic philosophy, historical experience and the mentality of our nation' (Karimov 1995, 124).

Bibliography

Abashin, S. 1997. Sotsial'nye korni sredneaziatskogo islamizma (na primere odnogo seleniya). In *Identichnost' i konflikt v postsovetskikh gosudarstvakh*. Edited by M. B. Olcott, V. Tishkov, and A. Malashenko. Moscow: Carnegie Endowment for International Peace.

———. 1999. O samosoznanii narodov Srednei Azii (kak Aleksandr Igorevich pospo-ril s djonom). *Vostok* 4, 207–20.

———. 2001. Islam i kul't svyatykh v Srednei Azii. *Etnograficheskoe obozrenie* 3, 128–31.

Abu-Lughod, L. 1993. Islam and the Gendered Discourses of Death. *International Journal of Middle East Studies* 25, 187–205.

———. 2005. *Dramas of Nationhood: The Politics of Television in Egypt*. Chicago: University of Chicago Press.

Adams, L. 1999. Invention, Institutionalization and Renewal in Uzbekistan's National Culture. *European Journal of Cultural Studies* 2, 355–73.

Akiner, S. 1996. Islam, the State and Ethnicity in Central Asia in Historical Perspective. *Religion, State and Society* 24, 91–132.

Arifkhanova, Z. 2000. *Sovremennaya zhizn' traditsionnoi makhalli Tashkenta*. Tashkent: O'zbekiston.

Aristotle. 1987. *Poetics*. Translated by R. Janko. Indianapolis: Hackett Publishing Company.

———. 1998. *Nicomachean Ethics*. Mineola: Dover Publications.

Asad, T. 1986. The Idea of an Anthropology of Islam. *Center for Contemporary Arab Studies, Georgetown University, Occasional Paper Series*.

———. 1993. *Genealogies of Religion: Discipline and Reasons of Power in Christianity and Islam*. Baltimore: The John Hopkins University Press.

———. 2003. *Formations of the Secular: Christianity, Islam, Modernity*. Stanford: Stanford University Press.

Bibliography

Ashwin, S. 2000. Introduction: Gender, State and Society in Soviet and Post-Soviet Russia. In *Gender, State and Society in Soviet and Post-Soviet Russia*. Edited by S. Ashwin. London: Routledge.

Babadjanov, B. 2001. O fetvakh SADUM protiv "neislamskikh obychaev." In *Islam na postsovetskom prostranstve: vzglyad iznutri*. Edited by M. Brill Olcott and A. Malashenko. Moscow: Carnegie Moscow Center.

______. 2004. Debates over Islam in Contemporary Uzbekistan: A View from Within. In *Devout Societies vs. Impious States: Transmitting Islamic Learning in Russia, Central Asia and China, through the Twentieth Century*. Edited by S. A. Dudoignon. Berlin: Klaus Schwarz Verlag.

Babadjanov, B., and M. Kamilov. 2001. Muhammadjan Hindustani (1892–1989) and the Beginning of the "Great Schism" among the Muslims of Uzbekistan. In *Islam in Politics in Russia and Central Asia (Early Eighteenth to Late Twentieth Centuries)*. Edited by S. A. Dudoignon and K. Hisao. London: Kegan Paul.

Bakar, O. 2005. Gülen on Religion and Science: A Theological Perspective. *The Muslim World* 95, 359–72.

Barth, F. 1993. *Balinese Worlds*. Chicago: University of Chicago Press.

Basilov, V. N. 1992. *Shamanstvo u narodov Srednei Azii i Kazakhstana* Moscow: Nauka.

______. 1996. Sunnat-toi v ferganskom kishlake. *Etnograficheskoe obozrenie* 3, 99–113.

Bauman, Z. 1993. *Postmodern Ethics*. Oxford: Blackwell Publishing.

Beatty, A. 1996. Adam and Eve and Vishnu: Syncretism in the Javanese Slametan. *Journal of the Royal Anthropological Institute (N.S.)* 2, 271–88.

Bellér-Hann, I. 2001. Rivalry and Solidarity among Uyghur Healers in Kazakhstan. *Inner Asia* 3, 73–98.

Bennigsen, A. A., and S. E. Wimbush. 1985. *Mystics and Commissars: Sufism in the Soviet Union*. London: Hurst.

Boddy, J. 1988. Spirits and Selves in Northern Sudan: The Cultural Therapeutics of Possession and Trance. *American Ethnologist* 15, 4–27.

Bowen, J. R. 1993a. *Muslims through Discourse*. Princeton: Princeton University Press.

______. 1993b. Return to Sender: A Muslim Discourse of Sorcery in a Relatively Egalitarian Society. In *Understanding Witchcraft and Sorcery in Southeast Asia*. Edited by C. W. Watson and R. Ellen. Honolulu: University of Hawaii Press.

______. 1997. Modern Intentions: Reshaping Subjectivities in an Indonesian Muslim Society. In *Islam in an Era of Nation-States: Politics and Religious Renewal in Muslim Southeast Asia*. Edited by R. Hefner. Honolulu: University of Hawaii Press.

Brenner, S. 1996. Reconstructing Self and Society: Javanese Muslim Women and "The Veil." *American Ethnologist* 23, 673–97.

Carrithers, M. 1992. *Why Humans Have Cultures: Explaining Anthropology and Social Diversity*. Oxford: Oxford University Press.

Casanova, J. 1994. *Public Religions in the Modern World.* Chicago: University of Chicago Press.

Comaroff, J., and J. L. Comaroff. 1999. Occult Economies and the Violence of Abstraction: Notes from the South African Postcoloniality. *American Anthropologist* 26, 279–303.

Comaroff, J. L., and J. Comaroff. 1992. *Ethnography and the Historical Imagination.* Boulder: Westview Press.

Csordas, T. J. 1994. *The Sacred Self: A Cultural Phenomenology of Charismatic Healing.* Berkeley: University of California Press.

Deeb, L. 2006. *An Enchanted Modern: Gender and Public Piety in Shi'i Lebanon.* Princeton: Princeton University Press.

Desjarlais, R. 1992. *Body and Emotion: The Aesthetics of Illness and Healing in the Nepal Himalayas.* Philadelphia: University of Pennsylvania Press.

DeWeese, D. 2002. Islam and the Legacy of Sovietology: A Review Essay on Yaacov Ro'i's Islam in the Soviet Union. *Journal of Islamic Studies* 13, 298–330.

Doumato, E. A. 2000. *Getting God's Ear: Women, Islam and Healing in Saudi Arabia and the Gulf.* New York: Columbia University Press.

Dragadze, T. 1993. The Domestication of Religion under Soviet Communism. In *Socialism: Ideals, Ideologies and Local Practice.* Edited by C. Hann. London: Routledge.

Dudoignon, S. 2004. Local Lore, the Transmission of Learning, and Communal Identity in Late 20th-Century Tajikistan. The Khujand-Nāma of 'Arifjan Yahyāzad Khujandi. In *Devout Societies vs. Impious States: Transmitting Islamic Learning in Russia, Central Asia and China, through the Twentieth Century.* Edited by S. Dudoignon. Berlin: Klaus Schwarz Verlag.

Dunn, S. P., and E. Dunn. 1967. Soviet Regime and Native Culture in Central Asia and Kazakhstan: The Major Peoples. *Current Anthropology* 8, 147–208.

Durkheim, E. 1964. *The Division of Labor in Society.* New York: The Free Press.

———. 1973. The Dualism of Human Nature and its Social Conditions. In *Emile Durkheim: On Morality and Society.* Edited by R. Bellah. Chicago: University of Chicago Press.

———. 2001. *The Elementary Forms of Religious Life.* Translated by C. Cosman. Oxford: Oxford University Press.

Edel, A. 1962. Anthropology and Ethics in Common Focus. *Journal of the Royal Anthropological Institute* 92, 55–72.

Edel, M., and A. Edel. 2000. *Anthropology and Ethics: The Quest for Moral Understanding.* London: Transaction Publishers.

Eickelman, D. F. 1978. The Art of Memory: Islamic Education and Its Social Reproduction. *Comparative Studies in Society and History* 20, 485–516.

______. 1982. The Study of Islam in Local Contexts. *Contributions to Asian Studies* 17, 13–28.

______. 1992. Mass Higher Education and the Religious Imagination in Contemporary Arab Societies. *American Ethnologist* 19, 643–55.

Eickelman, D. F., and J. Piscatori. 1996. *Muslim Politics*. Princeton: Princeton University Press.

el-Zein, A. H. 1977. Beyond Ideology and Theology: The Search for the Anthropology of Islam. *Annual Review of Anthropology* 6, 227–54.

Ewing, K. P. 1990. The Dream of Spiritual Initiation and the Organisation of Self Representations among Pakistani Sufis. *American Ethnologist* 17, 56–74.

______. 1997. *Arguing Sainthood: Modernity, Psychoanalysis, and Islam*. Durham: Duke University Press.

Fathi, H. 1997. Otines: The Unknown Women Clerics of Central Asian Islam. *Central Asian Survey* 16, 27–43.

______. 2006. Gender, Islam, and Social Change in Uzbekistan. *Central Asian Survey* 25, 303–17.

Faubion, J. 2001. Towards an Anthropology of Ethics: Foucault and the Pedagogies of Autopoiesis. *Representations* 74, 83–104.

Fitzpatrick, S. 2000. Ascribing Class: The Construction of Social Identity in Soviet Russia. In *Stalinism: New Directions*. Edited by S. Fitzpatrick. London: Routledge.

Foucault, M. 1990. *The History of Sexuality Volume 1: An Introduction*. London: Penguin Books.

______. 1994. The Subject and Power. In *The Essential Foucault: Selections from Essential Works of Foucault, 1954–1984*. Edited by P. Rabinow and N. Rose. New York: The New Press.

Gaffney, P. D. 1991. The Changing Voices of Islam: The Emergence of Professional Preachers in Contemporary Egypt. *The Muslim World* 81, 27–47.

Gardner, K. 1999. Global Migrants and Local Shrines: The Shifting Geography of Islam in Sylhet, Bangladesh. In *Muslim Diversity: Local Islam in Global Contexts*. Edited by L. Manger. Richmond: Curzon.

Geertz, C. 1968. *Islam Observed: Religious Development in Morocco and Indonesia*. Chicago: University of Chicago Press.

Geiss, P. G. 2001. Mahallah and Kinship Relations: A Study on Residential Communal Commitment Structures in Central Asia of the 19th Century. *Central Asian Survey* 20, 97–106.

Gellner, E. 1981. *Muslim Society*. Cambridge: Cambridge University Press.

Good, B. 1994. *Medicine, Rationality, and Experience: An Anthropological Perspective*. Cambridge: Cambridge University Press.

Greenway, C. 1998. Hungry Earth and Vengeful Stars: Soul Loss and Identity in the Peruvian Andes. *Social Science and Medicine* 47, 993–1004.

Gross, J. T. 1982. A Note on the Nature of Soviet Totalitarianism. *Soviet Studies* 34, 367–76.

Hallaq, W. B. 2005. *The Origins and Evolution of Islamic Law*. Cambridge: Cambridge University Press.

Hanks, R. 2001. Repression as Reform: Islam in Uzbekistan during the Early Glasnost' Period. *Religion, State and Society* 29, 227–39.

Haugen, A. 2004. *The Establishment of National Republics in Central Asia*. London: Palgrave Macmillan.

Heintz, M., ed. 2009. *The Anthropology of Moralities*. Oxford: Berghahn Books.

Henkel, H. 2005. Between Belief and Unbelief Lies the Performance of Salāt: Meaning and Efficacy of a Muslim Ritual. *Journal of the Royal Anthropological Institute (N.S.)* 11, 487–507.

Herzfeld, M. 1997. *Cultural Intimacy: Social Poetics in the Nation-State*. London: Routledge.

Hilgers, I. 2006. The Regulation and Control of Religious Pluralism in Uzbekistan. In *The Postsocialist Religious Question: Faith and Power in Central Asia and East-Central Europe*. Edited by C. Hann and the "Civil Religion" Group. Berlin: Lit Verlag.

Hirsch, F. 2005. *Empire of Nations: Ethnographic Knowledge and the Making of the Soviet Union*. Ithaca: Cornell University Press.

Hirschkind, C. 2001. The Ethics of Listening: Cassette-Sermon Audition in Contemporary Egypt. *American Ethnologist* 28, 623–49.

———. 2006. *The Ethical Soundscape: Cassette Sermons and Islamic Counterpublics*. New York: Columbia University Press.

Hoffman, V. 1997. The Role of Visions in Contemporary Egyptian Religious Life. *Religion* 27, 45–64.

Hoffmann, D. L. 2003. *Stalinist Values: The Cultural Norms of Soviet Modernity, 1917–1941*. Ithaca: Cornell University Press.

Horvatich, P. 1994. Ways of Knowing Islam. *American Ethnologist* 21, 811–26.

Howell, S. 1997. Introduction. In *The Ethnography of Moralities*. Edited by S. Howell. London: Routledge.

Human Rights Watch. 2004. *Creating Enemies of the State: Religious Persecution in Uzbekistan*. Human Rights Watch.

———. 2005. *Bullets Were Falling Like Rain: The Andijan Massacre*. Human Rights Watch 17(5D).

Hunt, L. 1998. Moral Reasoning and the Meaning of Cancer: Causal Explanations of Oncologists and Patients in Southern Mexico. *Medical Anthropology Quarterly, New Series* 12, 298–318.

Ilkhamov, A. 1998. Shirkats, Dekhqon Farmers and Others: Farm Restructuring in Uzbekistan. *Central Asian Survey* 17, 539–60.

______. 2000. The 'Uzbek Model' of Farm Economy: Formal and Informal Aspects. Paper presented at the conference on Informal Economies and Civil Society in Post-Soviet Eurasia, Centre for Russian Research and East European Studies, University of Michigan, 2000.

______. 2006. The Phenomenology of "Akromiya": Separating Facts from Fiction. *China and Eurasia Forum Quarterly* 4, 39–48.

Ingold, T., and E. Hallam. 2007. Creativity and Cultural Improvisation: An Introduction. In *Creativity and Cultural Improvisation*. Edited by E. Hallam and T. Ingold. Oxford: Berg.

Ingold, T., M. Strathern, J. D. Y. Peel, C. Toren, and J. Spencer. 1996. The Concept of Society Is Obsolete. In *Key Debates in Anthropology*. Edited by T. Ingold. London: Routledge.

International Crisis Group. 2005. *Uzbekistan: The Andijon Uprising*. Asia Briefing No. 38.

Jessa, P. 2006. Aq jol Soul Healers: Religious Pluralism and a Contemporary Muslim Movement in Kazakhstan. *Central Asian Survey* 25, 359–71.

Kamp, M. 2002. Pilgrimage and Performance: Uzbek Women and the Imagining of Uzbekistan in the 1920s. *International Journal of Middle East Studies* 34, 263–78.

______. 2004. Between Women and the State: Mahalla Committees and Social Welfare in Uzbekistan. In *The Transformation of Central Asia: States and Societies from Soviet Rule to Independence*. Edited by P. Jones Luong. Ithaca: Cornell University Press.

Kandiyoti, D. 1998. Rural Livelihoods and Social Networks in Uzbekistan: Perspectives from Andijan. *Central Asian Survey* 17, 561–78.

______. 1999. Poverty in Transition: An Ethnographic Critique of Household Surveys in Post-Soviet Central Asia. *Development and Change* 30, 499–524.

Kandiyoti, D., and N. Azimova. 2004. The Communal and the Sacred: Women's Worlds of Ritual in Uzbekistan. *Journal of the Royal Anthropological Institute (N.S.)* 10, 327–49.

Kapferer, B. 1997. *The Feast of the Sorcerer: Practices of Consciousness and Power*. Chicago: The University of Chicago Press.

______. 2003. Sorcery, Modernity and the Constitutive Imaginary: Hybridising Continuities. In *Beyond Rationalism: Rethinking Magic, Witchcraft and Sorcery*. Edited by B. Kapferer. New York: Berghahn Books.

Karimov, I. 1993. *Building the Future: Uzbekistan – Its Own Model for Transition to a Market Economy*. Tashkent: Uzbekiston.

———. 1995. *Uzbekistan: Along the Road of Deepening Economic Reform.* Tashkent: Uzbekiston.

———. 1997. *Uzbekistan on the Threshold of the Twenty-First Century: Threats to Security, Conditions of Stability and Guarantees for Progress.* Tashkent: Uzbekiston.

Karomatov, H., Z. Husniddinov, A. Hasanov, A. Abdullaev, O. Yusupov, A. Adhamov, and A. G'ofurov, eds. 2001. *Islom ziyosi o'zbekim siymosida.* Tashkent: Toshkent islom universiteti.

Kehl-Bodrogi, K. 2006. Who Owns the Shrine? Competing Meanings and Authorities at a Pilgrimage Site in Khorezm. *Central Asian Survey* 25, 235–50.

———. 2008. *Religion is not so Strong Here: Muslim Religious Life in Khorezm after Socialism.* Munster: Lit Verlag.

Keller, S. 2001. *To Moscow, Not Mecca: The Soviet Campaign against Islam in Central Asia, 1917–1941.* Westport: Praeger.

Kendzior, S. 2006. Inventing Akromiya: The Role of Uzbek Propagandists in the Andijon Massacre. *Demokratizatsiya: The Journal of Post-Soviet Democratization* 14, 545–62.

———. 2007. Poetry of Witness. *Central Asian Survey* 26, 317–34.

Khalid, A. 1998. *The Politics of Muslim Cultural Reform: Jadidism in Central Asia.* Berkeley: University of California Press.

———. 2003. A Secular Islam: Nation, State, and Religion in Uzbekistan. *International Journal of Middle East Studies* 35, 573–98.

———. 2007. *Islam after Communism: Religion and Politics in Central Asia.* Berkeley: University of California Press.

Khan, S. 2003. *Muslim Reformist Political Thought: Revivalists, Modernists and Free Will.* London: Routledge Curzon.

Kharkhordin, O. 1999. *The Collective and the Individual in Russia: A Study of Practices.* Berkeley: University of California Press.

Kleinman, A. 1988. *The Illness Narratives: Suffering, Healing and the Human Condition.* New York: Basic Books.

———. 1999. Moral Experience and Ethical Reflection: Can Ethnography Reconcile Them? A Quandary for "The New Bioethics." *Deadalus* 128, 69–97.

Koroteyeva, V., and E. Makarova. 1998a. The Assertion of Uzbek National Identity: Nativization or State-Building Process? In *Post-Soviet Central Asia.* Edited by T. Atabaki and J. O'Kane. London: Tauris Academic Studies.

———. 1998b. Money and Social Connections in the Soviet and Post-Soviet Uzbek City. *Central Asian Survey* 17, 579–96.

Kotkin, S. 1995. *Magnetic Mountain: Stalinism as a Civilization.* Berkeley: University of California Press.

Kreindler, I. T. 1995. Soviet Muslims: Gains and Losses as a Result of Soviet Language Planning. In *Muslim Eurasia: Conflicting Legacies*. Edited by Y. Ro'i. London: Frank Cass.

Laidlaw, J. 2002. For an Anthropology of Ethics and Freedom. *Journal of the Royal Anthropological Institute (N.S.)* 8, 311–32.

Lambek, M. 1988. Spirit Possession/Spirit Succession: Aspects of Social Continuity among Malagasy Speakers in Mayotte. *American Ethnologist* 15, 710–31.

______. 1990. Certain Knowledge, Contestable Authority: Power and Practice on the Islamic Periphery. *American Ethnologist* 17, 23–40.

______. 1993. *Knowledge and Practice in Mayotte: Local Discourses of Islam, Sorcery and Spirit Possession*. Toronto: University of Toronto Press.

______. 2002. Nuriaty, the Saint and the Sultan: Virtuous Subject and Subjective Virtuoso of the Postmodern Colony. In *Postcolonial Subjectivities in Africa*. Edited by R. Werbner. London: Zed Books.

Lapidus, G. W. 1979. *Women in Soviet Society: Equality, Development and Social Change*. Berkeley: University of California Press.

Launay, R. 1992. *Beyond the Stream: Islam and Society in a West African Town*. Long Grove: Waveland Press.

Lewis, I. M. 1998. *Ecstatic Religion: A Study of Shamanism and Spirit Possession*. London: Routledge.

Lindholm, C. 1996. *The Islamic Middle East: Tradition and Change*. Oxford: Blackwell Publishing.

Lindquist, G. 2001a. The Culture of Charisma: Wielding Legitimacy in Contemporary Russian Healing. *Anthropology Today* 17, 3–8.

______. 2001b. Wizards, Gurus, and Energy-Information Fields: Wielding Legitimacy in Contemporary Russian Healing. *Anthropology of East Europe Review* 19, 16–28.

Lobacheva, N. P. 1989. Znachenie obshchiny v zhizni sem'i (po materialam svadebnoi obryadnosti khorezmskikh uzbekov). In *Etnicheskaya istoriya i traditsionnaya kul'tura narodov Srednei Azii i Kazakhstana*. Edited by N. Palagina. Nukus: Karakalpakstan.

Louw, M. E. 2007. *Everyday Islam in Post-Soviet Central Asia*. London: Routledge.

Lubin, N. 1981. Women in Soviet Central Asia: Progress and Contradictions. *Soviet Studies* 33, 182–203.

MacIntyre, A. 2007. *After Virtue*. London: Gerald Duckworth and Co. Ltd.

Mahmood, S. 2005. *Politics of Piety: The Islamic Revival and the Feminist Subject*. Princeton: Princeton University Press.

______. 2006. Secularism, Hermeneutics, and Empire: The Politics of Islamic Reformation. *Public Culture* 18, 323–47.

Malashenko, A. V. 1994a. Islam and Politics in the Southern Zone of the Former USSR. In *Central Asia and Transcaucasia: Ethnicity and Conflict*. Edited by V. Naumkin. Westport: Greenwood Press.

———. 1994b. *Islam in Central Asia*. Reading: Ithaca Press.

Manger, L. 1999. Muslim Diversity: Local Islam in Global Contexts. In *Muslim Diversity: Local Islam in Global Contexts*. Edited by L. Manger. Richmond: Curzon.

March, A. 2003. State Ideology and the Legitimation of Authoritarianism: The Case of Post-Soviet Uzbekistan. *Journal of Political Ideologies* 8, 209–32.

Mardin, S. 2004. Religion and Secularism in Turkey. In *The Modern Middle East: A Reader*. Edited by A. Hourani, P. S. Khoury, and M. C. Wilson. London: I. B. Tauris.

Marsden, M. 2005. *Living Islam: Muslim Religious Experience in Pakistan's North-West Frontier*. Cambridge: Cambridge University Press.

———. 2009. Talking the Talk: Debating Debate in Northern Afghanistan. *Anthropology Today* 25, 20–24.

Masquelier, A. 2001. *Prayer Has Spoiled Everything: Possession, Power and Identity in an Islamic Town of Niger*. Durham: Duke University Press.

Massell, G. 1974. *The Surrogate Proletariat: Moslem Women and Revolutionary Strategies in Soviet Central Asia, 1919–1929*. Princeton: Princeton University Press.

Massicard, E., and T. Trevisani. 2003. The Uzbek Mahalla: Between State and Society. In *Central Asia: Aspects of Transition*. Edited by T. Everett-Heath. New York: Routledge Curzon.

Mattingly, C. 1998. *Healing Dramas and Clinical Plots: The Narrative Structure of Experience*. Cambridge: Cambridge University Press.

Maxwell, D. 2005. The Durawall of Faith: Pentecostal Spirituality in Neo-Liberal Zimbabwe. *Journal of Religion in Africa* 35, 4–32.

McBrien, J. 2006a. Extreme Conversations: Secularism, Religious Pluralism, and the Rhetoric of Islamic Extremism in Southern Kyrgyzstan. In *The Postsocialist Religious Question: Faith and Power in Central Asia and East-Central Europe*. Edited by C. Hann and the "Civil Religion" Group. Berlin: Lit Verlag.

———. 2006b. Listening to the Wedding Speaker: Discussing Religion and Culture in Southern Kyrgyzstan. *Central Asian Survey* 25, 341–57.

McIntosh, J. 2004. Reluctant Muslims: Embodied Hegemony and Moral Resistance in a Giriama Spirit Possession Complex. *Journal of the Royal Anthropological Institute (N.S.)* 10, 91–112.

Medlin, W. K., and W. M. Cave. 1964. Social Change and Education in Developing Areas: Uzbekistan. *Comparative Education Review* 8, 166–75.

Medlin, W. K., W. M. Cave, and F. Carpenter. 1971. *Education and Development in Central Asia: A Case Study on Social Change in Uzbekistan*. Leiden: E. J. Brill.

Megoran, N. 2002. The Borders of Eternal Friendship? The Politics and Pain of Nationalism and Identity along the Uzbekistan-Kyrgyzstan Ferghana Valley Boundary, 1999–2000. Ph.D. diss., University of Cambridge.

———. 2005. The Critical Geopolitics of Danger in Uzbekistan and Kyrgyzstan. *Environment and Planning D: Society and Space* 23, 555–80.

———. 2008. Framing Andijon, Narrating the Nation: Islam Karimov's Account of the Events of 13 May 2005. *Central Asian Survey* 27, 15–31.

Meyer, B. 1998. The Power of Money: Politics, Occult Forces, and Pentecostalism in Ghana. *African Studies Review* 41, 15–37.

———. 2004. Christianity in Africa: From African Independent to Pentecostal-Charismatic Churches. *Annual Review of Anthropology* 33, 447–74.

Middleton, J. 1963. Witchcraft and Sorcery in Lugbara. In *Witchcraft and Sorcery in East Africa*. Edited by J. Middleton and E. H. Winter. London: Routledge and Kegan Paul.

Milliy istiqlol g'oyasi: asosiy tushuncha va tamoyillar. 2001. Tashkent: Uzbekiston.

Moore, H., and T. Sanders. 2001. Magical Interpretations and Material Realities: An Introduction. In *Magical Interpretations and Material Realities: Modernity, Witchcraft and the Occult in Postcolonial Africa*. Edited by H. Moore and T. Sanders. London: Routledge.

Moryakova, E. 1998. Mahallah: The Traditional Muslim Neighbourhood Community in the Development of Uzbek Civil Society. In *Post-Communist Transformations: A New Generation of Perspectives*. Edited by D. Dornisch, P. Elvin, and R. Kania. Warsaw: IfiS Publishers.

Murray Matley, I. 1967. *Agricultural Development*. In *Central Asia: A Century of Russian Rule*. Edited by E. Allworth. New York: Columbia University Press.

Nadel, S. F. 1952. Witchcraft in Four African Societies: An Essay in Comparison. *American Anthropologist, New Series* 54, 18–29.

Nandy, A. 1998. The Politics of Secularism and the Recovery of Religious Toleration. In *Secularism and its Critics*. Edited by R. Bhargava. New Delhi: Oxford University Press.

Naumkin, V. V. 2005. *Radical Islam in Central Asia: Between Pen and Rifle*. Lanham: Rowman & Littlefield Publishers.

Navaro-Yashin, Y. 2002. *Faces of the State: Secularism and Public Life in Turkey*. Princeton: Princeton University Press.

Noori, N. 2006. Expanding State Authority, Cutting Back Local Services: Decentralization and its Contradictions in Uzbekistan. *Central Asian Survey* 25, 533–49.

Northrop, D. 2004. *Veiled Empire: Gender and Power in Stalinist Central Asia*. Ithaca: Cornell University Press.

Nourse, J. W. 1996. The Voice of the Winds versus the Masters of Cure: Contested Notions of Spirit Possession among the Laujé of Sulawesi. *Journal of the Royal Anthropological Institute (N.S.)* 2, 425–42.

O'Hara, S. L. 2000. Lessons from the Past: Water Management in Central Asia. *Water Policy* 2, 365–84.

Obeyesekere, G. 1981. *Medusa's Hair: An Essay on Personal Symbols and Religious Experience.* Chicago: The University of Chicago Press.

Ong, A. 1988. The Production of Possession: Spirits and the Multinational Corporation in Malaysia. *American Ethnologist* 15, 28–42.

———. 1999. Clash of Civilizations or Asian Liberalism? An Anthropology of the State and Citizenship. In *Anthropological Theory Today.* Edited by H. L. Moore. Cambridge: Polity Press.

Parkin, D., ed. 1985. *The Anthropology of Evil.* Oxford: Basil Blackwell.

Pelkmans, M. 2007. 'Culture' as a Tool and an Obstacle: Missionary Encounters in Post-Soviet Kyrgyzstan. *Journal of the Royal Anthropological Institute (N.S.)* 13, 881–99.

Pelkmans, M., and J. McBrien. 2008. Turning Marx on his Head: Missionaries, 'Extremists' and Archaic Secularists in Post-Soviet Kyrgyzstan. *Critique of Anthropology* 28, 87–103.

Peshkova, S. 2006. Otinchalar in the Ferghana Valley: Islam, Gender and Power. Ph.D. diss., Syracuse University.

Peters, R. 1980. Idjtihād and Taqlīd in 18th and 19th Century Islam. *Die Welt des Islams (N.S.)* 20, 131–45.

Pierce, R. A. 1960. *Russian Central Asia 1867–1917: A Study in Colonial Rule.* Berkeley: University of California Press.

Poliakov, S. P. 1992. *Everyday Islam: Religion and Tradition in Rural Central Asia.* London: M. E. Sharpe.

Privratsky, B. 2001. *Muslim Turkistan: Kazak Religion and Collective Memory.* Richmond: Curzon.

———. 2004. "Turkistan Belongs to the Qojas": Local Knowledge of a Muslim Tradition. In *Devout Societies vs. Impious States: Transmitting Islamic Learning in Russia, Central Asia and China, through the Twentieth Century.* Edited by S. A. Dudoignon. Berlin: Klaus Schwarz Verlag.

Qutb, S. 1990. *Milestones.* Translated by A. Z. Hammad. Indianapolis: American Trust Publications.

Rahman, F. 1966. *Islam.* Chicago: University of Chicago Press.

———. 1982. *Islam and Modernity: Transformation of an Intellectual Tradition.* Chicago: The University of Chicago Press.

Ramadan, T. 2004. *Western Muslims and the Future of Islam*. Oxford: Oxford University Press.

Rappaport, R. A. 1999. *Ritual and Religion in the Making of Humanity*. Cambridge: Cambridge University Press.

Rasanayagam, J. 2002a. The Moral Construction of the State in Uzbekistan: Its Construction within Concepts of Community and Interaction at the Local Level. Ph.D. diss., University of Cambridge.

———. 2002b. Spheres of Communal Participation: Placing the State within Local Modes of Interaction in Rural Uzbekistan. *Central Asian Survey* 21, 55–70.

———. 2003. Market, State and Community in Uzbekistan: Reworking the Concept of the Informal Economy: Max Planck Institute for Social Anthropology Working Paper No. 59.

———. 2006a. Healing with Spirits and the Formation of Muslim Selfhood in Post-Soviet Uzbekistan. *Journal of the Royal Anthropological Institute (N.S.)* 12, 377–93.

———. 2006b. Introduction to Special Issue: Post-Soviet Islam: An Anthropological Perspective. *Central Asian Survey* 25, 219–33.

Rassudova, R. 1969. Zanyatiya naseleniya. In *Etnograficheskie ocherki uzbekskogo sel'skogo naseleniya*. Edited by G. P. Vasileva and B. Karmysheva. Moscow: Nauka.

Reeves, E. B. 1995. Power, Resistance, and the Cult of Muslim Saints in a Northern Egyptian Town. *American Ethnologist* 22, 306–24.

Ricoeur, P. 1991. Narrative Identity. In *On Paul Ricoeur: Narrative and Interpretation*. Edited by D. Wood. London: Routledge.

Rizvi, S. H. 2005. Mysticism and Philosophy: Ibn 'Arabī and Mullā Ṣadrā. In *The Cambridge Companion to Arabic Philosophy*. Edited by P. Adamson and R. C. Taylor. Cambridge: Cambridge University Press.

Ro'i, Y. 1995. The Secularisation of Islam and the USSR's Muslim Areas. In *Muslim Eurasia: Conflicting Legacies*. Edited by Y. Ro'i. London: Frank Cass.

———. 2000. *Islam in the Soviet Union: From the Second World War to Gorbachev*. London: Hurst.

Robbins, J. 2004. The Globalization of Pentecostal and Charismatic Christianity. *Annual Review of Anthropology* 33, 117–43.

———. 2004. *Becoming Sinners: Christianity and Moral Torment in a Papua New Guinea Society*. Berkley: University of California Press.

———. 2007. Between Reproduction and Freedom: Morality, Value and Radical Cultural Change. *Ethnos* 72, 293–314.

Rorlich, A. A. 1991. Islam and Atheism: Dynamic Tension in Soviet Central Asia. In *Soviet Central Asia: The Failed Transformation*. Edited by W. Fierman. Boulder: Westview Press.

Rosaldo, M. 1984. Towards an Anthropology of Self and Feeling. In *Culture Theory: Essays on Mind, Self and Emotion*. Edited by R. A. Shweder and R. A. LeVine. Cambridge: Cambridge University Press.

Rosaldo, R. 1989. *Culture and Truth: The Remaking of Social Analysis*. London: Routledge.

Rotar, I. 2006. Uzbekistan: What is Known about Akramia and the Uprising?: Forum 18 News Service.

Roy, O. 2000. *The New Central Asia: The Creation of Nations*. London: I. B. Tauris.

Saroyan, M. 1997a. Ambivalence, Authority, and the Problem of Popular Islam. In *Minorities, Mullahs and Modernity: Reshaping Community in the Former Soviet Union*. Edited by E. W. Walker. University of California Press/University of California International and Area Studies Digital Collection.

———. 1997b. Islamic Clergy and Community in the Soviet Union. In *Minorities, Mullahs and Modernity: Reshaping Community in the Former Soviet Union*. Edited by E. W. Walker. University of California Press/University of California International and Area Studies Digital Collection.

———. 1997c. Rethinking Islam in the Soviet Union. In *Minorities, Mullahs and Modernity: Reshaping Community in the Former Soviet Union*. Edited by E. W. Walker. University of California Press/University of California International and Area Studies Digital Collection.

Scheper-Hughes, N. 1992. Hungry Bodies, Medicine, and the State: Toward a Critical Psychological Anthropology. In *New Directions in Psychological Anthropology*. Edited by T. Schwartz, G. M. White, and C. Lutz. Cambridge: Cambridge University Press.

Scheper-Hughes, N., and M. Lock. 1987. The Mindful Body: A Prolegomenon to Future Work in Medical Anthropology. *Medical Anthropology Quarterly, New Series* 1, 6–41.

Schubel, V. J. 1999. Post-Soviet Hagiography and the Reconstruction of the Naqshbandi Tradition in Contemporary Uzbekistan. In *Naqshbandis in Western and Central Asia: Change and Continuity*. Edited by E. Özdalga. Istanbul: Swedish Research Institute.

Scott, J. 1985. *Weapons of the Weak: Everyday Forms of Peasant Resistance*. New Haven: Yale University Press.

Shahrani, N. 1995. Islam and the Political Culture of "Scientific Atheism" in Post-Soviet Central Asia: Future Predicaments. In *The Politics of Religion in Russia and the New States of Eurasia*. Edited by M. Bourdeaux. New York: M. E. Sharp.

Shankland, D. 1999. *Islam and Society in Turkey*. Huntingdon: Eothen Press.

Sievers, E. W. 2002. Uzbekistan's Mahalla: From Soviet to Absolutist Residential Community Associations. *The Journal of International and Comparative Law at Chicago-Kent* 2, 91–158.

Simon, G. M. 2009. The Soul Freed of Cares? Islamic Prayer, Subjectivity, and the Contradictions of Moral Selfhood in Minangkabau, Indonesia. *American Ethnologist* 36, 258–75.

Slezkine, Y. 2000. The USSR as a Communal Apartment, or How a Socialist State Promoted Ethnic Particularism. In *Stalinism: New Directions*. Edited by S. Fitzpatrick. London: Routledge.

Smith, G. 1996. The Soviet State and Nationalities Policy. In *The Nationalities Question in the Post-Soviet States*. Edited by G. Smith. London: Longman.

Snezarev, G. P. 2003. *Remnants of Pre-Islamic Beliefs and Rituals among the Khorezm Uzbeks*. Berlin: Reinhold Scheltzer Verlag.

Sokolovski, S. V. 2005. Identity Politics and Indigeneity Construction in the Russian Census 2002 Halle/Saale: Max Planck Institute for Social Anthropology. Working Paper No. 77.

Ssorin-Chaikov, N. 2003. *The Social Life of the State in Subarctic Siberia*. Stanford: Stanford University Press.

Starrett, G. 1998. *Putting Islam to Work: Education, Politics and Religious Transformation in Egypt*. Berkeley: University of California Press.

Stephen, M., and L. K. Suryani. 2000. Shamanism, Psychosis and Autonomous Imagination. *Culture, Medicine and Psychiatry* 24, 5–40.

Tapper, N., and R. Tapper. 1987. The Birth of the Prophet: Ritual and Gender in Turkish Islam. *Man (New Series)* 22, 69–92.

Taussig, M. 1977. The Genesis of Capitalism amongst a South American Peasantry: Devil's Labor and the Baptism of Money. *Comparative Studies in Society and History* 19, 130–55.

Taylor, C. 1989. *Sources of the Self: The Making of the Modern Identity*. Cambridge: Harvard University Press.

Tett, G. 1995. Guardians of the Faith: Gender and Religion in an (ex) Soviet Tajik Village. In *Muslim Women's Choices: Religious Belief and Social Reality*. Edited by F. El-Solh and J. Mabro. Oxford: Berg.

Trevisani, T. 2007a. The Emerging Actor of Decollectivization in Uzbekistan – Private Farming between Newly Defined Political Constraints and Opportunities. Paper presented at the conference Cotton Sector in Central Asia: Economic Policy and Development Challenges, London.

_______. 2007b. Kolkhozes, Sovkhozes, and Shirkats of Yangibozor (1960–2002): Note on an Archival Investigation into Four Decades of Agricultural Development of a District in Khorezm. *Cahiers d`Asie Centrale* 15–16, 354–65.

Turam, B. 2004. A Bargain between the Secular State and Turkish Islam: Politics and Ethnicity in Central Asia. *Nations and Nationalism* 10, 353–74.

Vaisman, D. 1995. Regionalism and Clan Loyalty in the Political Life of Uzbekistan. In *Muslim Eurasia: Conflicting Legacies.* Edited by Y. Ro'i. London: Frank Cass.

Vishnevskii, A. 1996. Srednyaya Aziya: nezavershenaya modernizatsiya. *Vestnik Evrazii* 2, 136–59.

Werbner, P. 2003. *Pilgrims of Love: The Anthropology of a Global Sufi Cult.* London: Hurst.

———. 2005. Honor, Shame and the Politics of Sexual Embodiment among South Asian Muslims in Britain and Beyond: An Analysis of Debates in the Public Sphere. *HAGAR International Social Science Review* 6, 25–47.

White, J. 2002. *Islamist Mobilization in Turkey: A Study in Vernacular Politics.* Seattle: University of Washington Press.

———. 2005. The End of Islamism? Turkey's Muslimhood Model. In *Remaking Muslim Politics: Pluralism, Contestation, Democratisation.* Edited by R. W. Hefner. Princeton: Princeton University Press.

Whitlock, M. 2002. *Land beyond the River: The Untold Story of Central Asia.* New York: Thomas Dunne Books.

Wikan, U. 1989a. Illness from Fright or Soul Loss: A North Balinese Culture-Bound Syndrome? *Culture, Medicine and Psychiatry* 13, 25–50.

———. 1989b. Managing the Heart to Brighten the Face and Soul: Emotions in Balinese Morality and Healthcare. *American Ethnologist* 16, 294–312.

Williams, B. 1985. *Ethics and the Limits of Philosophy.* London: Routledge.

Yurchak, A. 2003. Soviet Hegemony of Form: Everything was Forever, until it was No More. *Comparative Studies in Society and History* 45, 480–510.

———. 2006. *Everything was Forever, until it was No More: The Last Soviet Generation.* Princeton: Princeton University Press.

Zigon, J. 2008. *Morality: An Anthropological Perspective.* Oxford: Berg.

Index

Index

Index

Index

Index

CPSIA information can be obtained at www.ICGtesting.com
Printed in the USA
BVOW020907151112

305643BV00004B/16/P

9 781107 411623